The Great Sophists in
Periclean Athens

JACQUELINE DE ROMILLY

The Great Sophists in Periclean Athens

Translated by Janet Lloyd

Clarendon Press · Oxford

1992

Oxford University Press, Walton Street, Oxford OX2 6DP

Oxford New York Toronto
Delhi Bombay Calcutta Madras Karachi
Petaling Jaya Singapore Hong Kong Tokyo
Nairobi Dar es Salaam Cape Town
Melbourne Auckland
and associated companies in
Berlin Ibadan

Oxford is a trade mark of Oxford University Press

Published in the United States
by Oxford University Press, New York

This English edition has been translated from the
original French publication Les Grands Sophists dans
l'Athènes de Périclès © Éditions de Fallois 1988
translation by Janet Lloyd © Oxford University Press 1992

British Library Cataloguing in Publication Data
Data available

Library of Congress Cataloging-in-Publication Data
Romilly, Jacqueline de.
[Grands Sophists dans l'Athènes de Périclès. English]
The great Sophists in Periclean Athens/Jacqueline de Romeilly,
translated by Janet Lloyd.
p. cm.
Translation of: Les grands Sophists dans l'Athènes de Périclès.
Includes bibliographical references and index.
1. Sophists (Greek philosophy) I. Title.
B288.R5513 1991 183'.1'09385—dc20 91-4759
ISBN 0-19-824234-4

Typeset by Best-Set Typesetter Ltd.
Printed and bound in
Great Britain by Bookcraft (Bath) Ltd,
Midsomer Norton, Avon

For Paul Lemerle

PREFACE

WHEN we think of the Athens of the fifth century BC, a host of illustrious names and dazzling works come to mind. It is well known that this was 'the age of Pericles' and that, following her achievements in the Persian Wars, Athens was the most powerful city in Greece: she embodied democracy, her navy ensured her command of the seas, she headed a veritable empire whose wealth she used to erect the buildings on the Acropolis, monuments to which people still flock today. It is well known that the sculptor Phidias was producing great works to adorn the Acropolis and that, at this point, just before the Peloponnesian War, which occupied the last third of the century, and throughout that war, Sophocles and Euripides were writing their tragedies, Aristophanes his comedies. The historian Herodotus came to live, at least for a while, in Periclean Athens, and Thucydides was about to write an audaciously candid history—this time devoted to the Peloponnesian War, in which Athens was pitted against Sparta, which started under Pericles, but was to last until the end of the century. It is also well known that at this time Socrates roamed the city streets, entering into discussion with young aristocrats and exposing them to new ideas which have been recorded for us by two of his disciples: Plato and Xenophon. It is well known that all this intellectual activity went on until the end of the century. At the time of Athens' defeat in 404, which brought the Peloponnesian War to an end, Pericles had been dead for twenty-five years, Sophocles and Euripides had died recently, Socrates was to be condemned to death in 399, and Thucydides was to disappear at about the same date. So this was a brief moment of capital importance for the history of Greek civilization and perhaps for the Western world as a whole. By contrast, not many people know very much about the Sophists. The names of Protagoras and Gorgias, let alone those of Hippias, Prodicus, and Thrasymachus, are mostly unfamiliar, except to specialists.

Yet it is not hard to see that, in this burst of creativity which was so astonishing, the role that they played was no less so. They seem to have influenced and had a hand in everything that happened. Everyone acknowledged their importance and all the writers of the time had been their disciples, learned something from them, imitated them, or argued about them.

Right from the start, the first of the Sophists, Protagoras, had close relations with Pericles, the most important figure in Athens. Plutarch's *Life of Pericles* describes the two men engaged in a day-long discussion over the question of the legal responsibility in a sporting accident. That may suggest an unproductive discussion over technicalities, a 'Sophistic' discussion, in the modern sense of the term. But it also involved an analysis of the concept of responsibility and reflection on the nature of law. Much of the development of Athenian law is there in embryo, as are all the debates of the orators, historians, and tragedians on the question of responsibility. Moreover, Protagoras, the Sophist involved here, emerges as a distinguished and respected figure. Indeed, in 443, when Pericles sent a Panhellenic expedition to establish a colony at Thurii, in southern Italy, he asked Protagoras to draft its laws: it was a heavy responsibility for a foreigner, and confirms the esteem in which he must have been held.

This handful of men exercised a considerable indirect influence on the fifth-century writers of Athens, and their fame is confirmed by the many allusions made to them by Aristophanes, who refers to them as to household names. The fact is that most of these writers were pupils of the Sophists. The evidence on this score is quite staggering. Euripides is said to have studied under not only Anaxagoras but also Protagoras and Prodicus, both of whom were Sophists. And it is quite true that his plays are full of ideas, problems, and stylistic features which appear to be derived from them. Thucydides is supposed to have been a disciple of three Sophists, Gorgias, Prodicus, and Antiphon. That may be a conclusion which rests on no more than the obvious similarities between his work and their teaching, but the similarities themselves are indisputable and impossible to overlook, whether they relate to methods of analysis, dialectical presentation, positivist attitudes, or even the cultivation of certain stylistic features. Socrates himself appears to have had many links with the Sophists. He treats some of them with considerable deference; and, in the *Meno*, Plato reports him as declaring himself to have studied under one, namely Prodicus. Certainly, in the *Cratylus*, he claims—as a joke, but not one beyond the bounds of possibility—that he attended not Prodicus' fifty-drachma lecture, but his one-drachma one (384 B). Later, Plato refers constantly to this group of men. He often introduces them in his dialogues, two of which are named after two of the first major Sophists, Gorgias and Protagoras. Finally, at the beginning of the fourth century, Isocrates, the founder of a new school of rhetoric and philosophy, defines it in relation to the Sophists, correcting some of their tendencies but certainly owing much to their spirit. He himself had studied under Gorgias, having travelled to Thessaly to attend his lectures. Everywhere, in the literature of the day, one is referred back to the Sophists, as if theirs was the decisive influence.

Given the circumstances, it would be extraordinary not to want to understand them. And specialists of Athens in the fifth century BC, who spend so long studying the texts of this period, must yearn to get back to these figures, who are so little known but so important; for, in truth, it is impossible to understand the age of Pericles and the 'Greek miracle' without a clear idea of the nature and scope of the Sophists' influence.

However, the task is as daunting as it is necessary. These influential men, who produced treatise after treatise in many different fields, turn out to be maddeningly elusive. We know more or less who they were. Apart from a few uncertainties, we know their names, their dates, and their reputations. They were teachers, who hailed from different cities, but who were all found teaching in Athens at one time or another in the second half of the fifth century BC or a little later. A number of texts tell us of their activities and their method of teaching. The difficulties start when we try to obtain a clearer view.

The paradox is that their works, their treatises, famous

though they were and written on such a wide range of subjects, have practically all been lost. Perhaps they were too
technical. But whatever the reason, from this vast mass of
texts only tiny fragments survive, most of them no more than
a few lines long, and those only saved from oblivion through
being cited by other writers.[1] The entire collection of fragments from the Sophists would amount to no more than
twenty pages. Furthermore, they reach us without a context.
Even if we suppose the quotations, noted down several centuries later, to be correct or faithful (which would be extremely
surprising), many are cited by authors who are totally unconcerned to record the Sophists' doctrines but are anxious to
give an example of the author's style, or to add some authority to their own ideas, sceptical in some cases, idealistic in
others. In other words, our first problem is one of interpretation. And every interpreter is bound to rely to a large
extent on his or her own imagination. Controversy inevitably
abounds. Of course, I would not deny the existence of a
certain amount of evidence. We are bound to think of Plato,
who, throughout his work, sets the Sophists on stage. He is
the best guide we have. But we are here confronted with
another paradox: our guide is quite clearly a biased one, for
although Plato sets the Sophists on stage, he has Socrates
refute their theses. We are accordingly bound to be wary of
following his testimony, sensing that the Sophists are in
danger of being ill served by this distorting spotlight.

It is thus no easy matter to reconstitute these debates, and
past attempts to do so have produced discouraging rather
than helpful results. Scholars have pored over every fragment;
they have translated them, produced commentaries on them,
emended them, and argued over them. They have done so

---

[1] All these fragments, most of which have come down to us as quotations,
have been collected together. The present work refers the reader to the
authoritative Diels–Kranz edition, *Fragmente der Vorsokratiker*, which is
used by all scholars and of which there have been many reprints, including
revisions from 1951 onward. Each Sophist is given a number, to which the
present work, contrary to philological custom, will not be referring. Citations
of the Sophists' texts are grouped under A, the fragments themselves under
B. B 4 would thus refer to the author's fourth fragment considered in the
Diels–Kranz edition.

with perspicacity and scholarliness. But, in many cases, they have run a double risk.

In the case of the more meticulous, the complexity of the problems and the multiplicity of controversial points have lent their discussions a somewhat indigestibly erudite character: the study of the Sophists has verged on esotericism, with all its attendant hazards.

In order to discuss these questions, one needed to be at once a philologist and a philosopher: two skills that are seldom evenly balanced. When a scholar's philosophical aptitude is uppermost, the problems raised naturally enough emerge from a way of thinking that is more specialized and more modern than the thinking of the Sophists. Thus, a particular fragment of Protagoras may, for example, be given a 'Hegelian' or a 'Nietzschean' interpretation. Hence, too, the custom of reading a particular ancient author 'in the light of' a philosopher of modern times. As a—virtually inevitable—result, each modern philosophical school tends to read these sparse fragments that have survived from the intellectual movement of the Sophists as a whole in such a way as to detect in them their own particular problems and prejudices. Some detect rationalism of the purest kind, others existentialism. Nowadays, the tendency—unsurprisingly—is to detect the elements of a Philosophy of language.[2]

Research of this kind—provided it is pursued with caution—may be generally stimulating and may open up suggestive perspectives. Clearly, however, it turns its back upon history as it was lived, within the framework of fifth-century Athens, by individuals in love with knowledge, in association with these teachers with a new inspiration. It is this history that provides the starting-point for the present work. This is what it seeks to rediscover, thereby approaching the Sophists from a rather different angle.

For this is a book about the history of ideas, in the widest

---

[2] This is paricularly noticeable in the two volumes of the proceedings of the recent Cerisy colloquium, edited by Barbara Cassin, *Le Plaisir de parler: Études de sophistique comparée* (Paris, 1986), and *Positions de la sophistique* (Paris, 1986). Some commentators, mindful of their own modern problems, try to read into these disjointed fragments a meaning which might have been implied by the Sophists.

sense of the expression. It is not a philosophical work, nor is it
written by a philosopher. It is, to be sure, impossible to study
classical Greece without being bathed in philosophy, for it
permeated everything at the time. But, after all, the pupils of
the fifth-century Sophists were not exclusively philosophers,
nor was the Sophists' influence limited to philosophers. Both
Thucydides and Euripides are deeply affected by their teaching, as, later, is Isocrates. Aristophanes refers to them, and,
when Plato sets them on stage, it is not necessarily in the
most austere of his dialogues. They are inextricably mixed up
in the life of the city. So it is perhaps not unreasonable for
someone who has studied the Sophists' disciples and those
who speak of them to try to assess their role. With such an
approach, it may be possible to grasp their thought as expressed in the very terms recorded in the works of their
contemporaries. It may also prove possible to define their
thought in the context of the extraordinarily momentous
period during which Athens first welcomed, then challenged,
and finally assimilated it. This work studies the Sophists in
relation to the Athenian culture upon which they left such an
indelible mark.

Such an approach implies on the one hand a number of
deliberate omissions, on the other a precise aim that defines
the project as a whole. The omissions are too numerous to
itemize, but let me point out a few of them.

In the first place, this work provides little in the way of a
bibliography of secondary literature, be it criticism or commentary. There are plenty of other works which provide these
tools of study for the benefit of specialists. Having, as far as
possible, read everything, I have decided to cite nothing. It is
hard enough to reach the Sophists, without setting up screens
of weighty erudition between us and them:

For the same reason, I have ignored secondary problems
which do not really seem to affect the message of these works.
I have not, for instance, attempted to tackle the problem of
whether certain titles relate to chapters or to entire works.

Nor does this book tackle the more technical side of the
Sophists' activities—and this is perhaps a more serious omis-
sion. Some—Hippias and Antiphon, for example—engaged in
mathematics, making new contributions to this field of study.

Some (e.g. Hippias, again) worked on the practice of certain mnemonic devices. Several made contributions to history, putting together records of facts. Such aspects of their work deserve to be remembered, but they are not studied in the present volume, partly to avoid distracting the reader and also to make it easier to grasp the general continuity of the intellectual adventure that was being played out.

Furthermore, for the same reasons, in interpreting the works of the Sophists, this book disregards the interpretations produced in the light of later philosophies. It endeavours to concentrate upon what contemporary readers seem to have understood. The strategy may appear somewhat limited, but it is at least more in conformity with a concern for historical truth.

In the name of that concern, I have not drawn upon what is sometimes known as the Second Sophistic, that is to say, the intellectual movement based upon the rhetoric of the fifth-century Sophists and inspired by their example. This Second Sophistic occurred in the second century AD, seven centuries after the movement with which we are concerned here. It was far more involved in rhetoric and far more affected by irrational tendencies, which were flourishing at that time. Here too, a comparison between the two groups of Sophists could be rewarding for those particularly interested in rhetoric and language. But it is irrelevant for those seeking to understand what was going on and being thought in fifth-century Athens.

My priorities have thus made for a number of omissions. On the other hand, they give rise to an aspiration, namely that of setting the record straight. For here lies the crux of the matter. These men were great teachers. But they have also been accused of being bad teachers. At various times, even in fifth-century Athens itself, they were publicly attacked. They were accused of . . . virtually everything: of destroying morality, of rejecting the truth, of sowing the seeds of bad faith, of fostering ambition, of bringing down Athens . . . Plato had a hand in this attack, but he was not alone. And as a result of all this denigration, the word 'sophistry', taken from the fine title of 'Sophists', experts in wisdom, that they had won, soon became and has to this day remained synonymous with crafty thinking. How did this come about? Were these men really so unworthy of their pupils? Were they really such miscreants? Or has there been some misunderstanding? And if so, where did it originate?

Over years of reading and research, these are the questions that have been at the back of my mind, stimulating and arresting my attention, and they constitute the subject of this book. They imply a concern about method, which is not characteristic of most works devoted to the Sophists. One of my major desires has been at all costs to avoid confusing the major Sophists with their all too self-satisfied disciples for, generally speaking, it was the latter who were the real, perhaps the only, amoralists. That is why it is important not to include Plato's Callicles among the Sophists, and there are no grounds for doing so. The differences that set the Sophists apart from the likes of him are sometimes of crucial importance and when, as all too often happens, all these figures are lumped together, there is a risk of falsifying the evidence. Similarly, however strongly Euripides may have been influenced by the Sophists, he was never one of them; and however close a contemporary philosopher such as Democritus may have been to them, the orientation of his thought was quite different, as was his field of activity. It is important not to blur these distinctions. Only so can we hope to shed clear light upon the Sophists in the true sense of the term, and discover how it was that their thought proved so easy to distort.

This seemed to me a chance not only to illuminate a crucial aspect of the history of Greek thought but also to make it easier to understand how something can go wrong in the dialogue between any school of dense theoretical thought and its contemporary public, which is only more or less well informed and capable of understanding it. These misunderstandings were possible in Athens; and, in our own day, we may be better informed but still not understand properly: the Athenian experience thus unfortunately takes on the character of a cautionary tale.

The aim of this book is to focus attention upon the dialogue that took place between the Sophists and Athenian public opinion, considering those Sophists in all their diverse roles, as teachers, as audacious thinkers, as lucid moral philosophers, and as political theorists. In each of these fields, a similar pattern of events is detectable: first of all we find bold discoveries, then scandalized response and criticism, finally a return to a modified acceptance of the ways ahead that the Sophists initially indicated.

They are, as we shall see, to a large extent the very same ways that we today, twenty-five centuries later, are still pursuing.[3]

[3] My warmest thanks go to Madame Jacqueline Salviat, who was kind enough to read and comment upon a first draft of this book, and also to Madame S. Saïd, who assisted me in correcting the proofs.

CONTENTS

1

The Rise and Success of the Sophists

WHO were these men whom we still, even today, refer to as 'the Sophists'?

The word itself means professionals of the intelligence. And they certainly set out to teach people how to use their intelligence. They were not 'sages', *sophoi*, a word which connotes not a profession but a state of being. Nor were they 'philosophers', for this word suggests a patient search for the truth rather than an optimistic confidence in one's own abilities. They knew certain methods and could teach them. They were masters of thinking, masters of talking. Knowledge was their speciality, just as the piano is the pianist's. One of them, Thrasymachus, hit on an admirable formula to convey this. The epitaph that he composed for his own tomb ran: 'Chalcedon was my country, knowledge my profession.'[1]

The meaning of the term 'Sophist' was in principle relatively wide. It could be applied to anyone thoroughly qualified to exercise his profession, be he a diviner or a poet.[2] In this sense, the term was sometimes applied to men such as Plato or Socrates. But it soon came to denote in particular the group of men who are the subject of this book and it remained associated with the kind of teaching that they provided. It was as a result of the reactions provoked by this teaching that the word, as used by Plato and Aristotle, acquired the derogatory undertones that it still has today. Much later on, notwithstanding, a group of teachers keen to draw inspiration from their example also adopted their name: this was the 'Second Sophistic', under the Roman Empire.

[1] A 8. In Greek: my *technē* is *sophia*.
[2] The noun appears in Pindar, meaning 'poet'; the verb *sophizō* was already used in Hesiod.

The above remarks give some indication of the importance of these early teachers, but they do not tell us what they did, only that they were teachers of a quite unprecedented kind.

They emerged in many different parts of Greece at about the same time; and they all taught for a while in Athens. It is in Athens, only, that we come across them and learn of them.

The greatest of them were Protagoras, who came from Abdera, in northern Greece, on the borders of Thrace; Gorgias, who was from Sicily; Prodicus, from the small island of Ceos; Hippias, from Elis, in the Peloponnese; and Thrasymachus, from Chalcedon, in Asia Minor. Others are known mainly just as names and hardly count. Among all these foreigners there were only two men who were natives of Athens, Antiphon and Critias, and neither—certainly not Critias—appears to have been a professional itinerant teacher. There were certainly other Sophists, such as the two brothers Euthydemus and Dionysodorus, whom Plato brings to life in his very comical dialogue named after the former. But they were not as eminent as the first group of masters given above: they were less innovative, less philosophical, less well known, and we know very little of them as individuals. The only Sophists we really know anything about are the ones in that first group, whose teaching and writing, quite apart from their performance as professionals, made them figure-heads.[3]

Protagoras must have arrived in Athens soon after 450, since we find him associated with Pericles in 443. Gorgias arrived in 427, after the death of Pericles. These two were older than the other Sophists, and Protagoras appears to have died in about 411. Gorgias, Prodicus, and Hippias were still alive at the time of Socrates' trial in 399. The movement thus belongs to the second half of the fifth century, which covers both Athens' greatness and its fall. Even if we extend the small group to include the authors of two treatises which have come down to us anonymously but which indubitably belong to the same movement of thought, the number of people involved is still very small: just a handful of men active for the span of roughly one generation.

[3] On the other hand, we do possess two anonymous passages of some length by Sophists. One is a whole treatise known as *Double Arguments* or *Dialexeis*; the other is by an unknown author (Anonymus Iamblichi) and is four or five pages long.

Thanks to Plato, we know very well who they were and what reactions their appearance had provoked. Let us allow him to describe their arrival upon the scene, for no one is in a better position than he to testify to the extraordinary fame of this group.

The *Protagoras* first presents a picture of the excitement that had seized the youth of Athens at the thought of hearing them. At the beginning of this dialogue, Socrates tells how one young man has rushed to visit him at break of day.

During this night just past, in the small hours, Hippocrates, son of Apollodorus and brother of Phason, knocked violently at my door with his stick and when they opened to him he came hurrying in at once and calling to me in a loud voice: Socrates, are you awake or sleeping? Then I, recognizing his voice, said: Hippocrates, hallo! Some news to break to me? Only good news, he replied. Tell it and welcome, I said: what is it, and what business brings you here at such an hour? Protagoras has come, he said, standing at my side. (310 A–B)

In the Greek language used, even the young man's breathlessness is conveyed. He is eager to become a disciple of Protagoras and he drags Socrates off forthwith, to meet the Sophists.

The Sophists have gathered in the house of the wealthy Callias, a member of one of the most noble families of Athens. They are there in force, surrounded by disciples and admirers. First we meet Protagoras, walking round the cloister escorted by disciples, many of whom are foreigners 'brought by the great Protagoras from the several cities which he traverses, enchanting them with his voice, like Orpheus'. Plato proceeds to describe the manœuvres of this chorus as it follows the master's every move and parts to allow him to pass through their midst.

Later, still in the same house, we meet Hippias, seated on a raised chair, facing a whole group of disciples crowded on to benches. 'Seated in his chair', Hippias replies to their questions. In another room is Prodicus: 'He was still abed, wrapped up in sundry fleeces and rugs, and plenty of them, it seemed.' Plato names the handsome, well-known Athenians clustered about him. We learn that Hippias was speaking of 'celestial matters', but there is no knowing what Prodicus is saying:

The subjects of their conversation I was unable to gather from outside, despite my longing to hear Prodicus; for I regard the man as all-wise and divine; but owing to the depth of his voice the room was filled with a booming sound which made talk indistinct.

The house is already full and becoming fuller. All the gilded youth of Athens has thronged to hear the masters. As Socrates and his young friend arrive, the handsome Alcibiades and Critias appear, two men with important roles to play in the history of Athens.

The picture that this dialogue presents is one not so much of the Sophists themselves, but of their incredible success. On the basis of this dialogue on its own, one might imagine it to be simply a fleeting fashion, a fad on the part of blind youth, groundlessly infatuated by these disturbing thinkers. But that hypothesis is belied beyond all doubt by the facts, for, as our Preface has pointed out, the influence that these men exerted upon the various authors of the fifth and fourth centuries BC was both enduring and profound. And the teaching of both rhetoric and philosophy was marked for ever by the ideas that the Sophists introduced and the debates that they initiated.

So we must accept the fact that one and all were swept off their feet by enthusiasm for the Sophists and that, at the height of its power and influence, Athens flung itself into the arms of these teachers with such fervour that its literature was to be marked by this for ever.

What did the Sophists bring that was so new and so marvellous? Why the fascination? What did they teach? It is time to discover and to move closer to these teachers whom we have glimpsed through Socrates and his young companion in the *Protagoras*.

Never before had such teachers been seen, never such teaching. Up until now, Athenian education had been the same as that of any aristocratic city in which values were transmitted by heredity and example. Now the Sophists introduced an intellectual education that would enable anybody with the means to pay for it to play a distinguished part in city life.

They were so confident of the effectiveness of their lessons that they insisted on payment for them. Nowadays this is common practice, but in fifth-century Athens it was a small scandal. They were selling intellectual skills, selling them dearly what is more.

The very principle was astonishing. As early as in the *Apology*, Plato's Socrates was waxing ironical about it. Feigning admiration for Gorgias, Prodicus, and Hippias, he exclaims:

Each of these men, gentlemen, is able to go into any one of the cities and persuade the young men, who can associate for nothing with whomsoever they wish among their own fellow-citizens . . . to associate with them and pay them money and be grateful besides. (19 E)

What is more, the fees asked were high. Although Socrates speaks of one lecture by Prodicus for which the modest charge was one drachma, he also mentions more expensive ones costing fifty drachmas, and that seemed exorbitant. We should remember that the *per diem* fee for citizens serving in the jury courts—which was considered so demagogic at the time and had so many repercussions—was set first at two, then at three obols, that is to say, half a drachma. Plato pulls no punches with either his adjectives or his comparisons. In the *Hippias Major*, Socrates says of Gorgias that 'by giving exhibitions and associating with the young, he earned and received a great deal of money from the city', and of Prodicus that 'in his private capacity, by giving exhibitions and associating with the young, he received a marvellous sum of money'. He continues that, in contrast to the sages of the past, who did not think it right to make money out of their knowledge, Gorgias and Prodicus were quite determined to do so, as was Protagoras before them (282 c–d). Tradition had it that Protagoras sometimes charged as much as 100 minai (10,000 drachmas). But he was so besieged with requests and his disciples were so delighted that they considered his charge extremely modest. When the lessons were over, if they could not agree on the sum to be paid, they declared, under oath, how much they thought them worth and, whatever the sum, Protagoras accepted the evaluation (*Protagoras*, 328 B). At all events, he grew rich. According to the *Meno* (91 D), Protagoras on his own earned more than Phidias and ten other sculptors put together.

We must not linger too long over the thought of this remarkable age when the arts appear to have epitomized lucrative activity. But Plato's scandalized comments testify to two
facts. In the first place, they provide further proof of the
extraordinary success enjoyed by the Sophists. They also
point to the innovatory nature of the idea that certain forms
of transmittable intellectual knowledge are directly useful.
The Sophists expected payment because they passed on
knowledge as professionals. Their attitude was justified by
the idea of the professionalism and the specialized skill, or
technē, that their very name suggests. And the fact is that
every last professor teaching today has benefited from the
claims which shocked Plato so deeply when the Sophists first
made them.[4]

What did the Sophists want to do? First and foremost, they
wanted to teach people how to speak in public, how to defend
their ideas before the Assembly of the people or in a court of
law. In the first instance, then, they were teachers of rhetoric.
At a time when everything—lawsuits, political influence, and
State decisions—depended on the people, and the people
depended on speech, it was essential to know how to speak in
public, how to argue one's case and advise one's fellow citizens
on political issues. It was all part of the same syndrome and
was the key to effective action.

This explains the different definitions given of the term
'Sophist', where nuance is of the essence. In Plato, Gorgias
describes himself as a master of rhetoric, while Protagoras
claims to be a teacher of politics. The one speaks of the art of
rhetoric, *rhetorikē technē* (in Plato's *Gorgias*, 449 A), but allows
that, in the last analysis, what matters is to be able to argue
one's case in a court of law and in the Assembly. The other
declares that what he teaches is the art of politics, *politikē
technē* (in Plato's *Protagoras*, 319 A), going on to explain that
this involves knowing how to administer one's own affairs
and those of the city, while the art of making decisions and
giving advice to others depends upon being able to argue

---

[4] In the definitions given in the course of the dialogue entitled *The Sophist*,
the lucrative aspect is repeatedly emphasized. The Sophist is 'a hunter
interested in wealthy people', a 'merchant of knowledge', and 'sells speeches
and teaching relating to virtue'.

one's case. Protagoras had written a great deal on the subject of argument. There can be no doubt that the different definitions chosen by the two men reflect the different nature of their preoccupations. But equally certainly, rhetoric and politics were closely connected, for the purpose of rhetoric is to prepare the way for politics and to provide it with its weapons. To this end, it evolves rules, strategies, and techniques. The word *technē*, used in both definitions, reflects the aims of both these Sophists and their common sense of having developed a method.

Practical success was thus the essential aim of this teaching. With its claim that anybody could learn and profit from it, it opened up to all citizens careers in public speaking. In reality, the nature of the Sophists' clientele indicates that there was, in practice, no true social renewal, but the potential certainly existed. In the meantime, a new discipline had been established and was already codified.

But practical success was not the only aim of the Sophists, nor was this twofold discipline the only new side to their teaching. When Protagoras speaks of good management of one's own affairs and those of the State, his words presuppose an intellectual content, a wisdom and experience that is produced by the art of organizing one's ideas successfully. It is an intellectual content that is inseparable from rhetoric, for two good reasons.

In the first place, the possibility of analysing a situation by arguing it through enables one to come to one's own decisions as well as to win over other people. Protagoras seems to take that for granted. And a little later, Isocrates was to make the point in no uncertain terms and with considerable dignity, in a passage of praise for the power of speech which appears twice in his works:

The same arguments which we use in persuading others when we speak in public, we employ also when we deliberate in our own thoughts; and while we call eloquent those who are able to speak before a crowd, we regard as sage those who most skilfully debate their problems in their own minds. (*Nicocles*, 5–9, and *The Antidosis*, 253–7)

Furthermore, the ability to analyse a situation presupposes a certain number of observations and items of knowledge summed up in commonplaces that can be applied to a whole range of different circumstances. All arguments must rest upon likelihood, and this in itself implies the power to reason and a clear view of normal, accepted, and reasonable human behaviour. All demonstrations of a legal or political nature were based upon the notion of likelihood. In a given situation, was it normal to make the decision that one made? When subjected to certain pressures, was it normal to make the mistake that one made? If one adopted a particular solution, was it normal to anticipate success? Those were the lines of reasoning that one had to learn always to follow. The practice of rhetoric and politics thus brought in their train yet another *technē*: a knowledge of modes of human behaviour. It is fair to say that, in practice, all the general reflections upon which Thucydides' orators and Euripides' characters base their arguments are a direct product of this passion for a new understanding of human beings and their behaviour.

It was this desire for knowledge that led these teachers of fifth-century Athens to note down and classify a whole mass of data relating to all areas of life: hence the somewhat surprising range of the titles of certain minor treatises: alongside the major treatises on rhetoric and politics, we find essays on wrestling (*Protagoras*), onomastic (*Gorgias*), the names of different peoples and a list of Olympic victors (*Hippias*), dreams (*Antiphon*), and constitutions (*Critias*).

We know that in the case of one of the Sophists, Hippias, this zeal to learn everything resulted in a remarkable encyclopaedism that even included the skills of craftsmen. Plato tells us that one day, at Olympia, he boasted of having made his own clothes, his own ring, his own seal. He claimed also to have made his shoes and woven his cloak; he had with him poems, epics, and other works that he had written. And (still according to Plato) he also claimed to know more than anyone else about rhythm, grammar, mnemonics . . . His claims were certainly exceptional but, in the last analysis, they simply reflected his extraordinary but characteristically human desire to master every conceivable branch of knowledge.

But all these skills were just by-products and spin-offs, for rhetoric was by no means the only subject taught by the Sophists. Their range of activity extended much further. As can well be imagined, in these debates in the course of which responsibilities, arguments, and criticisms were all turned inside out, it became customary always to consider the possibility of a contrary thesis: everything was open to criticism; everything could be called into question. The mind discovered new paths to explore. Respect for rules gave way to confrontation. In the Sophists' intellectual world, where nothing was accepted a priori any more, the only sure criterion was immediate, concrete human experience. Gods, traditions, and mythical memories no longer counted for anything. Our own judgements, our own feelings and interests now constituted the sole criteria. 'Man is the measure of all things,' Protagoras used to say. For these trained minds, it was easy to make out what, in the traditions and rules of the city, was purely a matter of convention. Much, indeed, was exactly that, as the Sophists were eager to demonstrate, to the great excitement of their public. They wrote metaphysical treatises, analysed concepts, and reflected on justice. They were not just teachers of rhetoric but philosophers too, in the strongest sense of the term, philosophers whose doctrines, by virtue of the very point of view adopted, liberated and stimulated people's minds, opening up new avenues of exploration. These new philosophers—not to be confused with those of the twentieth century—sparked off a veritable intellectual and moral revolution.

For us, the landmarks in that revolution are represented by the memory of the Sophists' great metaphysical and moral treatises, now lost. Plato has commented on them and discussed and refuted them so often that we do have some means of gauging their importance. We shall have to endeavour to define their critical and negative side as precisely as possible, but also try to re-establish their more positive aspects.

It was the critical side which, by provoking such keen reactions, attracted the most attention. This was what Plato discussed and what listeners who were not true philosophers rather hastily seized upon. But we should not allow its brilliance to obscure the fact that these treatises also undertook to reconstruct certain values upon totally new bases.

Our task will be to pinpoint these different aspects of the work of the Sophists, both as teachers and as thinkers. As we do so, it is important to recognize that each of them was original in his own way. Some were interested above all in rhetoric, others in moral philosophy. Some were more radical than others in their criticism of traditional values and their analysis of knowledge and the world. Others were more traditionalist. Some devoted themselves mainly to over-throwing or refuting the theories of the past, others to re-constructing them. In every chapter, we shall accordingly have to keep returning to individuals. But on the whole, the aspects of their activities mentioned above were common to them all: all were innovative as teachers and all were harshly critical of all kinds of transcendentalism, making a more or less clean sweep of the values of the past and replacing them, also more or less uncompromisingly, with new values founded on the needs of human life and city life. It is this common element, the 'Sophistic' spirit, that we shall be concerned, above all, to define. For that is what accounts for the deep excitement caused by these men. They enjoyed a resounding success, but provoked an equally resounding scandal.

Some idea of this is conveyed by Aristophanes' *Clouds*. The comedy, presented in 423, is entirely devoted to the new education. Of course, the play is very unfair, for Socrates, who sought for the truth rather than for success, is presented as one of the Sophists. After all, he too spent his time discuss-ing ideas and calling into question what people thought they knew; and he too offered a purely intellectual education. A comedy was allowed to make such conflations 'in fun'. And in truth, the play is just as unfair to the Sophists. But what it does is symptomatic, for its major targets for attack are the rejection of traditions, the rejection of morality, and the lying art of defending one's own interests by specious argument.

Put on three years after Gorgias' arrival in Athens, the play at any rate shows how very much the whole city was by now aware of the crisis in values that these new philosophers had brought with them, and of the revolution that they had introduced in people's minds. They had brought both good things and bad, marvellous knowledge but undeniable moral risks—and all of it was new.

But once that point is made, two questions immediately

arise. You cannot help wondering where the new ideas orig-
inated and how it was that different individual minds, from
separate far-flung Greek cities, all entered upon roughly
parallel lines of thinking; and you cannot help wondering
why it was in Athens in particular that they all made such an
impact.

In a sense, what needs to be explained is the exceptional
cultural development that fifth-century Athens enjoyed and,
over and above that, the mechanisms of the great mutations
that sometimes take place in the history of ideas.

First, the Sophists clearly fulfilled an expectation and were
part of a deep process of evolution that was finding expression in many different fields at this time. Thinkers and writers
in Greece were now tending to allot a greater place than
before to human beings and to reason.

The history of philosophy is revealing in this respect. Philosophy shifted its attention from the universe to man himself,
and from cosmogony to morality and politics. Up until the
first third of the fifth century, philosophy, whether in Ionia or
in Magna Graecia, had sought to reveal the secrets of the
universe. That is true not only of Thales, Anaximander, and
Anaximenes, but also of Heraclitus, Parmenides, and
Empedocles. But by Pericles' time, the age of these 'masters
of truth' was over.

Anaxagoras was one of a number of known masters whose
teaching Pericles followed. He was born in Asia Minor, but
had come to live in Athens. In his *Life of Pericles*, Plutarch
presents Anaxagoras as a rationalist. He tells us the story of a
single-horned ram whose head had been brought to Pericles.
The diviner Lampon interpreted the phenomenon as an omen,
but Anaxagoras opened up the head and produced a purely
physiological explanation. Where the one saw a divine action,
the other used science and observation. The same rational
tendency reappears at the end of the *Life of Pericles*, when,
using the corner of his cloak to demonstrate how an eclipse
works, the statesman shows a helmsman that he should not
be frightened by it. The mid-fifth century was shedding its
superstitions. On the other hand, while Anaxagoras, like his
predecessors, had a system of the world to offer, for him what

made that system work was not the elements, chance, or necessity, nor even love or strife, but Mind (*nous*). And this was close to an idea of intelligible causes and explanations that are accessible to human reason. In the *Phaedo*, Socrates gives an entertaining account of his delight when he came across this theory of Anaxagoras'. He thought that it would now be possible to explain everything by showing what was for the best in each particular case and working out comprehensible intentions. In other words, Socrates, who for his part was soon to try to evolve a philosophy entirely centred upon man, thought that he had discovered in Anaxagoras a guide and a philosophy to show him the way forward. But he went away disappointed. There had certainly seemed to be a hint, a possibility; but, later, this text, still maintaining the same light tone, records Socrates' discomfiture as he reads on, abandoning his high hopes when, instead of final causes, he finds Anaxagoras putting into play a variety of irrational material elements. Those material causes come as a disappointment to him. He fancies that if the question were put why Socrates is sitting in this particular place, Anaxagoras would rake together a thousand and one material explanations, saying that his body is composed of bones and nerves and functions in such or such a fashion, but he would fail to produce the true reason, namely that, under sentence of death, he, Socrates, has deemed it best to sit here, right to remain here to wait for the death sentence to be carried out.

His hopes were thus raised only to be dashed. This remarkable passage in the *Phaedo* certainly shows that Anaxagoras represented a measure of progress towards human and rational explanations, but also that that progress was deemed insufficient by his successors.

Another example of a development that is sketched in but soon superseded is presented by Diogenes of Apollonia, a less well-known philosopher who also came to live in Athens and whose interests are believed to have lain in the medical field as well as in teleological explanations.

Soon, however, the crucial step was taken. Democritus of Abdera was one of the fathers of atomism, a man who was still seeking to explain the universe but this time in an objective and materialist fashion. Moreover, as well as a treatise on the order of the universe, he had written one on the human order. This compatriot of Protagoras can thus, like Socrates, be accounted a moral philosopher.

Clearly, the influence of the 'Physicists' was still felt. That is why, in *The Clouds*, Aristophanes lumps their preoccupations together with those of Socrates and presents the latter as being absorbed in 'celestial matters' (thereby completely missing Socrates' originality).

For with Socrates, everything changed: now all that counted was man and the ends that he proposed; what mattered was the good. In a single generation, philosophy moved into a different domain and set off in a different direction. In fact, the change was so fundamental that it has become customary to refer to all the philosophers before Socrates as a group, as the pre-Socratics—a term in which the Sophists tend to be included, even though Socrates was their contemporary. (He was twenty years younger than Protagoras, the eldest, and twenty years older than the youngest of them.) Yet they were moving in the same direction as he was and the parallelism between them testifies to a deep-seated tendency towards an increasingly human and rational philosophy. The fact that the movement affected a series of thinkers hailing from different cities explains how the burgeoning philosophy started to develop simultaneously in a number of locations quite distant from one another. The ground was already prepared.

Meanwhile, as the reader will possibly have realized, descriptions of the universe were, for their part, becoming more scientific and rational. At the very moment when Socrates' philosophy was turning to man himself, thereby carving out a new domain for itself, another birth was taking place: the birth of scientific medicine.

At first, medicine had been largely religious or magical. It was supposed to have begun with the god Asclepius and for a long time was based on drugs handed down by tradition or discovered by chance. In the fifth century, people began to want to understand, to know about the human body and how it functioned. It is impossible to say exactly when this happened, for the interest must have developed gradually. For us, medicine as a science begins with Hippocrates. But Hippocrates, who came from Cos, seems to have been born in about 460, as were Thucydides and Democritus. So he cannot have been the first to arouse interest in medicine in the authors of the time. As we have noted, Diogenes of Apollonia took an interest in the human body. (A fragment by him on the veins has come down to us.) More certainly still, Thucydides was at pains to give a careful, clinical description of the plague which broke out at the beginning of the Peloponnesian War, listing all the symptoms that might lead to a diagnosis. But he cannot have been influenced by Hippocrates, who must have been about 30 years old at the time. Likewise, Thucydides' orators repeatedly refer to the model of medicine to justify their political actions. But again, it cannot have been Hippocrates who inspired them to do so. He must have had predecessors.

There had been earlier indications of a new spirit of enquiry and new aspirations. A desire for a better understanding of the physical nature of human beings had clearly been growing over the past decades. Hippocrates was the final product of an evolution in this domain, just as Socrates was in the domain of moral philosophy. From that moment on, rationality and method are explicitly recommended. Some treatises in the so-called Hippocratic Corpus react against the superstitious interpretations of certain diseases. Some elucidate the rules of a rigorous and cautious method. Others explain climatic influences. Yet others set out to describe how the human body functions in a way that was startlingly new at the time, however old-fashioned it inevitably seems to us today. The doctors' concern to be scientific corresponded to their desire to establish a *technē*, just as the Sophists were doing in the political field.

The Sophists had nothing to do with the new burst of activity in the medical field. The continuity of this medical progress and the probable date of the activities of those involved rule out any such possibility. However, the principles underlying medical science, imperfect and inaccurate though this was, may well have attracted and inspired the future Sophists, just as they may have helped to dispose the public kindly towards them. A common spirit prompted the two new movements and inspired the parallel ambitions of the founders of these *technai*.

Significantly enough, the brother of the Sophist Gorgias was a doctor, and Gorgias seems to have had relations with medical circles, which placed him in an advantageous position to assess the roles of on the one hand orators, on the other doctors. That, at least, is what Plato has him say (*Gorgias*, 456 B).

Meanwhile the spirit of *technē* was spreading to an area even closer to the Sophists, namely literary activities. Rhetoric and *technai rhētorikai* certainly existed in Sicily before the Sophists. Corax and Tisias may be little more than names to us, but we know that they were already using arguments based on likelihood and were doing so in a fashion that Socrates calls 'expert and full of skill': *sophon* and *technikon* (*Phaedrus*, 273 B).

Aeschylus, the oldest of the tragedians, died in 456, that is to say, before the middle of the century, and his *Prometheus* contains a passage in praise of all the discoveries that the Titan bequeathed to mankind: ingenious inventions, devices, arts, and means (*sophismata, mēchanēmata, technai, poroi*: the terms crowd one upon the other, to be summed up in line 506 as all the *technai*). Prometheus' discoveries included a variety of material inventions; also, in addition to divination, upon which Aeschylus insists with piety, there were more rational discoveries such as the art of counting and, of course, medicine.

It was a theme so much in keeping with the spirit of the age that both Sophocles and Euripides were soon to take it up themselves, each emphasizing different discoveries and achievements but both, in their own particular ways, celebrating the marvels of civilized life and the skills and techniques upon which it depended. It is a fifth-century leitmotif to which several of the Sophists were also to return. In Plato's *Hippias Major*, Hippias compares the progress of his own skills to the progress of the other arts, which he cites as obvious, and claims that the *technē* of the Sophists is much more scientific than that of the ancients (281 D).

But we anticipate. To return to Aeschylus, it is fair to say that, quite apart from the passage on the triumphant *technai* in the *Prometheus*, the whole of his *œuvre* indicates that the new spirit was already widespread, even in the first half of the century.

His plays are still religious and dominated by the action of the gods: they are, after all, but the starting-point for the tragic genre. But they also raise questions, with the chorus doggedly seeking to understand the idea that the gods are just, and to determine whether there is any truth in it. The old ideas about *hubris* are re-examined in the light of the new faith; arbitrary behaviour on the part of the deity is severely criticized. Moreover, Aeschylus is obsessed with the problem of wrongdoing and punishment. The entire *Oresteia* trilogy seeks to reject the old retributive *lex talionis*, assess responsibility more fairly, and ultimately make men themselves and the city responsible for the maintenance of justice. Behind the plays, we sense a mind in quest of a moral philosophy, and institutions taking shape and becoming more human.

After Aeschylus, it is clear that, while Sophocles' tragedies still convey a strong sense of the sovereignty of the gods, they are concerned not so much with their reasons but rather with how men should respond to them. With tragic heroes, interest is centred upon human action. The strong, uncompromising forces set in opposition in these plays represent different and contrasting attitudes, as might speeches for the prosecution and the defence in a court of law. The focus is definitely shifted from the gods to human beings. Now, when the first of the major Sophists arrived in Athens, Sophocles was already about 50 years old. In his later works, the new fashion may have influenced his style or choice of words here or there, but his basic inspiration clearly owed nothing to the Sophists. This is borne out by the contrast between him and Euripides, for when a dramatist truly was influenced by the Sophists, there was no mistaking the fact.

The evolution of the tragic genre shows that, while a marked step forward may have been taken at the point when the Sophists' influence came to make itself felt, the trend towards human interest and rationality had set in long before, without any involvement at all on the part of the Sophists. On the contrary, the evolution of tragedy itself prepared the ground for the Sophists' actions and for their success.

A similar situation obtained where history was concerned. Herodotus presided over the beginning of the historic genre just as Aeschylus did over the beginning of the tragic. Though still packed with legends, gods, and oracles, his *Enquiry* (as *Historiē* still meant in his day) is the first true work of history; and that is because Herodotus pursued two aims. The first was to produce a rational record of recent events which related not to legend, but to the human world. The second was to submit the statements of the various witnesses to a critical and judicious investigation. Before Herodotus, accounts relating to the past had been chiefly concerned with the founding of towns and the genealogies of heroes. Then Hecataeus of Miletus had tried to adopt a more critical approach, but it still did not occur to him to centre his work upon a specific and coherent sequence of human behaviour. Both early tragedy and Herodotus' history were founded on the principle of concentrating upon human behaviour under pressure from difficult circumstances and irrationality.

It should be added that, like so many other writers, Herodotus ended up in Athens and that the last part of his work, in which Athens itself is the main protagonist, is also the part in which politics and military strategy are the most clearly analysed and irrational legends are remarkable chiefly for their absence or brevity.

True, this was not the critical, positivist kind of history, proudly committed to human reason, that was to be produced by Thucydides, writing after the Sophists. Thucydides' work also marks a definite step forward. All the same, although Herodotus' history reflects the influence of the Sophists only indirectly and in isolated passages, it expresses even in its internal development the very same aspiration towards rationality and human endeavour as is detectable in all the works produced in this century.

If we also remember that this enquiring traveller amassed all kinds of information about the customs of various peoples and, by comparing them, developed a keen sense of their relativity, we shall see, even in the case of his least systematic enquiries, that the spirit informing them led directly on to the relativism of the Sophists and may well have provided them with either a starting-point or at least a justification.

The new spirit of enquiry was putting out shoots in all directions, upsetting the old balance and displacing the old interests. Even the figurative arts testify to that, for in the

first half of the century monsters and all other animals except
the horse disappeared, leaving pride of place to the human
figure, now captured in all its vibrant reality. It was precisely
around 450 that the style known as 'classical' took over. Like
Anaxagoras and Protagoras, Phidias was a friend of Pericles;
and he it was who discovered how to endow to human figure
with a supernatural majesty. His virtuoso technique produced the major chryselephantine, gold, and ivory masterpieces of classical sculpture.

Fundamental changes were thus taking place in every field.
They had long been detectable but became more marked
from the beginning of the fifth century. They may have been
encouraged by the development of political life, which
heightened the citizens' sense of the importance of human
action. Or, alternatively, it may have been the experience of
common, responsible action during the Persian Wars that
speeded up the process. In any event, the new tendency,
which is one of the essential characteristics of Greek civilization, now became particularly noticeable.

That is the only possible explanation for the appearance of
the Sophists' theories at virtually the same moment in places
as distant from each other as Sicily, Abdera in northern
Greece, and Asia Minor. All these thinkers, with their new
ideas, were borne along by the same impetus, an impetus that
accounts for their common success.

But the fact remains that it is in Athens that we find them
all. It was to Athens that they came, here that they found a
welcome, and here that they exerted a profound influence.
Were it not for Athens, we should probably not even know the
name 'Sophist'. And even if we did, it would have no meaning
or interest. Without doubt, the vogue for the Sophists only
came about thanks to a catalyst which Periclean Athens alone
could provide.

The concentration of thinkers and artists in Athens is certainly a striking phenomenon. As we have seen, Anaxagoras of
Clazomenae and Diogenes of Apollonia both settled in the city
and Herodotus lived there for long periods. It was hardly
surprising that they were followed by the Sophists, flocking
in from the Aegean, Sicily, and the islands. Protagoras,

Gorgias, Prodicus, Hippias, and Thrasymachus all lived for long periods in Athens, receiving a princely welcome. It was here that they attracted the disciples who are known to us; here that their influence began to spread, thanks to which other writers preserved such passages from their works and such glimpses of their thought as we possess. The Sophists were part of a general convergence on to the city which certainly played a greater part than anything else in producing the unprecedented flowering of Athenian literature. In the early years, Athenian literature had been of less significance than the works that came out of Asia Minor and the islands. But with all the talent that it managed to attract in the fifth century, Athens now assumed pride of place.

The general movement towards Athens was not prompted solely by the presence of the Sophists; and although the other reasons for the congregation of so many writers at the foot of the Acropolis may be obvious, it is worth pausing to consider them. The first reason is clearly power. Athens had emerged from the Persian Wars as the major victor. During the wars, she had assumed the place of leader of all the Greeks engaged in the struggle against the barbarians, and she had retained that position ever since. She had organized the former allies into a confederation—the Delian League—and gradually, being the only wealthy State as well as the only one with a navy, she had seized the chance of the slightest show of recalcitrance to impose her law by force. The confederation had become her empire. The federal exchequer had found its way to Athens, where each federated city duly presented its tribute. In return for guaranteeing the freedom of the seas, Athens used that tribute as she saw fit: to fund the construction of the Acropolis, for instance. Furthermore, Athens had become the major centre of maritime trade and this brought her even greater wealth. She had established delegates, or even colonies, in the islands. In all kinds of litigations, the island inhabitants had to seek justice before the Athenian courts. Within a space of fifty years, Athens had become the principal city in the whole of maritime Greece. The fleet, which had always been maintained by the contributions from her allies, which were mainly devoted to that end, had become so powerful by the beginning of the Peloponnesian War that Pericles could boast that nothing could challenge her supremacy.

Athens devoted much of her wealth to beauty, luxury, and all the trappings of an agreeable life. The funeral speech that Thucydides attributes to Pericles for those fallen in the war makes that point forcefully:

We have provided for the spirit many relaxations from toil: we have games and sacrifices regularly throughout the year and homes fitted out with good taste and elegance; and the delight we each day find in these things drives away sadness. And our city is so great that all the products of all the earth flow in upon us. (2. 38)

Not surprisingly, all this power and luxury attracted hordes of foreigners—just as any big city attracts people from the provinces.

Moreover, Athens' victory in the Persian Wars, the source of all its later power, still surrounded her with an aura of incomparable prestige a whole generation or half-century after the event. All the Greek cities had had cause to fear the barbarian foe and all regarded Athens as their liberator, the city which, through her courage and resolution as much as by the force of her arms, had earned the gratitude and admiration of all. All the orators' speeches in Thucydides and all the praises showered upon Athens even in the fourth century revert constantly to that moment of glory and the wish to be associated with it. When a writer such as Herodotus, in Asia Minor, decided to devote himself to the history of the Persian Wars, he could not but have wished to live in the city that was the heroine in that struggle. Another who must have done so was Gorgias, who hailed from one of the States of Magna Graecia that had taken part in the war, sending ambassadors to Athens to request her aid—Gorgias, who was later to argue for a new Greek union. Men such as these must also have wanted to stay on in Athens, in the city that was the very embodiment of their ideal. The capital of Greece and its islands was also the guardian of the Panhellenic tradition which the Peloponnesian War was to cloud somewhat in the last third of the century but which, under Pericles, still retained all its force. So, in 443, when Pericles conceived the plan for a Panhellenic colony at Thurii, it was certainly not by mere chance that Herodotus volunteered for the expedition and became a citizen of the new colony, while Protagoras was responsible for devising its laws.

The wealth and prestige of Athens were two of the causes for the great concentration of talent in the city under Pericles. But there were others. Athens stood not only for Greek liberty from barbarian interference but also for political liberty pure and simple, for since the beginning of the century it had been striking out along the then uncharted paths of democracy. The most decisive reforms in this respect took place in 460, which was also the year in which Pericles came to power. It was a moment when everything seemed a new invention, a new discovery. As contemporary writers have noted, the empire and the fleet no doubt played a crucial role in this evolution, for the sailors were men of the people who had by now become more important than the knights and the hoplites. In any event, democracy was becoming increasingly firmly established. Even the building of the Acropolis was partly undertaken to provide work for the people, as Plutarch has pointed out in his *Life of Pericles*. The programme as a whole has sometimes been described as Periclean 'state socialism'.

Small wonder that such a way of life and such a spirit of liberty attracted to the city those frustrated by the oppression of tyranny or the rigidity of oligarchy in their own home-lands. Small wonder that it also attracted men interested in political problems and anxious to understand the possibilities of liberty and the means of safeguarding it. It must even have drawn those who were already becoming alarmed at the risks attendant upon excessive liberty. Above all, of course, it must have acted as a magnet upon those whose very activities were justified by the role that was now conferred upon citizens: namely the Sophists, who taught men how to distinguish themselves through speech and for whom Athens was the perfect place in which to exercise their profession.

Finally, we should also bear in mind one particular feature of the Athenian spirit of freedom, namely the fact that all these gifted and brilliant men from the rest of the Greek world were at liberty to come to Athens and settle there, if they wished to do so. Athens had always taken pride in the welcome and hospitality that it extended to foreigners. This is not the place to study the contributions made to Athens' wealth and size by marriage, adoption, and naturalization long before, in the distant past. Since then, a certain retrenchment had taken place; and, as citizens acquired ever more important rights, Athens became increasingly fastidious in the granting of citizenship. On the other hand, the city welcomed foreigners with open arms. They were allowed to settle there and, short of becoming citizens, could participate fully in Athenian life. Such was Athens' deliberate policy, and she took pride in it. She even boasted of this difference between her and Sparta, where the expulsion of foreigners (*xenēlasia*) was common practice and regarded as a method of preserving law and order and also of protecting the city's defence secrets. In the same funeral speech that celebrates the brilliance and luxury of Athenian life, Thucydides draws attention to this characteristic:

We are also superior to our opponents in our system of training for warfare, and this in the following respects. In the first place, we throw our city open to all the world and we never by exclusion acts debar any one from learning or seeing anything which an enemy might profit by observing if it were not kept from his sight. (2. 39. 1).

Hospitality of this kind can be as important as power to a country's well-being. Throughout history, it can be observed to have happy effects for the States which practise it, one example—*mutatis mutandis*—being the twentieth-century United States of America, where European intellectuals and professors play a role of such importance.

Perhaps it could be objected that Athens' record for hospitality towards foreign intellectuals is not unmarked by moments of crisis. With Pericles at its head, the democracy possessed an educated and aristocratic leader. He liked to surround himself with brilliant people and gave them his protection. He was friendly with everybody who was anybody in the domain of thought and art. But, for that very reason, when he himself ran into difficulties and, later, when he died, his brilliant entourage had to pay the price, and came under attack for impiety. When times were hard for the people, they turned against the innovators and rejected them. Aspasia, the

cultivated Milesian woman whom Pericles loved, was prosecuted for impiety; and later, Protagoras seems to have
fallen under similar attack, with his books being condemned
to be burned in public. But that is what tends to happen
anywhere in times of political upheaval and war. The foreigners did not come under particular fire *qua* foreigners: in fact,
we know of only two cases in which the death sentence was
passed on intellectuals and both were Athenians. The first
was Antiphon, condemned to death in 411 for his part in the
oligarchic coup of the Four Hundred. The second was
Socrates, designated as the scapegoat for all the innovations
introduced by others, and executed in 399.

Thus Athens, well known for its great hospitality, turned
against the foreigners only in so far as they, alongside others,
had taken part in movements of thought which the city now
deemed to be linked to its misfortunes. Athens was never
xenophobic.

That absence of xenophobia was yet another factor in the
attraction that Athens exerted upon the most brilliant minds
from Greek cities all around. The consequences were clearly
incalculable: up to the fifth century, virtually the only
Athenian writer known to us is Solon; but between 450 and
350, Greece's greatest century, we know of hardly any texts
that are not Athenian: only one or two fragments of history or
lyric stand out from the surrounding darkness. Thanks to her
circumstances and the influx of talent from outside her,
Athens, for a few short years, *was* Greece. That is certainly a
fact of capital importance. But from our own present point of
view, the convergence of so many brilliant minds upon
Athens produced other consequences too. Not only did
foreigners flock to Athens, but they met one another there. In
the imaginary scene in Plato's *Protagoras*, we find several of
the greatest Sophists gathered in Callias' house: Protagoras,
Hippias, and Prodicus. The contacts that they made in Athens
must have stimulated all these thinkers, encouraging discussion, developing their ideas, or, alternatively, defining
their limits and fostering an abiding, if latent, spirit of competition. In the same dialogue, moreover, the foreigners are
surrounded by a whole group drawn from the Athenian élite
including, among others, the two sons of Pericles and

Eryximachus (the doctor) and the young Phaedrus. They were soon to be joined by Alcibiades and Critias. It is reasonable to suppose that Plato may have embroidered somewhat upon the real situation and that gatherings which included all these men at once were not necessarily daily events. However, there would be no point to the fiction had a wide range of contacts not truly constituted an essential factor in this intense intellectual ferment.

This brings us to the next point, which concerns not so much what it was that drew the Sophists to Athens, but what the Athenians hoped to gain from foreigners in general and the Sophists in particular. The expectations were high, both individually and on the part of the city as a whole. For each individual, as well as the city in general, desired urgently and ardently to learn how to engage in debate on political, legal, and moral problems.

Athens was a direct democracy. If he knew how to express himself, any of her citizens could make a name for himself and acquire influence. Whoever had a chance of making his name heard thus owed it to himself to cultivate his talents at all costs. By doing so, he would be in a position to air his views in the Assembly or plead a case before a court of law. As for citizens who were less well placed, they wanted to be trained to understand, to pass criticism, and to express approval. For at the end of the day, they themselves would have to cast their votes on political matters and legal cases. It was essential for the citizens of a city such as Athens to know how to argue their case and make up their minds on the rights and wrongs of the issues put before them; and this was particularly important for young men of talent who were capable of taking part in political struggles.

Many people have wondered whether the teaching that the Sophists brought to these young men favoured any particular line. It is a problem that we shall tackle in due course,[5] but in a sense it is a somewhat artificial one. After all, there is no reason why all the Sophists should have held the same views. Some belonged to Pericles' entourage; others were among those who promoted oligarchy. It is important to understand

---

[5] See Ch. 8.

that what they purveyed above all was a *technē* rather than a concrete political programme. And that *technē* was indispensable to anyone who wished to play his part as a counsellor of the people. It presupposed the existence of democratic institutions and of a group of aristocratic young men of means. In Athens, both were indeed present.

But merely to note these purely pragmatic aspects involving individual ambitions and careers would be to fail to do justice to the situation. The point is that, as they exercised their powers of argumentation and judgement, the Athenians were embarking upon a quest that all the existing circumstances predisposed them to pursue with passionate eagerness.

Athens had come to maturity amid the developments described above—developments which set an increasingly high value upon human beings and their faculty of reason. As its drama shows, it had turned its attention to problems concerning ethics, law, war, and peace. In the course of the Persian Wars and during the decades that followed, Athens had proved herself to be the major maritime power and was proud of her navy and her skills of manœuvre. Athens represented the spearhead of progress and *technē*, in contrast to the conservative Sparta. At the same time, she was coming to grips with all the problems of democracy. She was thus simultaneously discovering and trying to resolve all kinds of problems to do with institutions, wages, warfare, and strategy; and others too, concerning the administration of an empire, the relations between law and force, the validity of treaties, the exercise of supreme command by a single individual, and the effects of fear or naïve hope. A greater understanding of human nature was thus evolving with passionate haste. Meanwhile, greater understanding of human nature was also what the Sophists' teaching, starting with their rhetoric, was offering and establishing. What the Sophists had to offer was exactly what the Athenians were ardently seeking. Each side provided stimulus for the other. The Sophists seemed as essential to fifth-century Athens as brilliantly effective physicists would be in the event of an atomic war in the twentieth century.

The success of the Sophists was linked in every respect with the surge of Athenian democracy. Together with the other circumstances considered above, this fundamental connection explains the enthusiasm with which they were received in the second half of the fifth century in Athens, where the coincidence of a wide range of factors seems to have prepared the ground for precisely what they had to offer.

However, the very enthusiasm of their reception masked various dangers, the effects of which were soon to make themselves felt, in the form of critical or positively hostile reactions. It is natural for innovators to run up against resistance; and teachers who train people to be adept at arguing a case whatever the point of view, sweeping aside the most deeply rooted traditions in the process, particularly expose themselves to resistance. To be considered shocking may be the price of their success.

But there was more to it than that in the case of the Sophists. It is certainly no surprise to find Aristophanes mocking and attacking them. But Euripides, who was so strongly influenced by them, also criticizes them on a number of occasions. Socrates too spent time in their company, yet Plato's entire œuvre is devoted to showing them being confounded by him. And Isocrates, who followed in their footsteps, himself becoming a teacher of rhetoric, launched his own school with a publication entitled *Against the Sophists*. Athenian reactions to the Sophists thus amounted to rather more than the normal level of resistance to be expected in the event of any innovations of a somewhat daring nature. A positive movement of rejection is detectable, a desire to refute the Sophists, to warn against them, and to correct many of their theses.

It is perfectly possible to be welcoming to foreigners, open to new ideas, and ardently progressive, and yet still to react strongly—all the more so when (as in this case) the imported ideas affect traditions, beliefs, and the very bases of law and morality even more than was at first supposed. In all likelihood, the way that the situation developed soon had the effect of accentuating the differences between the new teachers and their public. It is not unreasonable to suppose that, carried away by their own success as well as by the boundless faith that they placed in their methods and in human reason, the Sophists may have become over-emphatic and, little by little, allowed themselves to go too far.

Curiously enough, though, neither Plato nor Aristotle nor Isocrates nor Xenophon ever attacks those major Sophists whom we have mentioned by name. But all do criticize the 'Sophists' in general or the 'Sophists of today'. This has already been demonstrated elsewhere in connection with Aristotle[6] and it is certainly also true of Plato. A curious text of Xenophon's (*On Hunting*, 13) makes the same point. It constitutes a (seemingly excessively) violent attack against the Sophists, containing passages such as the following:

I am surprised at the sophists, as they are called, because though most of them profess to lead the young to virtue, they lead them to the very opposite . . . the wisdom they profess consists of words and not of thoughts . . . The sophists talk to deceive and write for their own gain.

But this aggressive text twice specifies that it is aimed against 'the Sophists of our generation'. Furthermore, it claims that the Sophists have produced not a single text that suggests that it is our duty to be virtuous. Yet Xenophon himself respectfully recorded Prodicus' apologue showing why Heracles, faced with a choice between Vice and Virtue, opted for Virtue. The implication seems to be that the 'Sophists' of the fourth century were no longer all that their predecessors had been.

If it was simply a case of professional Sophists becoming degenerate, that would have been quite bad enough. But Athens was daily becoming increasingly aware of the danger inherent in theories introduced by them and subsequently exaggerated and distorted by young men of ambition. As we have seen, as early as 423 Aristophanes was criticizing teaching that promoted amoralism, teaching with which he associated not only the Sophists but also Socrates. It was not long before some people, carried along by the fashion of the

---

[6] See J. C. Classen, Aristotle's Picture of the Sophists', in G. B. Kerferd (ed.), *The Sophists and their Legacy*, Hermes Einzelschriften, 44 (Wiesbaden, 1981), 7–24.

moment, began to distort the teaching that they had received more or less directly, and to bring it into discredit.

As a result, the enthusiasm felt by some was soon matched by the violent irritation evoked in others. Plato tells us of this. The picture of the Sophists' devoted disciples painted in the *Protagoras* and cited earlier in this chapter is offset by that of the irritation so forcefully evoked in the *Meno*. When Socrates suggests that the Sophists might be cited as an example of masters of virtue, Anytus hits the roof. Anytus was a politician who was a strategos in 409 and was active in the restoration of democracy in 404. He is best known for having initiated the charges pressed against Socrates. His fury at the mere name of Sophists knows no bounds:

May no kinsman or friend of mine, whether of this city or another, be seized with such madness as to let himself be infected with the company of these men . . . [It is] the young men who pay them money [who are demented] and still more the relations who let the young men have their way; and most of all the cities that allow them to enter and do not expel them, whether such attempt be made by stranger or citizen! . . . Any Athenian gentleman will do [a young man] more good, if he will do as he is bid, than the sophists. (91 c, 92 A–B, 92 E).[7]

Anytus' reaction in this instance is as unjust as Xenophon's criticisms in *On Hunting* (and Plato implies as much, for he has Anytus confess that he has never met the Sophists in person). But it shows just how tempestuous relations between the Sophists and Athens sometimes were.

Yet the resentment and anger was never directed against the major Sophists, nor is it ever expressed by those who came into direct contact with them. The zeal of the Sophists' neophytes on the one hand, and the angry outbursts of their opponents on the other, should certainly not distract our attention from the teaching that must have been given, the debates that must have accompanied it, and the very real influence that it must have exerted. We must try to return to that teaching, try to make out what it was that made for both the success of these masters and also the reactions against them, and see how, little by little, the Athenians assimilated

---

[7] For an echo of this hostility, see the speech *Against Lacritus*, falsely attributed to Demosthenes (39–42).

much of their teaching, correcting and adjusting it as they did so.

Of course, it is a pity that the conditions in which we are forced to make our appraisal of the Sophists' teaching are so unfair to them. As we know, their own writing has disappeared. It never was aimed at a large public, so was seldom copied and did not circulate widely. As a result, it has all been lost. As for the teaching delivered orally, that is, their lectures, however brilliant they may have been, they were clearly ephemeral performances aiming for what Thucydides calls 'the pleasure of the moment'. Lasting concern for humanity and beauty or to produce a 'treasure for always' is not a quality that can be attached to any of the Sophists' writings.

As a result, these masters, one of whom at least declared that for us the only truth lies in appearance, are destined to be known only through the distorting, partial, and biased vision of others who (some of them centuries later) cited occasional sentences from the Sophists in order to criticize or interpret them. For us, they are thus themselves reduced to these relative appearances.

The unfairness of all this is perhaps what strikes us most forcefully about their role in relation to Athens. For whatever has come down to us from their teaching and influence has perforce done so through the mediation of the Athenian authors who assimilated, modified, and rethought their ideas with other, new ends in view.

It is a situation that renders the dialogue with the Sophists particularly difficult to reconstruct, albeit all the more fascinating for that very reason. Their fate is perhaps one that no author would relish but that teachers ought to hope for. For the Sophists were, *par excellence*, the teachers of the age of Pericles.

2

A New Teaching

To appreciate what the Sophists' teaching represented, it is important to understand its great novelty. There was nothing that even remotely resembled what we call further education in Athens; there was, indeed, very little intellectual teaching of any kind.

For the moulding of the young, an aristocratic society depends, first and foremost, on heredity, with the aid of the models that are provided by ancestors, family, and tradition. In such a society, courage and various physical attributes tend to be valued above all else, and so it was with Athens. It had been warfare that, in the first instance, set a high value on these attributes; later, they gradually came to be associated with sport and athleticism. The youth of Athens continued to be brought up in this spirit, even after the establishment of democracy. Literary sources tell us of the various teachers to whom a child would be entrusted. The nature of their specialization is extremely revealing.

First there was the *paidotribēs*, 'the one who trains children'. It was, of course, an athletic training. It took place in the *palaistra* and included all the forms of sport whose importance was emphasized in competitions and games: running and jumping, throwing the javelin and the discus, and certain kinds of wrestling. The essential role of the *paidotribēs* or gymnastic trainer is indicative of the importance attached to physical education. A body that was perfectly formed, strong, supple, and graceful was a major element in the human ideal.

A figure slightly—but only slightly—more familiar in our own idea of education was the *kitharistēs*, or music-master. Of course, the cithara was one particular instrument, but the training associated with it embraced a number of skills. Children learned to sing and dance, nearly always as a chorus. Singing and dancing were also noble activities that were part of the life-style of aristocratic society. Besides, these studies under the *kitharistēs* were expected to produce more than musical competence: they also engendered a sense of discipline and harmony together with all the concomitant moral sensibilities.

We know all this from Plato, who himself, as late as the mid-fourth century, still grounded the education of the Guardians of his ideal city upon music and gymnastics, in accordance with a tradition which had, he said, 'been established in the course of ages'. In *The Republic*, he not only adopts the same programme, but also emphasizes its good sense and effectiveness. In this connection, it is interesting that even at the end of his life, in *The Laws*, he describes men incapable of taking part in a chorus as uneducated (654 A–B). He also explains the decadence of an Athens beset by anarchy as resulting from the lack of discipline that has crept into music (700–1). These two major focuses for the education of children had clearly remained virtually unchanged ever since the fifth century.

In all fairness, however, we should recognize that there was at least a modicum of intellectual education for children. It was dispensed by the *grammatistēs*, the master in charge of reading and writing. But that was the lot: just three teachers, as Socrates reminds us at the beginning of the *Protagoras*, when he speaks of the instruction received from the *grammatistēs*, the *kitharistēs*, and the *paidotribēs* (312 B).[1] All the same, as early as the fifth century, reading and writing involved a study of the poets, that is to say, Homer and the lyric poets. The pupils would copy passages out and learn others by heart. And just as music was expected to inculcate a sense of morality, knowledge of the poets was deemed an initiation into wisdom, morality, politics, and an understanding of living creatures and the world. Protagoras himself says as much, in the dialogue by Plato which bears his name: when the schoolmaster sees that the children have learned their letters, they are

---

[1] This explains why the debates on teaching contain so many references to learning to read and write. Isocrates was later to criticize the Sophists' claim to be able to teach the art of public speaking using the same methods as for the letters of the alphabet (*Against the Sophists*, 10, cited at the end of this chapter).

furnished with works of good poets to read as they sit in class, and are made to learn them off by heart; here, they meet with many admonitions, many descriptions and praises and eulogies of good men in times past, that the boy in envy may imitate them and yearn to become even as they. (325 E – 326 A)

Homer's works, above all, constituted a bible for the young. The Athenians had learned something that we ourselves tend all too often to forget: literature can teach us to live better in our own times.[2]

There is no lack of evidence for this, especially as customs did not greatly change. In Egypt, a schoolboy's papyrus has been discovered in which Homer is used in exercises of writing, paraphrase, and transcription into the modern Greek of the Hellenistic period. Among highly educated people, meanwhile, familiarity with Homer—and memorizing exercises—were so much cultivated that one character from Xenophon's *Symposium* boasts of knowing the entire text by heart, from start to finish. Rhapsodes were in the habit of giving frequent performances of a more or less mimed recitation, so this form of instruction continued and was encouraged even among the adults of privileged circles.

The trouble was that such circles were virtually alone in benefiting from some kind of ongoing instruction. As a general rule, once a young man was educated up to this point, he learned nothing more, except from his experiences in daily life.

In intellectual circles there was, however, one exception to that general rule: philosophers attracted disciples; sometimes the ancient texts even refer to them as 'pupils' (Zeno was Xenophanes' 'pupil'; Gorgias was Empedocles' 'pupil'; and so on). However, we should not give such words too modern an interpretation. The young men no doubt extracted from their master all that he had thought and understood: knowledge and theories concerning the universe, and religious, moral, and even political doctrines. But it is not hard to see that it was a matter of no more than small groups of future

---

[2] The Sophists themselves used the poets as commentaries to their lectures and discussions. Protagoras apparently considered it essential to 'be skilled in the matter of verses' (*Prt.* 338 E). See also the more detailed remarks recorded in e.g. A 29 and 30.

philosophers, prompted by curiosity or admiration, but with no practical aim and submitted to no regular curriculum. These were private relations which only existed within extremely limited circles.

Apart from these exceptions to the rule, there was nothing. Young Athenians could learn a trade from a master specializing in medicine, sculpture, architecture, navigation, or one of a number of the other technical skills that Plato so frequently uses as points of comparison in his dialogues. But they received no systematic intellectual education. They learned simply by living and keeping their eyes open.

Suddenly, these ambulant teachers appeared upon the scene, offering, or rather selling, an education. They taught how to speak, how to reason, how to make decisions—all things that citizens would be expected to do throughout their lives. And they purveyed this knowledge to young people who had already gone through the traditional education. Now something other than athletics and music was available, even something other than the study of the poets of the past. The Sophists gave them arms to win the kind of success that did not depend on strength or courage, but on the deployment of their intelligence.

The philosophers also made use of their intelligence, of course. But, with the Sophists, intelligence was deployed within a new framework and for different ends. Unlike the philosophers, the new teachers were not disinterested theorists in quest of metaphysical truths. The teaching that they dispensed had a practical side to it and was designed to be just as useful in life as any other professional skill or *technē*. But the range of this training was wider than that offered for other professions, for it was the *technē* for citizens.

Hence the difficulty that the Athenians of the day appear to have experienced in defining this teaching; hence the hesitancy of the young man in the *Protagoras*, despite his eagerness to seek it out; hence too the variety of descriptions that the masters themselves applied to their teaching. These new features also account for remarks such as those made by Protagoras at the beginning of the dialogue that bears his name. He explains that the Sophists' art is ancient, but had previously gone unrecognized under a number of disguises:

poetry, initiations, and prophecies, even gymnastics and music. Since the teaching of the Sophists was teaching *par excellence* and the true education for human beings, elements of it could be said to lie unrecognized in every kind of instruction that already existed. But Protagoras is the first to claim for his own art a special place and an independent status.

The prevailing situation in Athens also explains how it was that the Sophists felt doubly confident. To the extent that they had neither rivals nor predecessors to contend with in this domain, they considered themselves masters qualified to provide the whole of man's intellectual education. In contrast to the teaching available for other professions and skills, the lessons that the Sophists gave were designed to produce not more Sophists but brilliant orators, competent citizens, and sharp minds. They set no limits upon their *paideia*. On the other hand, they meanwhile credited themselves with the ability to transmit their teaching in a direct and effective fashion; and they would speak of the *technē* of oratory or politics as they would speak of any particular *technē* with known rules that could easily be learned.

That is why they introduced the innovation of fee-paying, a feature that marks a clear difference between them and Socrates. To request payment would no more have occurred to Socrates than to any of the earlier philosophers whose conversation, of a totally private nature, enriched the minds of those who sought their company. The Sophists, for their part, claimed to possess an immediately effective and transmittable *technē* and the very fact that they demanded payment underlined the effective and practical nature of their lessons. The success that they promised was something that it was reasonable to expect to be paid for, whereas that did not apply to seeking for the truth.

Their teaching thus seemed to be altogether novel and also to answer many existing needs. It suited the new political conditions and fitted in with the current movement of thought in all fields. There had never been anything like it before. It was totally original. In his famous book *A History of Education in Antiquity*, H. I. Marrou has no hesitation in speaking of the Sophists' 'great revolution in teaching' (p. 47).

It is the utter novelty of the Sophists that explains both their extraordinary success and also the wave of euphoria that must have carried them along. There was no limit to their promises, no end to their claims. The Greek verb *epangellein*, meaning 'to proclaim, to promise', recurs time and again in their connection. Their promises do indeed betray an arrogant confidence. In Plato's *Protagoras*, Protagoras tells a prospective pupil:

Young man, you will gain this by coming to my classes, that on the day when you join them you will go home a better man, and on the day after it will be the same; every day you will constantly improve more and more. (318 A)

We will not, at this point, pause to define the term 'better', but simply note that in its ambiguity lies the seed of his differences with Socrates. But one thing is certain: namely, Protagoras' conviction that he will succeed, and succeed fast. In similar vein, when Protagoras is asked whether he is undertaking to make men good citizens, he replies, 'That is exactly the purport of what I profess' (319 A); and elsewhere he forthrightly declares:

Such a one I take myself to be, excelling all other men in the gift of assisting people to become good and true, and giving full value for the fee that I charge. (328 B)

Likewise, in the *Gorgias*, Gorgias is asked:

Is Callicles here correct in saying that you profess to answer any questions one may ask you?

and Gorgias confirms that 'indeed, I was just now making this very profession' (447 D).

They knew everything and taught everything, even the sciences. And in every case, what they offered was not a slow meditation upon principles, but immediate results: all you had to do was learn. It was so simple and it worked so fast: 'By Zeus, if you give him a fee and win him over, he will make you wise too' (*Protagoras*, 310 D). An ironic Socrates mockingly tells the two Sophists of the *Euthydemus*, 'this faculty of yours is such, and is so skilfully contrived, that

anyone in the world may learn it of you in a very short time'
(303 E).[3]

Of course, Socrates' irony renders this testimony suspect:
the two Sophists' claims were no doubt not quite as arrogant
as he makes out. But his words surely do convey the pride
of the new teachers and the amazement that they evoked
in their contemporaries. Some of the Sophists may have
lost their sense of proportion somewhat, for Plato sometimes depicts them as overweeningly arrogant or, as it were,
pontificating from on high.

The Sophists also clearly needed to advertise themselves.
They gave their lessons in the form of a series of talks grouped
around particular topics. But they also offered public sessions
which anybody could attend. These took the form sometimes
of speeches in imaginary cases, sometimes of direct lectures.
Frequently they solicited questions from the audience, and in
answering took the opportunity to develop their own ideas
and at the same time provide direct proof of the effectiveness
of their intellectual method.

The Athenians listened in wonder to these dazzling intellectual performances, regarding them as the most fascinating
of spectacles. Thucydides records Cleon as deploring the
pleasure thus afforded to the citizens, who, even when
attending the Assembly, fell into the habit of behaving as if
attending a Sophist's lecture. The upshot of it all was that a
new breed of men, the intellectuals, began to emerge from
amongst the initiates or semi-initiates. They were destined
for a fine future.

This new breed certainly was a novelty of considerable
proportions. But there was one man, at least, who was easily
confused with them. Socrates remained a philosopher in
the full accepted sense of the term. He charged no fee, nor
did he promise rapid progress. He did not prepare his
listeners for any practical action; on the contrary, he was
constantly restraining the young in their over-eagerness to
launch themselves forward. But he and the Sophists did share
certain characteristics, and he often mixed with them. At

---

[3] See also *Euthd.* 303 C: 'Ah, happy pair! What amazing genius, to acquire
such a great accomplishment *so quickly and in so short a time!*'

a time when the concept of human nature was becoming increasingly important, he too was concerned with human problems and moral ideas. Like them, he loved to argue, define things more closely, and confound his interlocutors. He opposed the Sophists' ends, but his means and methods resembled theirs. However, many Athenians seem to have been misled by appearances. In his attacks against the Sophists, Aristophanes, for instance, whether deliberately or not, lumps all the fashionable intellectuals of the day together with them. He portrays Socrates as being at one with them in all things, as sharing the same scientific interests as the 'Physicists' for example—interests which in reality some of the Sophists, in their quest for knowledge, certainly did embrace, but which the real Socrates rejected. Aristophanes also ascribed to Socrates the avowed ends of the new masters of rhetoric and the famous views expressed by Protagoras. He was not concerned to make fine distinctions; and the Athenians of the day were, in general, probably incapable of doing so. To an outsider, Socrates' group seemed to behave in a similar fashion to the Sophists—which is precisely why Plato is at such pains to point out the differences between them.

One result of this situation was that the new teaching gave rise to two kinds of negative reaction. There were some who deplored the activities of both the Sophists and the philosophers, resenting the prerogatives of all this intellectual society. Others, on the other hand, aimed their criticisms at the Sophists alone, attacking the very characteristics which set them apart from the philosophers. If we bear in mind, furthermore, that their extravagant promises posed fundamental problems of the very possibility of such a training proving successful, it is easy to see that the impact of the new teaching was bound to be a source of fascinated speculation for a long time to come. The written texts that survive from this period are full of such controversies.

The most obvious was constituted by the open clash between intelligence and sport. The emphasis that the Sophists laid on the mind rather than on training young people in the *palaistra* and preparing them for competitive athletic games was the most immediately striking aspect of the new teaching. We know through Aristophanes that simple folk were perturbed about it.

In *The Clouds*, Aristophanes draws attention to the lamentable physical form of the fashionable intellectuals. He describes them as 'palefaced' (102), and has one youth refuse to join their school because he does not want to face the knights with 'all my colour worn and torn away' (120). Elsewhere we are told that they look like 'those Spartans whom we brought from Pylos' (prisoners of war) (186), and that they cannot 'expose themselves too long to the open air' (199). Furthermore, the contrast between the two types of education, the old and the new, is constantly represented as an opposition between the wrangling of intellectuals and the traditional physical training. It is true that the old education promoted self-control and modesty, but *The Clouds* does not so much dwell on those virtues as paint one physical portrait in order to contrast it with another. The text is so telling and so charming that it is worth citing it at some length, in particular the passage describing what awaits the young man if he makes a wise choice:

> You'll excel in the games you love well,
>   all blooming, athletic and fair;
> Not learning to prate as your idlers debate,
>   with marvellous, prickly dispute,
> Nor dragged into Court day by day to make sport
>   in some small disagreeable suit;
> But you will below to the Academe[4] go
>   and under the olives contend
> With your chaplet of reed, in a contest of speed
>   With some excellent rival and friend,
> All fragrant with woodbine and peaceful content
>   and the leaf which the lime blossoms fling,
> When the plane whispers love to the elm in the grove
>   in the beautiful season of Spring.
> If then you'll obey and do what I say,
> And follow with me the more excellent way,
> Your chest shall be white, your skin shall be bright
> Your arms shall be tight, your tongue shall be slight,
> And everything else shall be proper and right.

---

[4] Academe: i.e. the gymnasium.

But if you pursue what men nowadays do,
You will have, to begin, a cold pallid skin,
Arms small and chest weak, tongue practised to speak,
Special laws very long, and the symptoms all strong
Which show that your life is licentious and wrong.

(1002–19)

Without even touching upon the moral considerations involved, Aristophanes here caricatures the intellectual in contrast to the comely youth who is a product of the traditional education.

The antipathy comes over loud and clear. It no doubt reflects the considerable degree of suspicion with which these debaters with their free-wheeling minds were regarded. All sorts of other details convey a definite resentment and alarm. The word *amathia*, which constituted a convenient shorthand for both ignorance and stupidity, was obviously designed to be derogatory and was almost always used with that sense. But those who were hostile to the new Sophistic spirit now, by way of reaction, began to sing the praises of *amathia*. In Thucydides' *History*, the King of Sparta praises the education of his fellow citizens because it fosters a sufficient degree of *amathia* to prevent them from ever deeming themselves above the laws (1. 84. 3); and the Athenian Cleon declares that he prefers *amathia* accompanied by wisdom to a combination of cleverness and too much freedom (3. 37. 3). There must have been plenty like him who reserved their praises for good old-fashioned common sense in reaction to these disturbing, individualistic intellectuals. Such reactions reflect the gap that was opening up.

Conversely, some Athenians now began to lampoon the athletes. They would probably not pick upon a young man as accomplished as the one portrayed by Aristophanes. But just as *The Clouds* mocked the professional intellectuals, these critics now derided the sports enthusiasts who set such store by physical strength, sportsmen who, as it happened, were tending more and more to become specialized professional athletes. Euripides thus frequently derides sheer physical strength which is nothing really, or may even be positively harmful when marked by *amathia*. One of our most telling texts here is a long fragment from a satyrical drama, the *Autolycus*, which constitutes a powerful attack against the athletes: 'Of all the evils from which Greece suffers, none is worse than the race of athletes.' All they can think of is their training; they have no idea of how to live. So the Greeks are quite wrong to flock to admire them:

> It would be better to crown men of worth[5] and appreciate those who know how to act for the good of the city and use their words to shield it from evils.

Two life-styles are set in contrast: on the one hand that of the professional athlete, on the other that of the citizen who is capable not only of thinking but also of expressing his thoughts. It is interesting to note a characteristic shift of expression in the Greek here: to describe those who are 'gentlemen', Euripides eschews the traditional 'handsome and good' and coins another expression which evokes intellectual qualities too. He calls such people 'knowledgeable and good'.[6]

In other plays, the opposition between physical strength and intellectual qualities can also be detected, albeit in relation to rather different problems. The theme constitutes a visible thread that runs through all kinds of different contexts. One example is constituted by the famous argument in the *Antiope* cited, in point of fact, in the *Gorgias*. Here, two brothers represent two contrary ways of life, the one active, the other contemplative. Amphion, the 'contemplative' brother, is unaffected by the teaching of the Sophists: he believes in artistic gifts; he does not seek success at all, preferring a life of retirement, in the old manner. Yet he also favours wisdom and reflection, rather than physical strength, and he regards *amathia* as a terrible scourge. Even this, rather different, debate, in which we can sense a measure of disillusionment on the part of the author, testifies to the abrupt change of orientation effected by the introduction of

---

[5] Isocrates, similarly, begins his *Panegyricus* by expressing his astonishment that athletes are honoured with crowns rather than those who serve their country through good judgement and speech.

[6] In the Greek, the first term is *sophous*.

the Sophists' new teaching, a change to which their promises and demands had suddenly drawn attention.

Setting a higher value upon intellectual qualities and regarding them as more useful than anything else may have constituted a kind of revolution and that revolution may indeed have stirred up a certain unease. However, that does not mean to say that unanimous agreement existed about the correct role of those qualities or how they should be used. In this connection a different set of questions was raised and other protests were made, this time by the philosophers. Provided they were paid, the Sophists promised relatively prompt practical success. In the eyes of the philosophers, that is Socrates and his disciples, this was misguided, for it meant turning one's back upon the true and the good, in short following quite the wrong path.

Neither Socrates nor Plato, who followed him, despised the activities of a citizen and his participation in the city's affairs. But such activities depended upon obtaining a certain maturity, through a lengthy and disinterested preparation, and they felt deeply hostile towards the suspect haste encouraged by the Sophists.

In the last analysis, this is the issue which introduces the note of bitterness into the clash between Callicles and Socrates, in the *Gorgias*. Callicles, whose hospitality Gorgias enjoys, is full of indignation at the sight of Socrates continuing, at his age, to philosophize, instead of launching himself into an active life. Philosophy is recommended for the young,

> but when I see an elderly man still going on with philosophy and not getting rid of it, that is the gentleman, Socrates, whom I think in need of a whipping. For as I said just now, this person, however well endowed he may be, is bound to become unmanly through shunning the centres and marts of the city in which, as the poet said, 'men get them note and glory' (485 C–D)

and he reminds Socrates that if charges are ever pressed against him, he will not know how to defend himself, and will be condemned to death. Socrates counters with the view that death is not necessarily the worst thing that can happen to a man. He suggests that the success that Callicles seeks may involve him in slavery and corruption:

Let us therefore take as our guide the doctrine now disclosed, which indicates to us that this way of life is best—to live and die in the practice alike of justice and all other virtue. (527 E)

It is hard to imagine two points of view more profoundly and dramatically opposed.

Of course, as we have already noted, Callicles is not himself a Sophist (and this is a point to which we shall be returning). But his ambition and his desire for fame and glory are characteristic of what the youth of Athens expected from the Sophists. And while the Sophists themselves may not have displayed such a passionate egoism as their ardent pupil, they were clearly not moved solely by a desire for the truth. As they were the first to admit, their teaching, as a *technē*, had first and foremost a practical end.

Could things conceivably have been otherwise? Who could blame them? No city can consist purely of philosophers meditating on the essences of things. It needs a certain sense of the realities to flourish in it too. It needs capable people trained to take part readily in its political deliberations and also men competent to defend themselves with a certain fluency before a court of law. It needs citizens who 'know about everything'. True, anyone who reads the dialogue is bound to side with Socrates against Callicles, is bound to be against ambition and for philosophy. Yet, in the last analysis, Socrates' ideal turns out to be as exceptional as it is admirable. No one, in any city state, would dream of extending it to all and sundry.

Plato deliberately set out to make fun of the Sophists' pragmatism and the quick results that they were expecting. In doing so, he made use of irony in every form imaginable, from the most obvious to the most subtle. Following Aristophanes' sarcastic sallies at the intellectuals, and Euripides' at the athletes, it was now a philosopher's turn to aim his irony at these teachers concerned with practical skills. Athens seems to have been a place where it was difficult to introduce new ideas without attracting mockery from all sides.

Plato's ironical sallies follow hard one upon another as he

describes the promises held out by the Sophists, their confidence, and their success. He is perhaps at his sharpest when
he is concerned with Sophists of the second rank. His picture
of the two brothers in the Euthydemus is as hard-hitting as a
satirical comedy. But in this same dialogue, he cloaks his
sarcasm more subtly to describe the new teachers as operating
on the borders between philosopher and politician (305 c) and
scores a point against them remarking that the position of
any intermediary is bound to be no more than approximate.
The expression was one that he had borrowed from Prodicus,
and it is one that is echoed in the sally aimed at Isocrates, at
the end of the *Phaedrus*. Isocrates, he notes, inspires a measure of hope, for his mind does possess 'some philosophy'
(the point being that Isocrates was extremely old at the
time). Such remarks convey a good enough idea of the
difference—and the disagreement—between the Sophists
and the philosophers.

At any rate, one way or another, be it through spirited
criticism, falsely patronizing airs, sarcasms, or indirect
allusions, the Sophists were under attack from all sides. The
constant reproach against them was that they thought they
were teaching something useful, but in reality only true
philosophers are capable of doing so.

The confusion that threatened to mislead the public, which
was inclined to lump Socrates and the Sophists all together,
undoubtedly made Plato all the more anxious to draw a clear
distinction between them, and to emphasize it in such a way
as to get people to accept it. As we have seen, that confusion is
apparent in Aristophanes; but what is more, to a large extent
it lay behind the accusations which were later made against
Socrates (of corrupting the young and not believing in the
city gods), and we should not forget that it was Anytus, who
attacks the Sophists so violently in the *Meno*, who was behind
those accusations. Plato is no doubt being less than ingenuous
when he makes Anytus admit that he has never personally
encountered any of the Sophists, so his violent attack on them
may well be quite unjustified—as are the barely veiled
threats that he directs at Socrates himself. However that may
be, though, it is perfectly understandable that Plato should
have determined to clarify all these confusions—as indeed

did Xenophon, who in the text from *On Hunting* cited earlier, is careful to make it clear that he is referring to 'the sophists, not the philosophers'.

However, it was not just a matter of personalities. The distinction between the two groups was absolutely fundamental. It is even fair to say that Plato's deep sense of that distinction stamped its imprint upon the whole of his thought. It was partly in reaction to the Sophists that he, for his part, determined to establish the principles of a rigorous, even absolute idealism. Two different ways of thinking and teaching thus emerged in opposition to each other. As against the practical haste of the Sophists, Plato rallied to the word first launched by the Pythagoreans: he declared himself to be not a wise man (*sophos*) or a 'master of wisdom', but a 'philosopher', that is to say, 'a lover of wisdom'. In contrast to the confidence that the Sophists placed in practical results, he would accept only one objective, however arduous the quest that it involved, namely the truth. These very different ends corresponded to two equally different systems of thought.

Plato never represented his Socrates as treating the great, early Sophists with disdain. However, Plato himself does not rest until he has clearly defined and stigmatized all that the Sophists in general, and even 'the Sophist' as a philosophical concept, represented. The distinction between Sophist and philosopher dictated the orientation of not only his own thought, but Greek thought in general.

The criticisms that he formulates against the Sophists thus help us to understand not only his own radical demands, but also, conversely, the originality of the ambitions that inspired the teaching of the Sophists.

The very ambitions of the Sophists posed a number of problems, one of which might be regarded simply as a preliminary one. In fact, however, it is essential. Given the context of fifth-century Athens, it is not surprising to find that this problem, more widely debated than any other, is also the most abstract and the most fundamental of all. It calls into question the very possibility of any kind of teaching being so effective.

As we have already noted, in an aristocratic society virtue is regarded as innate. If one possesses it, it is either a chance of birth or, more usually, a result of heredity. The way to strengthen it in practical life is to imitate one's ancestors. This idea frequently recurs in Pindar; and Sophocles was still defending it at the time of the Peloponnesian War. His Electra and his Ajax owe their greatness to that of their forefathers. Even more clearly, his *Philoctetes* shows how, despite Odysseus' influence, the true nature of the son of Achilles will out in the end in all its force. 'Nature' is a word that is used again and again in this play, and the young man's sudden decision is presented as a triumph for hereditary virtues: 'You have shown your nature and true origin' (1310). Perhaps Sophocles' very insistence upon this point betrays his need to react against the new ideas that he had seen to be spreading. The Sophists' most revolutionary innovation was, precisely, that, faced with nature, they set up teaching to counteract it and considered that virtue could be learned by attending their classes.

In the eyes of modern readers, the question as thus posed may seem somewhat theoretical, almost pedantic, even purely scholastic. But set in the context of fifth-century Athens, with its new school of teaching and the social innovation that this implied, the problem becomes a burning and pressing issue.

It had arisen directly from the bold new venture of the Sophists. At least, it was that venture and its success that gave the issue a degree of urgency which it is perhaps difficult to appreciate today. Can virtue really be taught, can it be learned? Is teaching more important than heredity? Overnight everyone in Athens became obsessed with this problem. The terms and questions in which it is expressed are always the same, whether they occur in the treatises of philosophers or in literary works, and whether the latter take the form of tragedies or histories. The all-pervasive character of this closely argued debate is a measure of the excitement aroused by the confidence that the new teachers professed in the success of their teaching.

This is, in fact, the very question that constitutes the subject of the dialogue that Plato devotes to the first of the great

Sophists: the *Protagoras* openly debates the question of 'whether or not virtue can be taught'. It is a subtle dialogue and somewhat disturbing, precisely because Socrates, too, is of the opinion that virtue can be taught, since it is a matter of knowledge. But he does not believe that it can be taught in the fashion advocated by Protagoras, nor that it is as simple a matter as the latter believes. Socrates is doubtful about the Sophists' programme as a whole, and it is to this somewhat preliminary critique of his that Protagoras attempts to respond, drawing first upon myth, then upon argumentation.

We will not go into the details of the discussion, the reference to the education provided by the city, Protagoras' promises, or his embarrassment when required to produce a strict definition of this virtue that he is proposing to disseminate (is there one kind or are there many?) or to answer other thorny questions that Socrates sets before him. The important thing is for us to register the fundamental problem that is so clearly presented here and is so closely bound up with the claims of the great Sophist.

Moreover, another dialogue, the *Meno*, is from start to finish concerned with the same problem. The very first words are:

Can you tell me, Socrates, whether virtue can be taught, or is acquired by practice, not teaching? Or if neither by practice nor by learning, whether it comes to mankind by nature or in some other way? (70 A)

Here too the answers take a nuanced form. But here too they are clearly aimed at the Sophists (and we have already noted the indignation with which Anytus sounds off against them on this occasion).

It is quite clear that this was a topic that aroused an unprecedented degree of interest and that the programme put forward by the new teachers provoked a huge intellectual reaction. Nor was the excitement limited to philosophical circles. It affected all kinds of thinkers. For every one of the thinkers of the period, Sophists and non-Sophists alike, there is evidence—a fragment, an indirect report, an allusion, or some other indication—to show that they were, to a greater or lesser degree, involved in the controversy in which heredity was opposed to education. Everyone seems to have wanted to have his say on the extent to which virtue was teachable. The anonymous text known as *Double Arguments*, which seems to be by one of Protagoras' disciples,[7] is entitled 'On Wisdom and Virtue: Whether they can be Taught'. By way of summarizing the views of those who do not believe such teaching to be possible, it sets out several of the arguments that Plato uses in the *Protagoras* (where are the teachers? why have eminent men not taught these virtues to their sons? how is it that some pupils follow instruction without result, while others distinguish themselves without ever having been taught how to? and so on). The author then briefly refutes these objections and, with regard to the anomalies evident in results, remarks that natural talents clearly do play their part: 'Of course, nature does come into it too.' Then, in one brief sentence, he uses the argument to be found developed at great length in Plato's *Protagoras*, which describes the anonymous education that is provided for children by the city. In itself, this text is not of great interest: it seems to be a collection of arguments that were already well known. However, set alongside the *Protagoras*, it provides startling proof of the extent to which Plato was reproducing discussions that really had taken place and theses that had in truth been defended. Furthermore, the very terseness of the style of the *Double Arguments*, which gives the treatise its air of a school exercise, is an indication of the degree to which these debates had become regular practice.

It is even more interesting to note that they were by no means limited to philosophical circles, whether these were composed of the Sophists themselves or their adversaries. This debate, which seems to us so abstract, was taking place on all sides. It was surfacing in both literature and in the theatre and was determining attitudes to the political situation and to the moral aspects of life, as is shown by testimony provided in the first of those areas by Thucydides and in the second by Euripides.

Thucydides does not go into the theoretical problem. However, the pattern of his thinking about the war and his

---

[7] See below, pp. 76–77.

way of reporting it is altogether determined by an opposition
between two forms of excellence and two forms of courage.
The Athenians represent a lucid courage born of experience
and rational expertise. The Spartans' courage rests upon
innate valour and tradition. In the speeches in book 1, the
orators of the two camps set in opposition the respective
advantages of these two forms of excellence. And in the
speeches that they make to their men, the leaders who
confront one another in the first naval battle of the war
undertake lengthy analyses related to the same theme. On the
one side, courage is said to come from the confidence that
stems from experience; on the other, natural valour is
regarded as essential for the application of knowledge. The
burning question of the moment even creeps into the
exhortations delivered on the very field of action. Seen from
one point of view or from the other, the problem crops up
apropos of everything and sometimes apropos of nothing at
all.

As for Euripides, time and again he returns to the question,
sometimes at the most unexpected moments. The most
striking example comes in *Hecuba*. When the old queen learns
of the death of her daughter, slaughtered by the Greeks,
instead of the despair that one might have expected, after
four or five lines of lamentation, the audience is treated to a
meditation on the powers of education:

> But how strange it seems.
> Even worthless ground, given a gentle push
> from Heaven, will harvest well, while fertile soil,
> starved of what it needs, bears badly.

(In other words: whatever is later used to cultivate a field is
more important than the original quality of the earth itself.)

> But human nature never seems to change;
> evil stays itself, evil to the end,
> and goodness good, its nature uncorrupted
> by any shock or blow, always the same,
> enduring excellence.   Is it our blood
> or something we acquire? But goodness can be taught,
> and any man who knows what goodness is

knows evil too, because he judges
from the good.

The digression is so surprising that Euripides himself
indirectly acknowledges the fact: Hecuba breaks off, to return
to her grief, saying:

> But all this is the rambling nothing
> of despair.

> (592–602)

Coming as it does, at such a moment of pathos, a digression of
this kind would have been unthinkable had not Euripides
himself, and likewise his contemporary audience, been
positively obsessed with the problem. *Hecuba* is believed to
date from 424, when excitement over the Sophists was at its
peak.[8]

But this is by no means an isolated instance. At least a
dozen other passages from Euripides have come down to us in
which either his protagonist or the chorus return to the
question. The first of them come from his earliest plays such
as *Hippolytus* and some of the tragedies which have been lost
(*Phoenix, Pelaeus*); the rest, later than *Hecuba*, come from *The
Suppliant Maidens* and later tragedies such as *Electra* and
Iphigenia at Aulis.[9] Even without seeking to reconcile all these
different statements (although it would be possible and useful
to do so), we can see that the problem pervades the whole
œuvre of Euripides and is of fundamental importance to him.
When a hero performs either an admirable or a criminal act,
the poet's reaction is to ask himself why, and the question is
always posed in the same terms: is nature responsible, or
education?

All this is a measure of the astonishment and perplexity
caused by the Sophists when they suddenly replaced nature,
or *phusis*, by teaching, or *didachē*. But did they really replace
it? The audacity with which they conferred this all-important

[8] The Naupactus debate belongs to a slightly earlier period. *The Clouds*
appeared one year later.

[9] Apart from *Hecuba*, cited above, see: *Hipp.* 80 and 917; *Supp.* 911–17; *El.*
369–70; *IA* 569–567; and fr. 516, 617, 810, 1027, 1068. These texts do not
include those which mention heredity or natural qualities without, however,
setting them in contrast to education (e.g. *Hec.* 380, and fr. 75, 232, 333, 495).

role upon teaching was such that the role of *phusis* may well have seemed discounted. But we should, in all honesty, recognize that that was probably not the true intention of the first Sophists. A fragment from Protagoras (B 3) indeed says as much: 'Teaching needs endowment and practice'; but also 'learning must begin in youth' (which clearly implies both training and habituation).[10] The words that Plato puts in Protagoras' mouth in the dialogue that bears the latter's name certainly acknowledge the part played by nature in the case of eminent men who do not trouble to teach their sons how to emulate them. Here, Protagoras speaks of sons who possess little or no aptitude (327 c). Similarly, the *Double Arguments*, referred to above, also, as we know, state: 'of course, nature also plays its part'.

The major Sophists of this early period thus appear to have adopted a qualified and reasonable position. However, given that the essential point of the whole exercise was the discovery of the importance of education, that balanced attitude was soon lost.

The moderate Sophists certainly continued to allow for qualifications. The Anonymus Iamblichi certainly seems to have been a Sophist yet is so little inclined to exaggeration that some scholars have suggested that he might be identified as the philosopher Democritus.[11] This author declares, with admirable clarity, that the first necessity is natural ability but it should be backed up by a desire for the good, a willingness to make an effort, and prolonged study (1. 2). All the same, the Sophists were undeniably prone to emphasize the role of education. Thus Antiphon states: 'The first thing, I believe, for mankind, is education' (B 60), while Critias observes: 'More men are good through habit than through character' (B 9). Moreover, quite apart from whatever theoretical position was adopted, the very confidence inherent in the promises that the Sophists made tended to obscure the roles of both nature and training, as is suggested by Socrates'

---

[10] Those three aspects (nature, teaching, training) are also mentioned in the course of the remarks that Plato ascribes to Protagoras, when he is distinguishing the qualities 'owed to nature and chance' from those that are 'taught and acquired after careful preparation' (323 D).

[11] Cf. below, pp. 169 ff.

words in the *Euthydemus* (304 c) when he refers to Sophists who boast of being able to teach anyone who can pay them, regardless of their 'character or age'.

In the case of many Athenians, who were certainly attracted but also alarmed by the Sophists' teaching, amazed yet at the same time inhibited by their own experience of daily life, it was this overweening assurance that provoked their antagonism. Euripides provides a good example. Faced with all the different passages in his plays that are devoted to this problem, some scholars have accused him of incoherence and contradiction. In truth, though, it would be fairer to praise his admirable appreciation of the complexity of the situation.

Admittedly, in the earlier plays especially, many of his characters refer to the important part played by heredity. Overall, however, the impression given is that of a man attracted by the new ideas, but whose own sense of human psychology tends to tell him that 'seeing where lies the good' is not enough. In fact, that is the basic difference between him and Socrates. Euripides is not an intellectualist. His Medea says:

> I know indeed what evil I intend to do.
> But my resolutions yield to my fury (*thumos*)
> Fury that brings upon mortals the greatest evils.
>
> (*Medea*, 1078–80)

Similarly, his Phaedra declares, equally forthrightly:

> We know the good, we apprehend it clearly.
> But we can't bring it to achievement. Some
> are betrayed by their own laziness, and others
> value some other pleasure above virtue.
>
> (*Hippolytus*, 380–1)

Education is a fine thing; learning can be very useful. But on its own, it is not enough. Euripides is a subtle psychologist and takes every opportunity to drive the point home with admirable subtlety.

Let us recall the passage from *Hecuba*, with its hesitant yet measured words, its reticence and its patient qualifications: But goodness can be taught ... We should also note the careful choice of words where she says that education helps one to *recognize* what is good and to *discern* what is evil. At no point does the text suggest that, once the lesson is learned, one necessarily acts for the good. In *Iphigenia at Aulis*, similarly, we are told that people's natural characters differ and that true nobility is always recognizable, but that education can *contribute* much to virtue, and again the text goes on to speak of *discerning* one's duty. Nature and education are given their due equally and the positive potential of teaching is recognized but scrupulously limited.

Similar limits are suggested elsewhere, in a fragment from the *Phoenix* which shows that education, however good, can never turn a base man into a good one and that, consequently, 'the crucial factor is nature' (fr. 810).[12]

Euripides also gives due recognition to the other irrational factor, namely training, the formation of habits. In *The Suppliant Maidens* and also in fragment 1027, Euripides even refers to the example of a small child who learns to say and understand things that he has never been taught to know: the child is trained by exercise (*askēsis*) and thereby contracts habits that he will retain throughout his life, habits which will become second nature to him.

It would be pointless to pile quotation upon quotation, digging out all the texts of the period which echo the above observations, for whether in the form of isolated remarks, reported testimony, or indirect allusions, there are so very many. Democritus, for instance, observes in fragment 242 that more men are virtuous as a result of their training than through their natural qualities. Gifts bestowed by nature no longer hold sway; on the other hand, he does not go as far as the intellectualism of the Sophists.[13]

In the long run, all these exchanges of views, all these hesitations, omissions, and rediscoveries, lead up to the attitude presented in Isocrates' programmatic speeches: it is moderate in spirit, even if peremptorily expressed. No more than half a century after the appearance of the Sophists,

---

[12] Cf. *Dictys* (333): 'The old saying is right: it is impossible to be good if one is born from a bad father.'

[13] For other references that are either less reliable or of a later date, see F. Heinimann, *Nomos und Physis: Herkunft und Bedeutung einer Antithese im griechischen Denken des 5. Jahrhunderts* (Basle, 1945), 101 n. 36.

Isocrates set up a school in Athens. His teaching, like theirs before him, was intellectual, designed to promote political action, and intended to dispense a general education. Yet his very first treatise for this new school, seemingly based on the model provided by the earlier Sophists, was entitled *Against the Sophists*. The first—and only—criticism that it makes of them is the very same as we have detected developing behind the reservations expressed in the fifth century. Isocrates takes the early Sophists to task for their exorbitant claims and because, in giving education priority, they did not ascribe enough importance to the two irrational factors constituted by natural talents and practical training. Such is the spearhead of his attack:

If all who are engaged in the profession of education were willing to state the facts instead of making greater promises than they can possibly fulfil, they would not be in such bad repute with the lay-public. (1)

And the same key terms appear, forcefully expressed:

they do not attribute any of this power either to the practical experience or to the native ability of the student, but undertake to transmit the science of discourse as simply as they would teach the letters of the alphabet. (10)

Isocrates goes on to point out—as did the author of the *Double Arguments*—that 'many of those who have pursued philosophy have remained in private life, others, on the other hand, who have never taken lessons from any one of the sophists have become able orators and statesmen' (14). Why is this? It is because:

Ability, whether in speech or in any other activity, is found in those who are well endowed by nature and have been schooled by practical experience. Formal training makes such men more skilful and more resourceful in discovering the possibilities of a subject, for it teaches them to take from a readier source the topics which they otherwise hit on in a haphazard fashion. But it cannot fully fashion men who are without natural aptitude into good debaters or writers, although it is capable of leading them on to self-improvement and to a greater degree of intelligence on many subjects.

A methodological change was inevitable at this point. What might be called practical exercises began to take over from the professorial lecture course.[14] But, most importantly, there is a palpable change of tone. It now becomes far more prudent and circumspect. The excessive confidence placed in the possibilities of an apprenticeship founded upon all kinds of intellectual techniques produced an initial sense of unease, which led to criticism and, eventually, revision.

However, this circuitous evolution (which the various chapters of the present book will repeatedly reflect) should not be allowed to obscure two important facts which emerge clearly from all our sources of testimony.

The first relates to Athens itself and to the characteristic tone of all these polemics. No sooner was an innovation launched than, as we can see, the Athenians—not just the philosophers, but other writers and dramatists too—all flung themselves into a debate which to us of the twentieth century seems incredibly abstract and philosophical. We ourselves would no doubt be interested in thrashing out the question of whether or not the pupils of any particular teacher were in fact 'successful'; but we would be unlikely to examine the problem a priori, in the most general of terms. Yet the Athenians blithely engaged in these abstract debates. For them, any subject, no matter what, was immediately regarded as a universal problem leading to the discovery of new ideas. In this instance, that enthusiasm was all the stronger given that the problems to be addressed seemed impellingly new. As we have seen, the very idea that intellectual teaching could have a practical use was a totally novel one to Athens. It was, furthermore, an idea that implied social change, and this caused the debate to grow ever more heated.

The question of the limits of education sometimes still crops up today, as does that of the usefulness of thoroughly understanding a situation in order to behave with courage;

---

[14] Thus Isocrates, *Against the Sophists*, 17: 'The student must not only have the requisite aptitude but he must learn the different kinds of discourse and practise himself in their use; and the teacher, for his part, must so expound the principles of the art with the utmost possible exactness as to leave out nothing that can be taught and, for the rest, he must in himself set . . . an example.'

and sometimes we try to define the parts played respectively by general training and by specialization in a course of intellectual teaching. Whenever we in the twentieth century tackle any such problems we inevitably fall back on the arguments that the ancient Greek texts marshalled, weighed up, and put together in the heat of the moment, twenty-five centuries ago.

The Athenians' inclination for debate may well have been encouraged and strengthened by the Sophists' art of explaining and discussing any- and everything. At any rate, the second factor that is so striking about these debates directly concerns the Sophists personally (and also concerns us). If we follow the controversy over the Sophists through from beginning to end, we can see that their totally novel ambitions marked an absolutely new point of departure in our history: an advance was made over ground that has never been lost since. As we have seen, the idea of an intellectual education from which each and every adult could benefit, an education designed to improve their aptitudes in every domain, thanks to intellectual techniques and human knowledge, was completely new. It was amazing; and it radically changed people's picture of human beings and what it was that determined the scope of their merits. In the years that followed, a number of corrections and modifications were suggested. But the fundamental notion has never, to this day, been rejected by any country in the civilized world.

At this point, let us return to Isocrates. It is quite true that he had qualifications to introduce and criticisms to make. But this was because he thought it the best way of safeguarding the Sophists' legacy. From time to time he says as much himself. In the *Antidosis*, written forty or so years later, his views were unchanged, for in this treatise he quotes at length from his earlier *Against the Sophists*, adducing new arguments to support his thesis. Nevertheless, he now declares the Sophists' new teaching to have been both good and useful:

who among you does not know that most of those who have sat under the sophists have not been duped nor affected as these men [who are hostile to the Sophists] claim, but that some of them have turned out competent champions and others able teachers; while those who have preferred to live in private have beome more gracious in their social intercourse than before, and keener judges of discourses and more prudent counsellors than most? How is it then possible to scorn a discipline which is able to make of those who have taken advantage of it men of that kind? (*Antidosis*, 204)

It was certainly not possible, and after this nobody presumed to try. Allowing for the later adjustments, Protagoras' new teaching truly leads straight to Isocrates, from Isocrates to Cicero, and from Cicero straight to us. We have Protagoras and his friends to thank for the fact that our own societies provide teaching for secondary schools, for students, and for those who, even in later life, are anxious to learn more about ideas and to make use of them.

There was reason enough for the fifth-century Athenians to be somewhat taken aback. But there is also reason enough for us to give these teachers credit where credit is due, even if their ambitions at the time were so overriding that, as we do so, we are also conscious of the echoes left by the controversy that their excesses inevitably provoked.

We have yet to consider the most controversial side of their teaching programme. It was daring enough to set out to teach political excellence, good judgement, and foresight. But it was still more audacious to seek to found all this upon instruction in the art of oratory. It is now time to recognize that this was indeed their claim.

3

Rhetorical Education

FOR the Athenians of the fifth century BC, and more generally for all Greeks of the classical period, the skill of 'clever speaking' or 'speaking well' was one that it was essential to acquire. In those days, an individual could make his voice heard directly and all major decisions were the outcome of public debates. Speech was thus an important mode of action, and it became increasingly so as democracy developed. Small wonder, then, that the art of the speaker, or rhetoric, was one of the foremost preoccupations of the Sophists' teaching. At the beginning of Plato's *Protagoras*, when the young neophyte who hastens to put himself in the master's charge is asked what the latter teaches, the first answer that rises to his lips is precisely that Protagoras is 'a master of making one a clever speaker' (312 D).

This was a skill that all the Sophists possessed; and to teach it was also the purpose of the movement that is known as the 'Second Sophistic', under the Roman Empire. The masters who belonged to it certainly regarded themselves as master-thinkers and were fully prepared to act in the capacity of councillors to cities or political leaders, but they were primarily masters of rhetoric and were keen to display their skill by discoursing upon the most paradoxical of subjects, thereby re-establishing their links with the first Sophists, those of fifty-century Athens.

The aim of their teaching was clear and easy to understand. Its content was more bewildering. Rhetoric could range from simple precepts to theoretical analysis, from style to thought, from practical effectiveness to intellectual training. Now when we examine the content of the Sophists' teaching and the spirit in which it was given, we soon detect a curious paradox. No doubt their very orientation seems to indicate a radical split between what we nowadays would call content and style. But in spite of that, the formal methods that they invented and propagated appeared in the first instance to be means of investigation and intellectual training.

The same no doubt holds true of any programme for the teaching of rhetoric, whether or not that is immediately apparent; but more so in some cases than in others. The Sophists of the mid-fifth century truly forged new instruments for the mind, and that is something we are bound to recognize when we appreciate the radical difference between them and their predecessors.

Broadly speaking, the first hesitant attempts of those who came before them stand in contrast to the two new tendencies in the art of rhetoric represented respectively by the two most famous early Sophists, namely Gorgias and Protagoras. After them, others continued what they had started, modifying and perfecting their methods. But all the foundations were laid in the two new stimuli for which these two grand masters of the fledgling art of rhetoric were responsible.

According to Aristotle, reported by Cicero (*Brutus*, 46), rhetoric was born in Sicily, following the expulsion of the tyrants, that is to say, in about the first third of the fifth century. He considers it to have been linked with the many lawsuits which took place at this time. The text in question clearly notes the pragmatic character of the new art and indicates how closely it was connected with the strictly defined world of lawsuits and legal chicanery.

Corax and his pupil Tisias were the two masters who attempted to codify the precepts of the new art, in Sicily. They could practically be accounted Sophists, already, for they were teachers who charged a fee for their labours, and they revelled in reasoned argument. Tisias, furthermore, seems to have been Gorgias' master and to have accompanied him on his embassy to Athens. Corax and Tisias had both written treatises or *technai*, and there are passages in both Plato and Aristotle which give us some idea of their contents, or at least the kind of argumentation adopted. It appears to have been terse, inflexible, and somewhat simplistic. Nevertheless, it relied heavily upon what was to become the very basis of argumentation for the Sophists, namely the

argument of likelihood. In these legal pleadings it is never the
truth that is in question (a circumstance that foreshadows
what was to be regarded as so shocking in the rhetoric that
was to follow). These rhetoricians knew how to exploit an
argument of likelihood both subtly and systematically. They
also knew how to make use of it at one remove, so as to
reverse its import. Plato comments upon the first of these
techniques as he summarizes the art of Tisias in the *Phaedrus*:

He wrote that if a feeble and brave man assaulted a strong coward,
robbed him of his cloak or something, and was brought to trial for it,
neither party ought to speak the truth; the coward should say that he
had not been assaulted by the brave man alone, whereas the other
should prove that only they two were present and should use the
well-known argument, 'How could a little man like me assault such
a man as he is?' (266 D)

The second technique is associated with Corax by Aristotle,
who is less censorious of the principle behind it and more
interested in the technique *per se*:

For if a man is not likely to be guilty of what he is accused of, for
instance if, being weak, he is accused of assault and battery, his
defence will be that the crime is not probable; but if he is likely to be
guilty, for instance if he is strong, it may be argued again that the
crime is not probable, for the very reason that it was bound to
appear so. (*Rhetoric*, 2. 24 D, 1402^a 18–20)

In short, within a modest framework, beyond which it did
not as yet occur to them to venture, these founding masters
had already marked out the path to be pursued. They had
defined the purpose of rhetoric and had given practical
demonstrations of how to use arguments based on the normal
reactions common to all men. Indeed, they may have done far
more, for their treatises in general had for some time (quite
how long we do not know) been considering many other
aspects of rhetoric which could not strictly speaking be
regarded as techniques of proof: narration, eulogy, personal
denigration, for instance.

The rhetoric taught by the Sophists was to continue along
the lines mapped out by their precursors. They would sketch
in a framework, then provide examples of different argu-

ments, types of reasoning, and commonplaces; and they would set up models and schemata. In the *Phaedrus* (266 D ff.), Socrates refers somewhat ironically to all these schemata, each with its own technical name. What he has in mind is oratorical training in general, but the Sophists certainly contributed to its design and no doubt employed techniques similar to those to which Socrates refers. Thrasymachus, for example, had written not only a *Treatise on Rhetoric*, but also collections of deliberative speeches and *Subjects for Oratory*. Two short examples of legal speeches by Gorgias have survived: *Helen* and *Palamedes*, to which we shall be returning. Protagoras had produced a collection of *Refutatory Arguments*, some of which were probably models of arguments to which no answers could be found.

The practical content of the Sophists' teaching may simply have developed and elaborated the aims of their precursors. However, it is quite clear that, with the advent of the first great masters, a change of perspective took place. The few sources of evidence that we possess prove beyond question that the study of the practical techniques that were on offer for disciples to learn was from now on inspired by a new spirit. Suddenly the new masters introduced the self-conscious analysis of speech in general, and set about exploring its full potential. This naturally enough provoked a reaction and launched an urgent debate on the relation of rhetoric to justice and truth. The question was posed, in the tightest possible terms, for the centuries to come, and the enthusiasm for the new ideas that it reflected confers upon these debates an ever-fresh sense of immediacy.

An examination of the contributions of the two greatest Sophists, Gorgias and Protagoras, reveals two new avenues of approach. The one discovers the magic inherent in speech and the potential power of style. The other establishes a method of argument and reveals the dialectic bases of all types of argumentation.

This is not to imply that Gorgias took no interest in argumentation. In fact, we possess two short treatises by him, composed as models (and, just for once, both are complete). One is his *Helen* (also designed as a defence for that heroine); the other is the *Palamedes*.[1] Palamedes was the very epitome of a man unjustly treated. Odysseus had levelled accusations against him before the walls of Troy, and, in the fifth century, Aeschylus, Sophocles, and Euripides each devoted a tragedy to him (all unfortunately lost).

It was here that the literary genre of the fictitious legal defence won its spurs: the masters of rhetoric proved their ability to defend any cause, no matter how difficult—in fact, the more difficult, the better. In later years, the exercise was to turn into a kind of game, to show off an orator's virtuosity. In the fourth century, Isocrates was to take part in it in his own particular fashion but at the same time complained of those 'who are filled with pride when, having chosen a strange and paradoxical subject, they manage to cope with it tolerably well'. We know of encomiums devoted to subjects such as salt (Plato pokes fun at them in *The Symposium*) and death (Alcidamas is known to have produced a work on this subject, in the fourth century).

The fashion, which was carried to extremes, testifies to the popularity of the fictitious examples composed by Gorgias. But it also points up a difference, for both the *Helen* and the *Palamedes* were *causes célèbres* which raised general questions of innocence and culpability of a quintessential kind.

Both these pleas for the defence, or rather models for them, written by Gorgias, follow the same style of argument. They proceed by drawing a priori distinctions and combine them with appeals to psychological verisimilitude. In defence of Helen's innocence, the author envisages four possibilities: either Helen followed Paris because fate or the gods dictated that she should do so, or because it was so decreed by an inevitable destiny; or else she was abducted by force, being either persuaded by words, or overcome by love for him. In none of these cases could she be held responsible, since in every one she was subject to a power so strong as to be irresistible. It is easy to understand the principle at work

[1] Gorgias had also written a *Treatise*, about which we know nothing (see A 3 and 4, and B 13) except that one of the subjects tackled was 'the right moment' (*kairos*). The authenticity of the *Palamedes* has sometimes been questioned. On these questions of rhetoric in general, cf. J. de Romilly, *Magic and Rhetoric in Ancient Greece* (Cambridge, Mass., 1975), ch. 1.

here. It is to deny responsibility by arguing that the accused had no choice. It is a principle repeatedly applied by the orators in Thucydides: they likewise claim that they were obliged to go to war, impelled to wield power by the force of circumstances; if a whole people is in the wrong, they declare that it had no option but to follow its masters or, if it invades another city, that it was invited to do so by the citizens. It is a principle that is also in constant use in the arguments of tragedy and later also in the speeches of the orators.

But in the case of Gorgias' defence of Helen, the argument is, as it were, four times as strong, as a result of this initial division into four alternatives. The impression given is that not a single possibility has been overlooked, and this makes the argument look like an impressive demonstration. The technique furthermore makes it possible to use general, theoretical arguments—definitely the hallmark of a philosopher. We are presented with a list of hypotheses rather than an analysis of the facts.

It was a new technique, and in the *Palamedes* it was again repeatedly used. Here it is combined with the argument of likelihood, with a view to setting aside all possible interpretations of the treachery that Palamedes was supposed to have committed. He might have committed treachery for wealth (15) or to acquire honours (16) or to save his skin (17) or to help his friends (18) or to avoid fear, trouble, or danger (19). But in each case, the orator shows that the explanation will not do: Palamedes is quite wealthy enough as it is and has few needs; he is already sufficiently laden with honours; concern for his own safety is ruled out since a traitor is always hated and spied upon by those around him; similarly, a desire to help his friends cannot be a motive for treachery (for it would be precisely them whom he betrayed); finally, nobody could point to any trace of fear or any danger to be avoided. Once again, the impression of having exhausted every possibility strengthens the speaker's arguments. At the same time, the distinction between the available hypotheses is noticeably based upon a lucid analysis of the major motives at work in human beings generally (wealth, honour, safety). In his justification of Athens' imperialism, Thucydides has his Athenians adduce the very same three instincts, declaring them to be fundamental: honour, fear, and self-interest (1.75.3 and 1.76.2). What is more, all except the last of the analyses in the *Palamedes* are based upon general reflections germane to the habitual behaviour of men in given situations ('it is not those who... but those who... honours come from... not from... for everyone, a traitor is...'). As is well known, this is precisely the technique that is used in Thucydides' speeches.

Gorgias' two fictional speeches for the defence are thus singularly important from the point of view of the argumentation employed. Not only do they reveal an already masterly ability to manipulate the argument of verisimilitude and human psychology in general; they also demonstrate a technique of a priori analysis that is nowhere else presented more clearly or more systematically and that may well have been peculiar to Gorgias himself. He was certainly more of a theorist and abstract thinker than the other Sophists. There is a fragment on the subject of non-being by him which provides dazzling proof of his virtuosity when it came to playing with intellectual concepts.

However, it was not to these procedures of argumentation that his contemporaries tended to draw attention. It was his style that seems to have been considered particularly important, and his name is still associated with the figures of rhetoric which gave it its exceptional sophistication. Even in the ancient world people would already refer to 'figures in the style of Gorgias'; and in all the various texts by him that have come down to us, every line is studded with them. Like many others, he frequently used antitheses, often seeking to render these more effective by all sorts of means designed to attract the reader's attention. Final assonances or rhymes, balanced numbers of syllables, the use of terms that were parallel either by virtue of form, or of sound or metre. Prose crafted like this, as if it were poetry, makes the reader feel that not a single syllable has been left to chance.

It was a revolutionary way of writing, but it must be admitted that the examples provided by the texts that have survived do not convey a particularly favourable impression. So much artifice makes the reader's head spin and somewhat tends to obscure the meaning. It is impossible to appreciate his writing fully in translation, since many stylistic effects are inevitably lost. However, the beginning of a fragment from his funeral speech may at least convey a general idea of the principle behind his style—and of its disadvantages. In an English translation, it has been rendered as follows:

For what did these men lack that men should have? What did they have that men should not have? Would that I could express what I wish, and may I wish what I ought, avoiding divine wrath, shunning human envy! For the courage these men possessed was divine, and the mortal part alone was human.

Towards the end of this one short page—the only one to have come down to us as an example of Gorgias' style—we find a series of adjectives, each coupled with one to complement it, arranged in two parallel groups and filling about ten whole lines:

Violent towards the violent... fearless towards the fearless... terrifying among the terrifying...

The passage is rounded off as follows:

Therefore, although they are dead, the longing for them has not died with them but immortal, though in mortal bodies, it lives on for those who live no more.

It does rather make one's head whirl. Of all the inventions of the Sophists, this bizarre, laboured style of Gorgias' seems one of the most artificial and fanciful. Perhaps that is why none of his followers imitated the master's excesses.

It has to be said, however, that he did have his imitators, but they were considerably more measured. First and foremost amongst them was Thucydides. When he employs this style in particularly insistent fashion (in the funeral speech delivered by Pericles and, as such, a text comparable to that of Gorgias), it produces shocked reactions in the commentators,[2] who deplore the complication of passages such as the following:

[2] Dionysius of Halicarnassus produced a stringent analysis of all these stylistic experiments, in which he drew attention to the influence of Gorgias and other Sophists: 'Ostentatious figures of speech are also to be found... in no small number. I mean those parallelisms in length and sound, word-play and anti-thesis, which were excessively used by Gorgias of Leontini, by Polus and Lycymnius, and by many... other contemporaries' (*Th.* 24).

We are lovers of beauty, yet with no extravagance, and lovers of wisdom, yet without weakness. Wealth we employ, rather as an opportunity for action than as a subject for boasting. (2. 40. 1)

However, here the rhymes and parallelisms (which it is impossible to render in translation) not only lend brilliance to the style but also strengthen the effect of the antitheses. The forcefulness of the style seems to impart a greater density of thought. In other passages, which are quite free from over-emphasis, this is even more striking. Thus, in the famous comparison between Sparta and Athens in book 1, such stylistic ploys abound. But their effect is to render the contrast more acute and more forceful, as in the famous sentence which, I suggest, might be translated:

They like innovation, are quick to form new plans as well as to act as they have thought fit; You keep what you have, devise nothing new, and, in your action, do not even achieve what needs to be done. (1. 70. 2; translation: J. de Romilly)

In the Greek, Thucydides' analysis contains rhymes, echoing prefixes, and many other ploys, and it is a whole page long; yet there is nothing artificial about it and the stylistic effects are neither wearisome nor overdone.

Gorgias should thus be recognized as the inventor of an extremely refined prose style. The examples of it that have come down to us from him may be somewhat artificial and forced, but when carefully and consciously employed it could be most effective. This is the first instance that we have come across in which an innovation introduced by a Sophist only revealed its full potential when it was cast in a different, less ostentatious mould, as it was in Attic literature.

However, his taste for rhetorical figures of speech was but one aspect of Gorgias' contribution to the creation of an elaborate prose style capable of indirectly affecting people's minds and emotions. It was just one of a number of self-conscious responses inspired by his wonder at the power of words.

Here we get to the crux of the matter. As it happens, we do possess a text written by Gorgias himself, in which he celebrates with panache the quasi-magical power of words. The passage comes from the *Helen*, where it constitutes his defence of Helen in the event of her having been 'won over by speech'. The passage suddenly seems to strike a more personal note: it is, after all, precisely to rhetoric, the agent of persuasion, that Gorgias has devoted his entire life. The spell-binding powers that he celebrates here have occupied his every moment.

What he fastens upon above all—characteristically enough—is the ability of words to work upon the emotions. He writes as follows:

Speech is a great power, which achieves the most divine works by means of the smallest and least visible form; for it can even put a stop to fear, remove grief, create joy, and increase pity.

To illustrate this description, he immediately produces a comparison in which he associates speech in general with poetry. It was quite a bold comparison to make. Until then, poetry had been considered the only noble form of expression, partly for the very reason that it was linked with inspiration and the Muses. Now Gorgias was claiming the same powers for speech of any kind. He regarded and defined poetry as a whole as 'speech that is metrically ordered'. All types of speech now acquired the same prestige as poetry; hence, presumably, his taste for stylistic experiments designed to bring prose closer to poetry.

But soon the metaphors and comparisons in this text move beyond poetry to suggest, instead, magic. The terms it uses evoke incantations, magic, charms, drugs, witchcraft. The implication can only be that, by seemingly irrational means, words have the power to enthral the reader, affecting him despite himself.

Gorgias then produces an analysis of knowledge designed to explain this magical power that words possess. Knowledge is in general unsure and affected by subjective elements; memory is similarly limited; so we are forced to fall back upon mere opinions, which are invariably fragile and changeable. That is why speech is important, for it has the power to affect people's opinions, to modify them or to carry listeners along—as can be seen from the debates in which wise men, orators, and philosophers express their opposed views. The use of rhetoric is justified by the uncertainty of knowledge. It works because our knowledge is imperfect.

That is how speech comes to acquire such absolute power. In the last part of this text, Gorgias leaves behind the two earlier comparisons and goes so far as to credit speech with necessary and compelling powers: one no longer has any choice in the matter; all one can do is agree. In such circumstances, it is speech alone that is responsible for one's actions. If Helen was persuaded to follow Paris, she was simply obeying the compulsion of all-powerful speech. From poetry, to magic, to constraint: in the space of a single page, we have moved on from a kind of emotional pleasure to a power of persuasion that nothing can arrest.

On the face of it, this short text would seem to be simply about Helen's mistakes and the part played by her bad advisers—a common enough excuse offered by many a guilty party. But the analysis takes in much more, introducing many new arguments. In effect it expresses an amazed recognition of the potential powers of discourse, potential powers that rhetoric can develop to their utmost. In passing, it is also interesting to note that Gorgias twice uses the word *technē* to describe the techniques of language. Under the guise of justifying Helen, the master of rhetoric proclaims his pride in his skills.

Now everything became grist to his mill: not just rational argumentation, but any and every irrational means capable of sustaining the magic of speech. Gorgias is known to have set great store by the art of seizing the right moment and making the most of an opportunity when it presented itself (*kairos*, to the Greeks). And we know that, according to Plato, Thrasymachus was

also a genius, as he said, at rousing large companies to wrath, and soothing them again by his charms when they are angry, and most powerful in devising and abolishing calumnies on any grounds whatsoever. (*Phaedrus*, 267 c)[3]

---

[3] In this part of the *Phaedrus*, Plato refers to the various parts of discourse that are subtly distinguished by Evenus of Paros, Tisias, and Gorgias. Alongside the major Sophists, he also mentions works by Polus, Gorgias' disciple, who is supposed to have written *Oratorical Sanctuaries of the Muses* and studies on emphasis, the sententious style, and the imagistic style. (*Phd.* 267 c).

The practitioners of the new art played with men's passions. They could arouse or quell them at will, exploiting the fragility of men's opinions in order to do so. In fact, their entire art depended upon that exploitation.

Already, we are conscious of a number of alarming features. Passions are dangerous things; and all this manipulation of people's opinions suggests that truth and justice may be given short shrift. In the *Helen*, Gorgias himself recognizes the dangers, for, according to him, if Helen fell victim to the power of speech, on this occasion the said speech was treacherous and led her into culpable behaviour. Gorgias makes it quite clear that, in a case such as this, the persuasion is evil and the deception flagrant (in fact he says as much not just once, but three times, in paragraphs 8, 10, and 14). His repeated criticisms contrast this use of speech with the 'divine incantations' which constituted our point of departure. Now we detect a new trend in Gorgias' ideas about rhetoric. This time it involves the ambivalence of rhetoric, and its dangers. If even he, the master, entertained such thoughts, there was, as can be imagined, plenty here for others to worry about.

The fact is that oratory is an essentially deceptive art; and its faults soon became apparent to many. The Athenian democracy was soon in thrall to men of 'fine words', and writers began to complain. In day-to-day life too, clever advocates, who could make people believe anything, became a scourge and voices were raised in protest on all sides. Even Euripides changed his tune. He had been deeply fascinated by the Sophists' discoveries and had presented in his plays the oratorical debates in which speakers defending opposite points of view were pitted one against another. He had so much enjoyed the game of arguing responsibilities away that he had ascribed precisely to Helen a whole speech that laid the responsibility for her errors at the door of either the gods or the unfortunate Hecuba, thereby proving her own innocence—all very much in the spirit of Gorgias. Yet even Euripides often regarded this rhetoric with unease, especially when it was used by the demagogues. In his *Hippolytus* (two years before Gorgias' arrival in Athens), Theseus is already bewailing the fact that, despite the many marvellous new inventions, nobody is concerned to inculcate wisdom (916–

20); and a few years later, in *Hecuba*, his criticisms of Odysseus are even more bitter: he is a 'hypocrite with honeyed tongue', a 'demagogue' who knows how to manipulate the army by means of persuasion (131–3 and 254–7). In fact, Euripides' tragedies are full of unscrupulous characters who justify their egotistical behaviour all too easily. Every time they do so, either the chorus or the victim in question laments the fact that the skills of the orator are out of all proportion to the worthiness—or lack of it—of the cause.

The teaching of rhetoric and the fashion that it set gave rise to the problem of its relation to justice and truth. This was a problem that inevitably brought about a head-on clash between the masters of rhetoric and philosophers like Socrates.

The opposition is first expressed, and with considerable force, by Xenophon in the chapter already mentioned in his *On Hunting*. The severe judgement passed upon the Sophist masters of rhetoric is hardly surprising coming from this sports enthusiast, who is, moreover, a disciple of Socrates. He makes no bones at all about accusing them of deliberate deception, pure and simple. But Plato's *Gorgias*, produced at about the same time as Xenophon's *On Hunting*, is the major text devoted to the clash between philosopher and master of rhetoric. The subject is of such central importance that, before moving on to consider the more technical innovations linked with the name of Protagoras, we must pause to consider this essential question which arose in connection with the great rhetorician Gorgias.

The position that Gorgias himself adopts in the dialogue is clearly identical with the one reflected in his *Helen*. Rhetoric, like speech itself, may be employed either for good or for evil, and Plato lends his Gorgias the same neutrality. He has him declare that rhetoric 'comprises in itself practically all powers at once' (*Gorgias*, 455 A); but also makes him admit that the power of rhetoric can be made to serve evil as well as good. The same can be said of many techniques:

Our use of rhetoric should be like our use of any other sort of exercise. For other exercises are not to be used against all and sundry.

So too with rhetoric:

If a man becomes a rhetorician and then uses this power and this art unfairly, we ought not to hate his teacher and cast him out of our cities. For he imparted that skill to be used in all fairness, whilst this man puts it to an opposite use. (457 A–C)

Gorgias' own attitude was reasonable enough. But that made little difference to the ambitions of other masters of the new school, and this was deeply disturbing. So, in this dialogue, Plato portrays a somewhat hesitant Gorgias who, after making all these fine declarations, nevertheless clings to the idea that, after all, his pupils do also derive a sense of justice from him and learn to respect it (460 A). But the claim is made somewhat uneasily. And the fact is that the real Gorgias seems to have been extremely reticent on this point. We are told in the *Meno* (95 c) that he himself made no promises to teach virtue and that he poked fun at other Sophists who did make such commitments. For himself, all he aimed to do was produce good orators. However, faced with Socrates' questions, he could hardly refuse to acknowledge that his rhetoric did imply some familiarity with the concept of justice. Neither in this dialogue nor elsewhere is he ever presented as an amoralist. Hence his unease, craftily conveyed by Plato through expressions such as 'it would appear that', 'the fact of the matter does seem to be'. And a little further on in the dialogue, Plato has the Sophist's less circumspect disciples take over from him. These, unlike their master, frankly abandon justice. Plato could not have ascribed to Gorgias ideas that the latter himself, as was publicly known, would have disavowed. But, by various means, Plato does manage to suggest what the new art was likely to lead to.

In this dialogue, Gorgias thus hands over to a younger speaker, Polus, who admits that, as he sees it, every guilty individual who avoids punishment is to be considered happy. Polus, in his turn, then gives way to an arrogant youth called Callicles, who goes further, arguing that the law of the stronger rules the world and that the idea of justice is just a convention established by the weak. Delving into the implications suggested by rhetoric, we thus discover justice to be rejected, a fact that the Sophist's disciples are quite prepared to accept. Rhetoric is in league with injustice.

Socrates could clearly not accept this. If rhetoric was seen to imply such a tendency, he was bound to reject it. This was no science, for its methods did not stem from clearly reasoned principles; no science, since it was not aimed at either the truth or the good. It was nothing but an art of blandishment, like cooking or dressing up. It had no serious purpose. And its defenders were bound to recognize that the ends that they had in view were hardly moral ones. A true philosopher had no choice but to condemn them in the strongest possible terms.

It is true that subsequently, in the *Phaedrus*, Plato was to recognize another kind of rhetoric, a science of dialectics this time. The contrast constituted by that future project emphasizes the inadequacies of the rhetoric of the Sophists; but it certainly does nothing to diminish the force of Plato's first reaction as expressed in the *Gorgias*, where, in the name of morality, he wanted to reject rhetoric utterly.

Gorgias, with his unqualified view of rhetoric, was thus on the one hand outstripped by his own disciples, both close and distant, through whom he was linked with immoralism, on the other condemned by those who insisted upon a quest for goodness and truth. It was an impasse; and for rhetoric, caught between the two extremes, the outlook seemed bleak.

Was there really no hope of a healthy kind of rhetoric? No chance of reconciling it with morality? The solution—once again—came from Isocrates. Somehow he contrived to be profoundly loyal both to his master Gorgias' faith in his art and to his hesitancy. While he did not condemn opinion as Plato did, like Gorgias he did acknowledge its fragility. On the whole, though, he reckoned it healthy, considering it to be, in any case, all we have, for to him the great truths pursued by Plato seemed far too distant. This, then, was the solution: if opinion is healthy, an orator, in his efforts to influence his audience, must clearly take account of it. To make a good impression on his public, he must win its approval by putting across ideas accepted as valid. His concern to make a good impression will generally lead him to what, so far as one can see, is indeed the truth, as will be manifest from the approval that it elicits from the audience. Of course, this is not the good or the truth of philosophers such as Plato; but it is the good and the truth as ordinary people see them. Speaking of the philosophers, Isocrates thus writes as follows:

> They exhort their followers to a kind of virtue and wisdom that is ignored by the rest of the world and is disputed among themselves; I, to a kind which is recognized by all. (*Antidosis*, 84)

Rhetoric and virtue are now in partnership.

To provide an example, Isocrates, in his turn, now also chooses the theme of Helen, using it to clarify his position *vis-à-vis* Gorgias. He takes Gorgias to task for leading the reader to expect an encomium when all he produces is a legal type of defence.[4] To make his point, he then launches into a eulogy of everything about Helen that could possibly be considered admirable: her divine birth, the exploits of those who sought to win her, her beauty with its universal power, the cult devoted to her, and her actions which finally had the effect of uniting the Greeks against the barbarians. There is no hint of the testy subtleties of his master Gorgias; instead, everything about Helen that could conceivably be considered desirable is carefully adduced. The orator able to argue his way out of a tight corner has been replaced by a committed teacher.

The loss involved can be offset against the gain. Launched in fifth-century Athens as the key to all success, rhetoric soon gave rise to unease and disagreement over its relation to justice. It was to an Athenian master and erstwhile disciple of Gorgias that it fell to mediate between on the one hand the power of speech, on the other practical and traditional morality. It is thanks to Isocrates that rhetoric itself survived, as did the idea of the crucial importance of opinion, which remained associated with it.[5]

Also instrumental in preserving the legacy of the Sophists

---

[4] The distinction is made in the manner of Prodicus (see below, pp. 74–5).

[5] The problem does not seem to have been of essential importance to Aristotle, who tried to make rhetoric more scientific and at last turn it into a real *technē*, but did not condemn it outright as Plato did.

was the practice, which survived down to quite recent times, of combining the study of 'rhetoric' with that of 'philosophy', or rather of having the former lead on to the latter. During Gorgias' own lifetime, however, it would have been unreasonable to expect the new and practical invention of rhetoric to be fully appraised and its full potential and all its limits clearly delineated. It was too soon for rhetoric to know its place.

What made it all the more difficult for it to do so was the fact that, for a Greek, *logos* also meant thought; and rhetoric did indeed include the art of reasoning, discussing and reaching a conclusion, as the work of Protagoras was soon brilliantly demonstrating.

Just as Gorgias manifested a measure of interest in argumentation, Protagoras was not uninterested in formal expression. But whereas Gorgias was concerned with the magic of style, Protagoras was more concerned with the rigour of language. Language fascinated him, as it did Gorgias. But Protagoras pursued his linguistic analyses further, regarding language as a tool for thought and seeking to understand its full potential and improve its precision. We know that he took an interest in grammar. Aristotle tells us that he established distinctions between the genders of nouns and the tenses of verbs. And, in the *Phaedrus* (267 c), Socrates credits him with the introduction of *orthoepeia*, or the 'propriety of expression' into the study of rhetoric.

Protagoras' point of view was quite different from Gorgias', for Gorgias was chiefly concerned with the effect produced on the listener, Protagoras with the precise correspondence between thought and expression. There is from the outset a more scientific air to the work of Protagoras. In truth, virtually nothing is known of his studies in this field, except that they existed.

Nor do we know anything about the work of other Sophists in this area. All we know is that it implied some kind of philosophy of language: an astonishingly modern innovation. They investigated both the potential of language and its imperfections. Protagoras seems to have shared Democritus' belief that the names of things were invented by human beings and possessed no natural roots. But unfortunately it is difficult to form any idea of their doctrines without modernizing them greatly and exaggerating their importance at the time. The Sophists' interest in language was essentially limited to a desire to teach people how to use it as effectively as possible. Protagoras' remarks on such and such an imperfection in Homer, or on problems connected with the gender of certain nouns, appear to have had no other purpose. Similarly, we know that Hippias wrote works on grammar and prosody, concentrating on syllable quantities, rhymes, and metre, although none of these have come down to us. We do not even know whether the other Sophists who concerned themselves with rhetoric—Thrasymachus, Theodorus of Byzantium, and Evenus of Paros, for example—ever addressed themselves to these problems. What is clear, however, is that it was the Sophists who first established the philosophy of language as a specific branch of knowledge, and some modern scholars have considered their investigations precise enough to warrant references to 'the beginnings of philology' or 'pioneers in the field of philology and grammar' (the phrases appear in the titles of works by Diels and P. B. R. Forbes, published in 1910 and 1933 respectively).

Prodicus is the only one of these men about whom anything is known—even indirectly—in this connection. He provides an excellent example, however. He too was concerned with 'propriety of expression' and set out to improve the precision of vocabulary, making careful distinctions between almost synonymous terms. The many references to him by other writers give some idea of how important this kind of work was in the elaboration of language in Athens.

Thucydides was a pupil of Prodicus', as was Euripides, and Socrates, somewhat ironically, claims the same distinction. Plato cites Prodicus or represents him over a dozen times in his dialogues. Invariably (except in one passage by Xenophon, which mentions his moral teaching), this Sophist is associated with the distinction of nuances of vocabulary. Plato makes fun of him, of course, treating his preoccupation as an inoffensive mania. He seems to have regarded Prodicus' verbal distinctions as a somewhat formal exercise, not really productive of true philosophical analysis. Be that as it may, by citing them so often, he draws attention to them. Time and again, he shows Prodicus establishing subtleties of meaning: to discuss is not the same as to argue; approval is not the same as praise; to want and to desire are not at all the same, nor are to be and to become, nor is fear the same as terror.

The *Protagoras* itself contains all the above examples. Plato records them there with a somewhat patronizing irony. His repetitive insistence in itself makes Prodicus' activity seem somewhat artificial. Yet its effects upon the development of rigorous language and assured thinking could hardly be overestimated. Thucydides, himself such a dense and profound writer, clearly owes much to it. The speeches that he records sometimes repeat distinctions credited to Prodicus. The latter had, for instance, drawn a distinction between 'discussion' and 'argument', and in book 1 of Thucydides' *History* the Corinthians declare:

Let no one of you think that these things are said more out of hostile feeling than by way of complaint; for complaint is against friends that err, but accusation against enemies that have inflicted an injury. (1.69.6)

Albeit adapted and made more specific, it is basically the same distinction. Furthermore, this is the principle at work each time that Thucydides uses specific contrasts and comparisons to illustrate and clarify particular concepts: to distinguish between fear and terror, for instance, but also between all the different forms of courage and boldness, between revolt and defection, hegemony and empire, and so on. The assurance of such thinking stems from the attention that Prodicus and Protagoras paid to the correct use of vocabulary.

That digression on Prodicus was prompted by Protagoras' investigations into language. We should remember, however, that, set in the context of Protagoras' work as a whole, those investigations were of a somewhat secondary importance. His major originality lay elsewhere, for his rhetoric was first and foremost a dialectic. Two of his ideas, preserved by the tradition on his doctrine, convey some idea of its nature.

The first was his invention of 'opposed speeches'. Diogenes Laertius and Clement of Alexandria refer to it in similar terms: 'Protagoras was the first to maintain that there are

two sides to every question, opposed to each other' (D.L.
9.51); and 'The Greeks claim, following Protagoras, that for
every speech there is one that is opposed to it' (*Stromates*,
6.65).

What are the implications here? The Greek word *logos* is
always difficult to interpret. Here, it may be understood in its
widest sense, and already the implications are considerable.
If the meaning is that every thesis may be countered by an
antithesis, and that the question of which of them to uphold
is purely a matter of choice, this marks the beginning of
the tradition of thrashing out ideas in debate, in *agōnes* in
which two contrary points of view were set in opposition and
argued in parallel speeches. As is well known, these debates,
often known as antilogies, are a constant feature of the writing of both Euripides and Thucydides. But in truth, despite
Diogenes Laertius' rather simplistic assertion, they were not
invented by the Sophists. They are already to be found in
Sophocles, and are a central feature of even the earliest
comedies. That is not surprising, for they were, after all, a
typical feature of legal debate. However, by developing this
technique, Protagoras converted it into as it were a method of
argument in itself, for which the rest of his teaching paved the
way. He is known to have written a *Method of Argument*[6] and
also two books of *Antilogies*. In other words, he taught his
pupils how to defend first one point of view, then its opposite,
how to praise and how to censure, how to present a prosecution and also a defence. These dialectical confrontations are
often referred to as 'double arguments'.

Such is the pattern followed in a short anonymous treatise
written a little before 400, which appears to constitute a
blueprint for teaching methods and in which the influence of
Protagoras is detectable. In fact, the treatise is frequently
cited as *Double Arguments* (*Dissoi Logoi*). It starts by declaring that there can be double arguments on good and evil,
the one holding that the two are confused since everything
depends on the circumstances, the other that they are distinct
from one another, for otherwise one would be faced with a

---

[6] In Greek, *technē eristikōn: eristikos* was to continue to be used by the
philosophers in its technical sense (see below, p. 82).

contradiction. The treatise then tackles the beautiful and the ugly, and the just and the unjust, in similar fashion. In each case, two theses are presented, the author first defending both, then choosing one in preference to the other. It has the air of an exercise in composition and probably reflects the teaching methods of the day.

But it was not a procedure reserved solely for the schools. A fragment from Euripides' *Antiope* declares:

On every subject, it would be possible to set up a debate of double arguments, providing one was skilled in speaking. (189 N).

What a novelty it must have seemed to be able to argue both for and against and to know how to refute any thesis you heard expressed. But how was it done? Here we come upon the other meaning of the word *logos*, and the more subtle side of the art of dialectics,[7] for it was not simply a matter of finding different arguments. The Sophists would counter every single argument in the first speech with its opposite, finding 'double arguments' in every instance. They did not merely refute arguments: they turned them to their own advantage. Perhaps this could be seen as a flowering and generalization of what earlier masters had taught about second-degree likelihood and the way in which it could be made to override immediate appearances: for example, a strong man would not attack, given that he knew he would be the first to attract suspicion. In this respect, Protagoras proceeded as a dialectician who may have been inspired by the methods of Eleatic philosophers. But he used those methods for practical purposes, thereby introducing a totally new technique. In Thucydides, we can appreciate the clever tactics which stemmed from a generalized use of Protagoras' methods. A single action is sometimes considered at different historical moments; two motives initially presented as contradictory are subsequently combined to complement each other; a fact is acknowledged but given a different interpretation. When Athens makes her intervention in Sicily, her adversaries try to stir up the towns against her:

---

[7] The double meaning of the word *logos* has often given rise to misunderstandings in the interpretation of Sophistic texts: see the good analysis by C. Natali, (Aristote et les méthodes d'enseignement de Gorgias', in B. Cassin (ed.), *Positions de la sophistique* (Paris, 1986), 105–16, 105–6.

One and the same design has guided them in acquiring their possessions over there and is now guiding them in their endeavour to acquire possessions here.

Athens' retort, in substance, is as follows: Yes, we do think of our empire but that leads us, here, to do the contrary of what we do in Greece proper, namely to defend people whose independence is profitable to us (6. 75–88). Furthermore, not just one adverse argument is overturned, but every argument conceivable. It was an elegant trick and the secret lay in knowing how to turn to one's own advantage the facts, the ideas, and the very words of one's opponent, making them point to altogether the opposite conclusion. It involved a combination of subtle shifts and reconstructions the secret of which—certainly held by Protagoras—a number of fascinated commentators have struggled to fathom.

This would suggest that the treatises cited above may have been more technical and theoretical than is sometimes supposed. It is also possible that a reflection of the technique of double arguments is discernible in the title *Kataballontes* or *Irrefutable Arguments*, which seems to have been given to the treatise also known as *Truth*.

That possibility sheds interesting light upon the second of the two ideas that tradition specifically associates with Protagoras. The idea was 'to make the weaker of two arguments the stronger'.[8] Aristophanes, who cites the expression in *The Clouds* (112 ff.), seems to understand it as referring to theses; and, in his view, to get the weaker thesis to defeat the stronger is to make injustice triumph. But Aristotle alerts us to a more technical meaning. He criticizes the principle on the grounds that it creates a misleading appearance of verisimilitude, the kind used in rhetoric and eristic. In all probability, when Protagoras boasted of being able to turn the tables against a superior *logos*, what he had in mind was precisely this technique of reversing arguments so that damn-

[8] 'Weaker' and 'stronger' clearly refer to the persuasive power of each argument. 'Stronger' does not mean 'the majority opinion', as is sometimes suggested. Rather, it is a matter of a reasoned, dialectical confrontation. On the other hand, nor does the term simply mean moral superiority (as Aristophanes suggests).

ing circumstances are converted into a justification, while favourable ones are turned into criticism. A simple, almost naïve example is provided by Thucydides: when the Athenians justify their imperialism by pointing to the glorious feats they performed in the Persian Wars, the ephor from Sparta retorts that, if they behaved so well then but are behaving badly now, 'they deserve two-fold punishment, because they used to be good and have become bad' (1. 86. 1). But subtle examples abound. Some take one by surprise for, at first sight, they can be most disconcerting.

It is important not to overlook the technical aspect of both the procedures ascribed to Protagoras, for to do so would be to convey a gravely distorted view of his teaching. On the other hand, in practice the two aspects probably overlapped: one thesis could be opposed to another all the better when opposed arguments were used. The weaker thesis triumphed because all along the line it 'refuted' the stronger. This surely explains why virtually every domain appears to have been affected by the principles of Protagoras' teaching, though these were applied with varying degrees of rigour and finesse. They became an integral part of contemporary rhetorical practice. The fictitious speeches of the orator Antiphon, which are typical of the spirit of the day, provide a good illustration.

These comprise three separate groups of four speeches each and are known as the *Tetralogies*. Each tetralogy consists of the drafts for four speeches relating to the same legal case (first one for the prosecution, then one for the defence, followed by a second for the prosecution and a second for the defence). In the first case, the speeches relate to an affair in which nothing can be proven and everything depends upon likelihood: the very model of a fine exercise in demonstration. The other two cases involve another exercise, in which the Sophists excelled: here, it is a matter of attributing and rejecting responsibility. The second tetralogy concerns an accident that occurred in a gymnasium. It is strongly reminiscent of the debate between Protagoras and Pericles, suggesting that this subject—like that of Helen—may have been regarded as a typical problem on which pupils could exercise their skills in school debates.

But these debates were more than formal exercises pure and simple. They reflected a new and important way of thinking about all problems connected with responsibility; and the art of dialectical argument that they deployed helped to set those problems out clearly. Killing by accident, through imprudence, against one's will, without being able to avoid it were all possibilities whose various implications were thrashed out and defined ever more precisely in the course of such debates, and gradually made an impact upon legal awareness.

But what is most immediately striking is the extraordinary agility of the technique. Antiphon's tetralogies provide a series of examples, demonstrating the art of switching from a thesis to its antithesis, at each turn presenting the facts in a new light: the victim cast himself upon the weapon, so was himself responsible; the instructor had already signalled that the weapons should be gathered up, so whoever flung the weapon should have paid attention; but the instructor who gave the order was more to blame than him . . . Amid all these reversals, which reflect the art of Protagoras, an untrained mind soon becomes bewildered. Furthermore, these speeches also draw upon Prodicus' technique of defining ideas more precisely by pointing out the antitheses between words whose meanings seem almost identical: impiety is not the same as error (1 α 3); bad luck is not the same as misfortune (2 γ 8 and δ 10). In the heady atmosphere engendered by the newly discovered techniques, all these methods are combined and complement one another.

It was heady stuff, no doubt, but alarming too. Such an ability to defend both points of view suggested a disconcerting unconcern for the truth. If it was a matter of defending opposite points of view equally well, justice was left with no role to play. Besides, the art of twisting arguments rendered the very principle of argumentation suspect. In fact, it made the reasoning of the Sophists look like precisely what we today would call 'sophistry'.

And the habit was spreading. Sophistry was thriving on every side. It was now possible to prove anything under the sun, to deny all the evidence and wriggle out of the tightest of corners. Even before the war broke out, the alarming aspect of this talent was recognized and was causing the Athenians concern. Plutarch cites the response of one of Pericles' opponents when asked which of the two of them was the stronger wrestler. His reply was, 'Whenever I throw him in wrestling, he disputes the fall and carries his point, and persuades the very men who saw him fall' (*Pericles*, 8).

With technical training and the growing popularity of the Sophists, such cleverness was gaining ground. The young man in *The Clouds*, still fresh from the Sophists' training, dazzles with consummate ease. And the theoretical writing of the day, exemplified by the short treatise known as *Double Arguments*, reflects these trends. Side by side, it notes down all the arguments that might be used—not only the ones employed by the best thinkers, which derived directly from philosophical thought, but also the most fantastic and artificial. The treatise declares that there is no absolute difference between good and evil since disease is a bad thing for the patient but a good one for the doctor as, similarly, death is a bad thing for the dying but a good one for the undertakers. The trouble with knowing too much about how to argue is that one tends to argue purely for the sake of argument.

So Plato, like Aristophanes, pokes fun at the Sophists. He dramatizes their passion for controversy, or eristic, portraying this as a meaningless game which provides an answer for everything. The two Sophists of the *Euthydemus*, so pleased with their ability to marshal artificial arguments, provide an excellent example.

Meanwhile, people were developing a taste for this game. They flocked to hear these argumentative confrontations as eagerly as we might to see a boxing match. Of course, Plato scoffed. At the end of the *Euthydemus*, after an argument even shakier than usual, which is nevertheless greeted with tumultuous applause, Socrates professes first to be 'knocked down', then to be crushed. Meanwhile the others praise to the skies both the arguments and the two foreigners: 'Everyone present . . . wildly applauded . . . till they all nearly died of laughing and clapping and rejoicing' (303 B).

The fashion for pointless argument was assuming dangerous proportions. In a passage from Thucydides to which we have already referred, Cleon begs the Athenians not to allow themselves to be seduced by a taste for the new arguments and warns them:

You are in thrall to the pleasures of the ear and are more like men who sit as spectators at exhibitions of sophists than men who take counsel for the welfare of the State. (3.38.7)

However, all this technical prowess was soon to be rejected and despised. Isocrates—in agreement, here, with Plato—frequently attacks those who indulge in these argumentative eristics, condemning their discussions as sterile, boring, and useless.[9] The word 'eristic' continued to be used in connection with the logicians of the Megara school, but the abuse of the procedure had discredited it in the eyes of the public, thereby sullying the reputation of the Sophists' rhetorical methods as a whole.

Besides, easy victories such as these tended to foster self-satisfaction and arrogance. Plato portrays Euthydemus, Dionysodorus, Thrasymachus, and Callicles all as ill-mannered and conceited. Their passionate desire to confound their adversaries renders them intolerant. As the love of truth went under, so did patience, courtesy, and meaningful dialogue.

It might be supposed, or hoped, that it was simply a matter of the professional distortions and predictable excesses to which new techniques often give rise. But a number of indications suggest that the problem was more serious.

In the first place, there is no denying that the technique rested upon a latent assumption that success mattered more than the truth. That went without saying. It was true of all rhetoric, even that of an oratorical or incantatory nature. But this rhetoric of argumentation truly affected the very workings of the mind. In the *Protagoras*, it is in connection with the success that this Sophist enjoyed in Athens that Plato warns the young man, or rather has Socrates warn him, that it is dangerous to deliver oneself up to the teaching of these masters without due caution; for what they teach

---

[9] Isoc., *Helen*, 1 and 6; cf. *Against the Sophists*, 3 ff.

penetrates their pupils' souls without the latter realizing it.

Aristophanes also points to the dangers of Protagoras' teaching. Strepsiades quotes virtually word for word the two formulas which seem to encapsulate Protagoras' teaching: first, he remarks with approval that two theses can be made out on any question, and that by attending the new masters' lessons one can learn how to make the weaker thesis prevail over the stronger. He then produces a statement that has misled plenty of people cleverer than the theatre-goers of the day. He declares the weaker thesis to be the one 'that says the things that are the most unjust' (115). Futhermore, we should not forget that the reason why first Strepsiades, and then his son, consult the new masters is to learn the secret of avoiding payment of their debts. Aristophanes' entire attack is thus directed against a rhetoric which serves solely as an acrobatic intellectual feat designed to promote the worst ends. The outcome is well known. The young man emerges from the professors' lessons equipped with a whole battery of arguments for not paying up, arguments which depend upon quibbling over the name of the day on which the debt falls due (1175–91). But he has also learned ingenious arguments to show that it is perfectly acceptable for a son to beat his father. This is Aristophanes' concrete illustration of the art of twisting arguments, so dear to Protagoras. Having sought to preserve his own interests by means of dishonest wrangling, Strepsiades finds himself ill used by the very person whom he has had instructed in this art.

We have already referred to the great debate in this comedy over the respective merits of the old education and the new. But this is the moment to fill in a few details relating to the circumstances in which the debate arose, for we are now in a better position to appreciate their significance. The debate is presented as an opposition between not two types of education but two *logoi*, the 'weaker' of which claims to be able to prevail (893–5); it will do so by using new arguments gleaned from the teachers of this art and thanks to a talent for countering ideas of justice through the art of antilogy (901). The 'just' speech is allowed the first say only to be subsequently overcome 'by the impact of little remarks and new ideas, like so many arrows'. Moreover, the 'weaker' argument achieves this without even attempting to conceal its true intentions:

> Why, I have been half-burst; I do so long
> To overthrow his arguments with arguments more strong.
> I am the weaker thesis? True: these schoolmen call me so,
> Simply because I was the first of all mankind to show
> How old established rules and laws might contradicted
> (*antilexai*) be.
>
> (1036–40) (Loeb translation adapted by J. de Romilly)

The whole of the argument that follows is inspired by the same amorality and a total contempt for truth.[10] Aristophanes' attack is direct and hard-hitting and is aimed against the redoubtable art of which Protagoras was the master. The protest of principle against the immorality of rhetoric here becomes more pointed and more pressing than hitherto.

What is more, unlike in the case of Gorgias, the attack here is not simply aimed against latent implications or insidious distortions. It takes as its direct target the shattering statements of Protagoras himself; and the great Sophist's ideas indeed appear to justify his attackers' worst fears. Protagoras was the author of a treatise entitled *On Truth*, which opens with the following declaration:

Of all things the measure is Man, of the things that are, that they are, and of the things that are not, that they are not. (B 1)

In other words, being can be reduced to seeming: there is no truth apart from sensation and opinion. This goes not only for what we feel but also for how we judge things. When we deem them 'beautiful' or 'ugly', 'just' or 'unjust', 'pious' or 'impious', our judgements are subjective and relative. They are valid only for ourselves.

These claims go considerably beyond the analysis in which Gorgias demonstrated the decisive role played by opinion. So grave were their implications that Plato returned repeatedly to discuss them (e.g. *Cratylus*, 386 A–E, and *Theaetetus*, 151 E–

---

[10] Anyone caught in adultery will start off by denying it (Aristophanes, *Clouds*, 1079–80), and later point out (as in Gorgias' *Helen*) that Zeus himself succumbs to love.

172 c). What Protagoras meant by these statements has been the subject of much debate, and we shall have to examine them more closely presently.[11] But their revolutionary character is immediately manifest: after centuries of religion and 'cosmic' philosophies, they introduced a total relativism that ruled out all theories of transcendency or certainty. Clearly, these ideas were closely connected with Protagoras' rhetoric. His doctrine, as expressed in *On Truth*, is, precisely, that theses and antitheses must coexist for ever in a confrontation to which there can be no resolution.[12]

The purely pragmatic trend of his rhetoric is, consequently, no accident. There can be no denying that it is not designed to discover either what is just or what is true. In Protagoras' view, it was pointless to seek the truth since it was no more than a snare and a delusion. That in itself would appear to provide philosophical justification for Plato's criticisms of a rhetoric that was opposed to the quest for truth. In all honesty, we are bound to recognize that rhetoric never fully recovered from his attack.

Rhetoric was not represented as being, in principle, a quest for the truth, nor—so far as Protagoras was concerned—could it possibly have claimed to be any such thing. However, that does not mean that, in practice, it did not help in distinguishing and understanding certain forms of the truth. For Protagoras, this was indeed precisely its role. The literature of the day confirms that fact, making it abundantly clear.

The time has come for us to emulate Protagoras himself and consider the situation from another point of view. Following the thesis, let us discover the antithesis. The thesis was conveyed by the theoretical debate on the relation of speech to truth; the antithesis is presented by texts whose authors are seeking to understand their experience of daily life. Here, we are in for a surprise, for in these texts rhetoric is put to serve ends very different from those imagined by Aristophanes. It appears to become the very key to the art of making good decisions. The fifth-century term for this was

---

[11] See below, pp. 97–103.
[12] Curiously enough, such scepticism, pushed to the limit, may turn against dialectic itself. According to Plato, Protagoras did not believe in the possibility of refutation. On this purely philosophical question, see Ch. 4.

euboulia, and it was an art by which the Sophists set great store.

Of course, it was possible to defend both a thesis and its opposite, and arguments could always be twisted: to that extent, anyone could justify anything. But the principle behind these debates was precisely that the two theses should be presented in a confrontation. The argument had to be set out together with the counter-argument, the one alongside the other. The very elements that might seem gratuitous and artificial when each side was considered in isolation became rigorous means of assessment and comparison once the two arguments were taken together.

After all, today still, if in defence of clients who are locked in conflict two advocates speak with equal eloquence, we do not consider this to hamper the judge and jury who must come to an enlightened decision. Quite the reverse. This is precisely the kind of situation that Athenian tragedy and works of history present. As in Antiphon's *Tetralogies*, the same author puts forward first one, then the other thesis. The two speeches are composed in conjunction, with the precise purpose of setting up a comparison between them.

Naturally enough, when the characters involved have particular personalities and pasts, some may resort to the kind of dishonest cleverness that Aristophanes targets. But in such cases, the text makes the matter clear and the sophistry rebounds against the cleverness of the guilty. In tragedy, for example, we understand the characters, we can distinguish the oppressed from the oppressors; our sympathies are steered to one side rather than to the other; or, if any doubt remains, the reactions of the victim guide us, as do the comments of the chorus. As we have seen, the lamentations of the chorus often testify to the dangers of rhetoric. But within the plays themselves, they also serve to palliate and offset those dangers. In the *Medea*, when Jason produces subtle arguments to justify his betrayal of his wife, the chorus-leader tells him:

> Jason, though you have made this speech of yours look well,
> Still I think, even though others do not agree,
> You have betrayed your wife and are acting badly.
>
> (576–8)

Likewise, in *The Trojan Women*, when Helen tries to prove her innocence with even greater subtlety, the chorus tells Hecuba that she must strive to resist Helen's persuasive words:

> Since she speaks
> well and has done wickedly. This is dangerous
> (966–8)

On this occasion, even the verdict condemns Helen. For the moment at least, Menelaus accepts the arguments of her accuser.

In these cases, the clever arguments backfire. Thanks to the contrast set up, they only succeed in revealing the inadequacy of their own foundations. But sometimes the scales are more evenly balanced and valid passions and memories weigh on both sides, as when Clytemnestra and Electra argue so bitterly over Agamemnon's murder, leaving us with a sense of unassuageable rancour in both women. In other clashes, the responsibilities on either side are equal, as in *Orestes*, where Tyndarus and Orestes argue over matricide. Both speak in general terms, pointing out the gravity and unacceptability of this action or that. Tyndarus shows that it is intolerable that a son should avenge his father directly, by killing his own mother: if everyone behaved in such a fashion, endless calamities would ensue. But Orestes argues that if a father's murder is allowed to go unpunished and his sons do not avenge him, the way will be open for a series of other, equally disastrous murders. Between the two of them they clearly set out the problem of what is right in all its gravity. The clash of arguments conveys the pressure of imperatives on both sides. This debate, which apparently leads to no conclusion, results in, not the discovery of some truth, but a tragic understanding of conflicting obligations.

This technique of assessing the situation in the light of all the different constraints affecting it is crucial to history as written by Thucydides.[13] Here, it is not a matter of speeches designed to reflect hypocrisy or passion; emotion does not

[13] On the antithetical speeches in Thucydides, see J. de Romilly, *Histoire et raison chez Thucydide* (Paris, 1976), ch. 3. On the influence of Prodicus, see J. de Romilly, 'Les Manies de Prodicos et la rigueur de la langue grecque', *Museum Helveticum* (1986), 1–18.

come into it. The sole concern is to analyse a situation using two opposite arguments, the two theses which, between them, cover every possibility.

When a speech is presented singly in Thucydides' *History*, it is usually because no adversary who possesses a clear view of the situation is present or, if one is, he is accounted of no importance. Pericles, for instance, is never contradicted, as if there simply could be no conceivable argument to oppose his. For the most part, though, speeches are presented in pairs, as two faces of a single block of stone, two contrary aspects of what is going on, and two opposed views of the best way to cope with it, both sensible and precise, and based on human experience, designed to complement each other, and linked by as many common details as possible. Thus combined, they enable us to see exactly where the argument can be reversed, where doubts lie, and what the outcome depends upon. The narrative then takes over, invalidating or—as the case may be—confirming the claims of the two speeches—and doing so with a far more convincing rigour than the somewhat vague appraisals made by a tragic chorus.

The clearest and most schematic models of this method of analysis are provided by Thucydides' accounts of battles such as the Battle of Naupactos, in book 2. Two antithetical arguments analyse everything that has a bearing on the battle, from the nature of courage down to the importance of military manœuvres. Then comes an account of the battle which seems at first to bear out the views of the Peloponnesians, then, thanks to a chance detail, confirms the Athenians' analyses on every point. In political analyses, the method is the same, the only difference being that the confirmation provided by the narrative may not follow on immediately or be developed so systematically. In all these cases, the use of pairs of arguments, or opposed *logoi*, and the technique of making the weaker seem the stronger—that is to say, the two procedures evolved by Protagoras—constitute means of enquiry and evaluation designed to make it possible to distinguish the true facts of a complex situation in a perfectly objective fashion, and thereby render them intelligible. It could equally be claimed, in point of fact, that Socrates' method of first posing questions, then following the answers up with refutations, also owes much to Protagoras' techniques.[14]

Everything depended upon the way in which the new art was practised. Gorgias had certainly made that point; but now the difference between the right way and the wrong way of using it was spelled out even more clearly and decisively. If, as in Aristophanes, it was a matter of defending a particular thesis chosen with a view to producing practical results and to justifying a particular line of selfish conduct, one's success clearly depended upon denying what was true and good. Used thus, the art fully deserved whatever criticisms it provoked. In contrast, used as an aid to serious thinking in which two contradictory theses were analysed, it made it possible to discover a truth more elaborate than either thesis. At the meeting point of two sets of 'appearances', two arguments, two theses, the Sophists' method operated as an intellectual technique which offered the best means of coming to a lucid understanding of the bewildering universe that surrounds us.

Admittedly, the truth discovered was never more than relative, linked as it was with 'seeming' and 'speech'. That is the chief point made by those who declare the truth of the Sophists to be merely a matter of words. But for those committed to reality and seeking for better judgement, the Sophists' techniques could be of incomparable use. For them, to study a rhetoric based on reasoning and dialectic, even if not directed towards the discovery of absolute truth, was one of the surest ways of achieving honest and rigorous thinking.

One might thus conclude that, although this method of argument provoked anxiety and scandal as soon as it was launched in Athens, at the same time, used to complement the huge curiosity that contemporary Athenians felt about human nature, for some it became a startlingly new and effective means of analysis. That would be a fair conclusion, but an incomplete one. At the end of the fifth century, the method of opposed argumentation was certainly still flour-

[14] See G. B. Kerferd, 'The Future Direction of Sophistic Studies', in the collective work, *The Sophists and their Legacy*, Hermes Einzelschriften, 44 (Wiesbaden, 1981), 4.

ishing on all sides; but soon it was abandoned. It even disappears from the history of rhetoric. We have seen how Isocrates rejected it. As for Aristotle, in his *Rhetoric*, he certainly studies different modes of reasoning and the circumstances which dictate their use, just as Protagoras did. But his purpose in doing so is to classify them. He is not concerned with practice, let alone the practice of double argumentation. Besides, once the different sciences were classified, the analysis of methods of making the weaker argument seem the stronger appeared to belong more to the category of logic than to that of rhetoric.[15]

Protagoras' art of opposed argumentation thus suffered the same fate as Gorgias' stylistic figures of rhetoric and his magical oratory. Introduced as exciting discoveries, the Sophists' lessons were initially hailed as magnificent and revolutionary; and they prompted a number of masterpieces. Then they were toned down; ambitions were tempered, and prudence took over. Their teaching was assimilated, moderated, and digested; but it was absorbed into our traditions.

The trouble is that today, when we come across the old weaponry of rhetoric as it was, and sometimes still is, used, we tend to forget the explosive discoveries and the struggles and efforts to which it owed its creation.

And there is something else that we forget and that it is time we remembered. When the tide ebbed, and things returned to normal, the wild ambitions of those early days bequeathed to the Sophists' successors not only the mature and useful science known as rhetoric but, alongside it, all the branches of research and the new disciplines that rhetoric had engendered. Grammar was one, with its enquiry into forms of speech and vocabulary, together with all the different studies connected with what we of the twentieth century have reverted to calling 'discourse', in the widest sense of the term. Another of rhetoric's legacies was logic, for it is quite clear that, in this field as in others, Aristotle's chief

---

[15] Aristotle regards what he calls 'dialectic' as part of the art of controversy. But, here again, he is not concerned so much with practicalities as with a theoretical analysis relating to the principles of a particular logic.

contribution—as he himself recognized[16]—was to draw theoretical lessons from the techniques which the Sophists had been the first to put to practical, empirical use.

Rhetoric also left behind some truly human sciences which it had invented to serve its own ends. One was psychology, the basis for all arguments of likelihood: the study of character, of people's normal reactions, their motives and weaknesses, and the constant features discernible in human behaviour. Palpable proof of that is provided by the general remarks with which the debates in Euripides and the speeches in Thucydides are studded, and is confirmed by the presence of a description of human characteristics and passions in Aristotle's *Rhetoric*. Once again, we are bound to note the ambitious confidence that the Sophists' contemporaries possessed: they did not doubt the possibility of establishing universal laws and a general science of human nature. Subsequently, those ambitions were modified: the Sophists' successors were content to observe and classify, recognizing that different cases and individuals could vary widely.

The science of psychology was frequently applied to cities, as can be seen in Thucydides and in Euripides too. An understanding of the rules that govern the behaviour of cities in times of peace and in times of war in its turn laid the foundations for the political and social sciences. Both make an appearance in Thucydides, chiefly in the speeches, where they supply a basis of argumentation for the orators' analyses. Political science and social science both sprang up in the wake of rhetoric, to serve and strengthen it.

The same goes for the science of military strategy, which is founded upon an analysis of the normal reactions of armies: 'after a victory, an army always...'; 'if he wishes to be successful, a leader always...'; 'a sea-battle always...', etc.: such are the general and somewhat simplistic reflections upon which the analyses of generals tend to be based.

---

[16] In his *Refutation of the Arguments of the Sophists* (183–4), he defines what it is that distinguishes him from the Sophists' type of rhetorical reasoning. In the first place, that type of reasoning only suits illusory probabilities, not the truth. Secondly, he is not describing a *technē*, but a series of applications (*ta apo tēs technēs*).

Strategy was thus yet another science born in the wake of rhetoric. One could make the same claim for other branches of study too, ones with more modern names such as politology, polemology, and so on, which are also hinted at in Thucydides. This is where everything started, under the impulse of rhetoric. Then, once they got going, all these human sciences shed their ties, and diversified, and they too became more empirical and more modest.

That is perhaps a timely reminder, for the distrust of rhetoric and all its lying ways that the Athenians developed could obscure these facts, as could the suspicion with which many people today regard studies of this kind. It was also a necessary reminder because, where the Sophists are concerned, it is so very easy to confuse the different categories. It was one thing to worry about the possible moral consequences of the use of rhetoric, quite another to react against explicit doctrines which denied the very existence of values.

Now, as we have seen in connection with Protagoras' treatise *On Truth*, in the case of the major Sophists the situation is complicated by the fact that they were not solely teachers of rhetoric. They were also, indeed first and foremost, thinkers; and, partly to show off their skills perhaps, but assuredly also to defend their doctrines, they were writers. Their theoretical works were well known, in fact famous, with an impact made all the sharper by their caustic, biting edge. Even without their rhetorical techniques, the Sophists' critical analyses would have been enough to sweep aside all earlier beliefs.

4

The Doctrines of the Sophists:
A *Tabula Rasa*

THE Sophists' written works, quoted extracts and summaries of which were circulating in the city, more than confirmed the fears of the Athenians. The doctrines that they reflected were by no means confined to the subject of teaching rhetoric: they boldly rejected the existing traditions, and their potential power to shock was considerable.

At this point, we enter upon new ground. These were truly philosophical doctrines, closely and confidently argued and every bit as audacious as the Sophists' activities in the sphere of teaching. It is important to make this absolutely clear, for the Sophists' doctrines should not be underestimated as a result of being associated with their teaching activities. Conscious of the practical aspect of the lessons that the Sophists gave and the arbitrary methods that, as masters of rhetoric, they used to show off their ability to defend an antithesis to every thesis, some critics have been led to minimize the importance of the Sophists' thought, despite the fact that it could hardly be more rigorous. Others have also been influenced by Plato and much affected by the contrast between his philosophical rigour and the more practical character of the Sophists' thinking. Hence the idea that has arisen that these teachers had no personal doctrines but just adopted those which suited their own professional interests.[1]

---

[1] Cf. H. I. Marrou, in his *A History of Education in Antiquity*, trans. George Lamb (London, 1977), where he comments that the Sophists were not, strictly speaking, thinkers and seekers after truth, but pedagogues. It is perfectly possible to be both at once. Others have dwelt upon the Sophists' sceptical side, with similar results, e.g. B. Cassin, 'Philosophie des apparences et apparence de la philosophie', in Cassin (ed.), *Le Plaisir de parler: Études de sophistique comparée* (Paris, 1986), 6.

I consider that view to be distorted and less than fair. It is perfectly possible to play a practical role and take an interest in the realities of day-to-day life while at the same time evolving a serious philosophy concerning the principles involved. And Plato's philosophy does not rule out alternatives. This chapter aims to show that, as abundant proof confirms, the Sophists were not content simply to conform with the facile attitudes of realists and pragmatists. The very tone of their statements, clear, definite, and bold, presupposes their adoption of a conscious position: they go straight to fundamental principles. What is more, they are completely coherent and closely argued. Finally, their very reception testifies to their importance and their indisputable originality. They were found both shocking and stimulating, and were cited, criticized, and discussed not only at the time but for centuries after.

Let us try to rediscover their ideas by sifting through the treatises that they composed. Virtually every one seems to have constituted a forthright attack against the major convictions of earlier thinkers. The written works themselves have, of course, been lost. But fragments survive, many of them statements of a revolutionary and uncompromising nature which it is not surprising to find reproduced in the work of Sextus Empiricus, the sceptic philosopher of the second century AD. No one could supply him with more effective ammunition in his struggle against dogmatism than this handful of philosophers of a new breed, who converged upon Athens seven centuries earlier and there subjected all existing beliefs to their ruthless analysis.

The Sophists' uncompromising contradictions and rejections stamp their mark upon every domain. In each, they become ever more radical as text succeeds text. No belief in the transcendental or the absolute is proof against the onslaught of the Sophists' reasoning, now supremely confident and ready to criticize any- and everything. Suddenly all the old notions seem to collapse: not only the idea of being, and the very existence of truth; but also assumptions that directly affect the way in which life is lived and that used to constitute the bases of religion and ethics: namely, the existence of the gods, and the meaning of justice.

It is sometimes hard to resist the doctrinaire interpretations and facile over-simplifications that have been put
forward in all these areas. But let us try to limit the Sophists'
declarations to their essential meanings. Even when scrupulously reduced to their exact implications, they retain a
disconcerting negative force.

Being and Truth

Being, in the metaphysical sense of the term, was a matter
that concerned only the professional philosophers. In this
area, the only attacks came from Gorgias. Gorgias arrived in
Athens several years after Protagoras. Let us notwithstanding
turn first to these criticisms of his, since the text in which
they appear is the only one which does not immediately
adopt a humanist point of view, but begins by considering the
philosophers of the past and establishes its own position in
relation to their problems. The earliest philosophers spoke
of the universe, affirming either its unity or its diversity. In
his great poem, *On Nature*, Parmenides defended its unity,
declaring:

Being has no coming-into-being and no destruction, for it is whole of
limb, without motion and without end. (fr. 8. 3–4)

and he maintained that non-being could not exist since it
could not be conceived.

Now Gorgias burst upon the scene. He is the only Sophist
to have left us a sample of writing that runs to several pages,
of a metaphysical nature, and conceived within the framework of earlier schools of thought. Significantly enough,
Gorgias hailed from Sicily, the home of Empedocles, where
he lived not too far from the town of Elea, the birthplace of
Parmenides. A relatively long fragment of his writing has
come down to us (thanks, of course, to Sextus Empiricus). It is
part of a treatise entitled—characteristically enough—'On
Non-being or Nature'. Like the works of earlier philosophers,
it is chiefly concerned with being and non-being, the possibility of understanding those concepts, and the beginnings of
being. It is, accordingly, not too surprising that a short,
comparative survey of the first century should have been

entitled 'On Melissus, Xenophanes, and Gorgias'. Melissus was an Eleatic philosopher of the same period as Gorgias, Xenophanes an earlier philosopher who also accepted the principle of indivisible and immutable being (although he did draw a distinction between knowledge and opinion). The fact that Gorgias is associated with these two authors is a clear indication of the close relation between the subject of his treatise and prevailing philosophical preoccupations of the day.

However, that is as far as the similarity goes. For though the problems may be old ones, Gorgias' solutions are altogether new. His rejection of earlier theories is radical and uncompromising. Gorgias presents three theses: (1) nothing exists; (2) if anything exists, it is incomprehensible; (3) if it *is* comprehensible, it is incommunicable. At a stroke, everything—not only being, but knowledge too—is rejected.

The demonstration is, admittedly, somewhat bewildering. Drily and tersely, it sets out a number of statements relating to the principle of contradiction (for example, if non-being is, it means both that it is and that it is not, and so on). But one striking point is that, rather as in the case of Helen's innocence, Gorgias proceeds by establishing a series of a priori distinctions (for example, if something is it is either being or non-being or being and non-being; if being is, it is either eternal or belongs to becoming or else it is both eternal and also belongs to becoming...); at every turn, a sort of logical game is played out, sustained by rapid-fire verbal flourishes.[2]

The method is that of the master of rhetoric, but behind it stands the philosopher. We sense that the text constitutes a kind of response to Parmenides, who held that being is and non-being is not, since we can have no concept of it. By introducing the notion of the beginning of being or that of its limits, Gorgias reveals contradictions that cannot be avoided. With his sequence of critical demonstrations, he establishes his dominant idea that it is impossible to know anything,

---

[2] To preserve this, the commentary here uses the word 'being' throughout, even where modern philosophers might make a distinction between 'being' and 'existing'.

maintain anything, or prove anything once and for all. It is not so much that he insists that nothing exists. Rather, he seeks to show that ideas about being can easily by reversed and are consequently essentially vain. Sextus Empiricus certainly understood what he was saying, for in his introduction to this text, he classified Gorgias among those who did away with the 'means of judging' (the *kritērion*).

Perhaps this eminently formal demonstration of Gorgias' contains an element of playfulness. Scholars still debate that question, even today. It has been pointed out that neither Plato nor Aristotle appear to have paid it serious attention, and that Isocrates, who admittedly was not much of a metaphysician, somewhat disparaged Gorgias' analyses.[3] Nevertheless, the exercise—if that is what it was—adopted an extremely negative and sceptical position *vis-à-vis* certain recognized problems, and the very fact that Gorgias was prepared to play about with such questions betrays a measure of scepticism on his part. In a context such as this, his irony in itself seemed to dismiss all the earlier theories about being.

Furthermore, the reservations that Gorgias expresses elsewhere about the possibility of knowledge seem to be echoed in an extreme form in this text. This possibly playful exercise in polemics is thus in line with more serious philosophical critiques, and implies a complete change of perspective. In that it sweeps aside everything that seemed sure or even thinkable, it opens the door to scepticism in all its forms. It is thus in profound agreement with one of the foremost doctrines of Sophistic thought: Protagoras' doctrine of relativism.

We have already come across[4] the treatise which Protagoras entitled *Truth*, which began by declaring, 'Of all things the measure is Man, of the things that are, that they are, and of

---

[3] *Hel.* 3: 'For how could one surpass Gorgias, who dared to assert that nothing exists of the things that are, or Zeno, who ventured to prove the same things as possible and again as impossible, or Melissus, who, although things in nature are infinite in number, made it his task to find proofs that the whole is one!' The frivolous aspect of Gorgias' text is recognized by both H. Gomperz and E. R. Dodds (Introduction to the *Gorgias* (Oxford, 1959), 6–10).

[4] Cf. Ch. 3, above, 85.

the things that are not, that they are not.' It is a declaration that we shall meet with again in this book, in connection with a wide range of ideas. It sounds the keynote to the Sophists' thought and dictates all the rest.

It is accordingly most important to assess its meaning and implications. The general sense is, of course, clear enough. It is still viable to speak of being and non-being, but questions of reality and truth are now superseded: all that remain are human impressions. Everything now depends upon man's feelings and opinions, feelings and opinions that can be neither challenged nor confirmed and vary from one person to another and according to circumstances. These are now the only criteria, the only yardsticks: 'Things are to me such as they seem to me', as Socrates sums up in the *Cratylus* (386 A). At a stroke, man becomes sole judge; and all about him all ideas begin to float free, with nothing to anchor them down.

The short treatise known as *Double Arguments* conveys some idea of this kind of relativism. Its arguments show that the good and the bad, the beautiful and the ugly, the just and the unjust become confused because they are only what they are according to one individual in a particular situation. The principle here was totally revolutionary and swept aside the very concept of objective truth.

Everything was immediately brought into question, starting with the possibility of any knowledge whatsoever and the very existence of error. One can see how it was that Plato, (in the *Theaetetus* in particular) determined to grapple with Protagoras' thesis. To judge by *Metaphysics*, book 3, even Aristotle seems to have been exercised by the problem. Protagoras had produced a philosophical thesis which was alarming and could not be ignored.

In an apparently paradoxical fashion, it seems to have involved the father of double arguments and antilogies in a philosophical quarrel in which he found himself in strange company: Plato calls Protagoras the kind of person who denies that it is possible either to speak wrongly or to refute (*antilegein*).[5] The disagreement was a famous one (Isocrates

---

[5] *Euth.* 286 B–C; cf. *Cra.* 429 D ff., and *Sph.* 237 A ff. A papyrus from Toura attributes the same thesis to Prodicus. Antisthenes seems to have continued

refers to it in the very first lines of his *Helen*). But the thesis as formulated seems to have linked on the one hand men such as Parmenides, who believed in the absolute unity of being (so that, according to him, it was impossible to speak of non-being) with, on the other, those like Protagoras, who did not believe in any truth at all (so that one could never claim to speak of being). For want of relevant texts, part of the polemic eludes us. But the echoes that it leaves at least provide added proof of the metaphysical significance of the statements made by Protagoras. Scholastic squabbles aside, there can be no doubt that his treatise postulated a world in which there was no such thing as truth. The step that Plato, following Parmenides, took when he proclaimed the existence of absolute, universal, and transcendental truth was certainly bold. But Protagoras' contrary and resolute denial of the very existence of truth was no less so. Much of Plato's philosophy is a response to Protagoras.

Given the importance of the thesis, it is a shame that nothing more definite can be said about it. Although its general orientation is patently clear, it is not easy to determine exactly how far Protagoras went. Some modern authors have zealously endeavoured to do so, but let us, for our part, limit ourselves to trying to discern its main arguments.

The first question which scholars have asked is whether 'man' is intended to denote one individual or human beings in general. If we accept Plato's testimony, there can be no doubt about the answer: when he refers to this doctrine in the *Theaetetus* it is the individual aspect that he repeatedly emphasizes. The examples that he cites relate to sensations which vary from one person to another (such as sweetness and bitterness); and he speaks of 'each person', 'each person for himself', and 'individual (*idiai*) sensations'. He also speaks of differences between 'one person' and 'another': 'each person differs immeasurably from every other in just this, that to one person some things appear and are, and to another person other things' (166 D). Perhaps Plato, who believed in

along this line. On this problem, see G. Binder and L. Liesenborghs, (Eine Zuweisung der Sentenz) οὐκ ἔϭτιν ἀντιλέγειν an Prodikos von keos', *Museum Helveticum*, 23 (1966), 37–43, repr. in C. J. Classen (ed.), *Sophistik*, (Wege der Forschung, 187) (Darmstadt, 1976), 452–62.

absolute essences that could be apprehended by the human mind, wished to make Protagoras' relativism seem as extreme as possible. Nevertheless, all the concrete examples that he cites in passing fit in with what Protagoras says, so there can be little doubt that Plato's account of what Protagoras meant was correct. Furthermore, Plato's interpretation is also in agreement with another fragment recently attributed to Protagoras, which states: 'To you who are present, I seem to be seated; to those who are absent, I do not: whether I am or not is not clear.'[6] The individual is clearly of primary importance in this doctrine.

Certain qualifications are nevertheless in order. Perhaps we should resist our modern inclination to decide categorically between the two possible interpretations. In the fifth century BC, nobody thought of the individual in isolation. And Protagoras himself possessed an exceptionally strong sense of the collective group.[7]

Furthermore, the notion of the collective group prompts other, still more important qualifications. According to the *Theaetetus*, Protagoras did acknowledge the possibility of convincing other people and also that some opinions could be more useful than others, both for individuals and for the group as a whole. His relativism thus recognized certain practical bounds. That is precisely the point that Plato seized upon in his attempt to refute the doctrine according to which man is the measure of all things. In some circumstances, Protagoras has to recognize the existence of a kind of wisdom which some possess in greater degree than others. Thus in the *Theaetetus*, where Socrates is imagining what Protagoras might have to say, Plato writes as follows:

I do not by any means say that wisdom and the wise man do not exist. On the contrary, I say that if bad things appear and are to any one of us, precisely that man is wise who causes a change and makes good things appear and be to him. (166 D)

---

[6] This fragment comes from a commentary on the Psalms, believed to be by Didymus 'the Blind'. Its authenticity is questionable and its meaning controversial. Some scholars, using different punctuation, regard the doubt as applying only to those who are absent (as the text says that it is not clear *to them*).

[7] See below, pp. 163–6.

That, he says, is exactly how a doctor proceeds with his patients or a Sophist with his pupils.

We must thus beware of drawing extravagant conclusions from Protagoras' somewhat peremptory statements. His rejection of truth leaves room for certain particular truths, or something of the kind. Nor can his thought be identified with later doctrines, whether labelled subjectivism or pure solipsism, which were to close the subject in upon itself.[8] A study of Protagoras' thought in other areas will help to make this clear, by confirming the importance that he attached to human relations. When seeking the origins of the doctrines of the Sceptics, Diogenes Laertius mentioned a host of ancient authors, but not Protagoras. Seen in the light of later attitudes, his relativism is not extreme.

Having made the above reservations, however, we are bound to recognize that, in its very principles, this relativism constituted a most daunting critical attack which clashed head-on both with philosophical doctrines which proclaimed that truth did exist and also with the barely conscious assumptions which afforded ordinary people reassurance through the notion of values which served to give their lives some foundation. Protagoras' trenchant declarations denied the validity of all those doctrines and undermined those foundations. All that was left was opinions, based upon feelings, and all subjective. It was now a matter of living in a world of appearances: seeming was all that could be known. One point of view could always be countered by another. The man who delighted in the clash of two contrary *logoi* ended up by offering a world in which that clash became law, and any one thesis was as valid as any other.

The importance of this doctrine to the history of Greek thought is considerable, as may be measured by Plato's reactions to it. Not only does he mention and criticize it repeatedly but he also seems to construct his own philosophy with these ideas in mind and in order to refute them. So much is clear from *The Sophist*, in which Protagoras himself is not

---

[8] See the recent observations of L. Rossetti, 'La Certitude objective inébranlable', in B. Cassin (ed.), *Positions de la sophistique* (Paris, 1986), 197–200.

named but Plato sets out to define Sophists in general. In order to do so, he is obliged to make a long digression which takes in Parmenides, so as to establish, in opposition to his views, the possibility of error—error which brings into being that which is not. The digression, which took in being and non-being, truth, and Parmenides, was a major and revealing one. Reacting against the thought of the Sophists, who, inspired by Protagoras, denied the distinction between error and truth, Plato used it, with determined rigour, to construct an altogether opposite philosophy.

The very terms used reflect the fundamental opposition. The word which has such a triumphant ring in Protagoras' statement is 'man': 'the measure of all things is man'. Man is what matters. What this means is that Protagoras jettisons all notions of being and truth that are in any way connected with the gods. In other words, at a single stroke he sets up a new universe in which the gods have no part to play. As a result of focusing upon the exact degree to which Protagoras' 'man' may be individual or collective, we have sometimes ended up by losing sight of this essential difference, which changed everything.

In this connection, Plato indulges in a moment of deliberate injustice when he jokingly has Socrates (still in the *Theaetetus*) say that he was surprised at the early part of Protagoras' treatise:

I don't see why he does not say in the beginning of his *Truth* that a pig or a dog-faced baboon or some still stranger creature of those that have sensations is the measure of all things. Then he might have begun to speak to us very imposingly and condescendingly, showing that while we were honouring him like a god for his wisdom, he was after all no better in intellect than any other man or, for that matter, than a tadpole. (161 C)

The text is lively and amusing. But, as used by Protagoras, the reference to 'man' was not at all arbitrary. he knew exactly what he was doing when he used it. He was rejecting the transcendent, limiting himself to a world of sensations, opinions, and interests—whether individual, collective, or general. But, as he did so, he retained the possibility of using this world as the foundation for an entire system of thought and morality which he would reconstruct without needing to resort to absolutes of any kind—whether ontological, religious, or ethical.

Everything rested upon that sentence: 'Man is the measure of all things'. So it is understandable enough that Plato—joking aside—should have sensed that it implied the crucial philosophical problem. It is thus by no means by chance that, in the last years of his own work, he wrote as follows in *The Laws*:

In our eyes God will be 'the measure of all things' in the highest degree—a degree much higher than any 'man' they talk of. (716 c)

The opposite poles of Western philosophy are summed up in those two contradictory statements.

The Gods

Protagoras' analysis of knowledge and truth implied resubjecting all religious beliefs to doubt. And we know that he also applied his critique to the domain of religion, an application which was at once central to his doctrine and dangerous from the point of view of Athenian public opinion. What is more, he was by no means the only Sophist to tackle the subject of religion. Most of the thinkers of the last quarter of the fifth century appear to have followed eagerly in his wake.

When the Sophists' critique affected themes upon which peoples' lives and behaviour depended, it proved even more resonant. It was taken over by other teachers, becoming stronger in tone or more radical in the process. For that very reason, it is important for us to examine it more closely. The effort will prove worth while. Only by dint of numerous comparisons is it possible to show that each step forward constituted a decisive new stage in the critique but one which was destined soon to be overtaken. Hence the repeated need to assess the distance covered and gauge how much further there is yet to go, to appreciate the boldness of the Sophists' venture but also its limits, to recognize its audacity at the same time as its relative prudence. In this way we shall, in the first place, avoid muddling up these teachers: for they were by no means interchangeable but were prone to take over from one another. Secondly, we shall avoid over-simplifying the Sophists' theses, which, because of their great impact and influence, have ever since antiquity so often suffered that very fate. We shall have to proceed very cautiously if we are to circumvent all the confusions, both ancient and modern, and rediscover the Sophists' thought in all its true rigour.

Actually, so far as Protagoras and the gods go, there is no great problem. On this subject, all that we possess is one statement, and its meaning is perfectly clear. The Christian writer Eusebius tells us that it was the opening sentence of Protagoras' treatise *On the Gods*, and it is attested by numerous citations. It runs as follows:

About the gods, I am not able to know whether they exist or do not exist, nor what they are like in form; for the factors preventing knowledge are many: the obscurity of the subject, and the shortness of human life. (B 4)

The last words have sometimes been omitted, but they are important. They indicate the ground upon which Protagoras took up his position and the nature of his agnosticism. All that mattered to him was what could be known; and the Greek word (*eidenai*) that is used twice in this sentence means, precisely, knowledge: not belief, not faith. Protagoras' point is that it is impossible to know anything about the gods. He does not say that they do not exist. That is an important difference. Cicero, in his treatise *On the Nature of the Gods* (1.1.2), was already concerned to draw a distinction between Protagoras' kind of doubt and genuine atheism. Some scholars hold that there is no reason why Protagoras should not have envisaged other bases for religion, and the remainder of this treatise may have explained what they were. But, as it stands, the sentence amounts to no more than a strict, perfectly clear analysis. Some scholars have used the word phenomenology in its connection.

The fact remains, however, that Protagoras' way, here too, of taking man as his starting-point and proceeding to consider only what man can or cannot know took on a revolutionary character when it came to the matter of the gods. From the point of view of knowledge, the statement that we cannot know whether the gods exist is indisputable, but it flies directly in the face of religious traditions, casting doubt upon them and condemning them. Because it opened up the way for impiety, it was considered scandalous.[9]

The matter is sufficiently important to warrant our seeking to establish the circumstances in which this agnosticism arose. The Greek religion incorporated no dogma and no priestly hierarchy. To express doubts where it was concerned was consequently less risky than it might be in the case of other religions. It was perfectly prepared to accommodate new gods: the divine myths acquired different versions at the hands of different authors and in the different places where their cult was celebrated. Several legends and several cults would be connected with each of the gods, and all this made for a general basic freedom. This found expression in increasingly discriminating ideas about the gods. Homer, even in his day, was covering up certain legends which were generally well known at the time (about Zeus' love affairs, for instance). Pindar himself agrees that he has in fact toned down certain stories about Pelops, because ill should not be spoken of the gods: 'Far be it from me to call any one of the blessed gods a cannibal!' (*Olympian Odes*, 1.35 and 52). Aeschylus, in his turn, makes an effort to gain a better understanding of the justice of Zeus, rejecting the notion of a virtually automatic nemesis sent to strike down wealth and greatness rather than wrongdoing and crime. And the philosopher Xenophanes, cited above in connection with Gorgias, went considerably further as early as the seventh century, refusing to envisage the gods in the anthropomorphic guise attributed to them by religion. He considered it deluded to give them clothes, voices, and bodies. In a sense, Protagoras' version of agnosticism constituted hardly more of an affront to the beliefs of his day.

Yet he did overstep one decisive mark. To modify, review, and correct the tenets of religion was a way of improving it from within. But to call the very existence of the gods into question was quite another matter. We must remember that,

---

[9] Protagoras had also written a treatise (or a chapter) entitled *On the Underworld* (or *On What Takes Place in Hades*). We know nothing of its contents; but the analysis is likely to have rested upon the critique and—so to speak—humanization of traditional views.

even if the Greek religion was free of dogma and a priestly hierarchy, it nevertheless was indissolubly linked with the life of the city. The gods protected the city and they also guaranteed morality, oaths, and the laws, the combination of which ensured that order was maintained in the city. Once it became accepted that the gods might not exist at all, the city's civic and moral foundations as a whole were in danger of crumbling away. As has already been noted, the city's response to this threat was to step up the pressing of charges of impiety.

The first wave of persecutions hit Pericles and his friends very hard. Pericles was friendly with Protagoras. He represented an enlightened attitude; and, as we have seen,[10] he preferred scientific explanations to omens. All this was acceptable. But when the difficulties with Sparta arose and hostility toward Pericles increased, those close to him were prosecuted, many of them for impiety. Aspasia, the woman he loved, was one, and Pericles was hard put to it to save her. Anaxagoras was the target of a decree announcing that all those who did not believe in the gods and who purveyed doctrines relating to celestial phenomena[11] would be accused of crimes against the State. Plutarch, who reports all this in his *Life of Pericles* (32), goes on to say that the author of that decree—a diviner, as it happened—'was aiming for Pericles, through Anaxagoras'. Pericles took the precaution of arranging for the philosopher to leave Athens. At this point, no specific mention is made of Protagoras (although Plutarch, in his *Life of Nicias* (23) connects his banishment with the arrest of Anaxagoras). But he too is said to have been later accused of impiety, and his books were publicly burned. Nor can we forget that the same accusation was subsequently levelled at Socrates, one of the charges being that of 'not recognizing the city gods to be gods, and introducing new ones'.

Protagoras' agnosticism thus led on to extremely dangerous ground, as is clear from the developments that followed. These show that the crisis then building up in Athens was of

---

[10] Cf. above, p. 11.

[11] Philosophers who concern themselves with celestial matters are assimilated to rationalists: the role of the clouds in Aristophanes' comedy presupposes a similar judgement.

the utmost gravity. In the wake of Protagoras, other Sophists went much further. Following the early surge of rationalism in the mid-fifth century, the wave of irreligiosity seemed to be gathering increasing momentum. It all happened within the space of twenty-five years.

Prodicus, who seems to have had so much in common with Protagoras in his concern for correct expression, was no revolutionary spirit, rather a man devoted to moral values. But on the issue of the gods, he appears to have followed in Protagoras' footsteps and even made matters worse. Prodicus no longer considers the subject of religion from the point of view of knowledge. As if belief in the gods were simply a phenomenon like any other, he offers an anthropological and positivist explanation for it. From the point of view of human enquiry and human knowledge, this marks an almost incredible leap forward. Meanwhile, from a religious point of view, the gods—many of them, at least—are reduced to the status of human inventions. In a fragment (cited, needless to say, by Sextus Empiricus, but also known to us from other sources), Prodicus declares that: 'The ancients accounted as Gods the sun and moon and rivers and springs and in general all the things that are of benefit to our life, because of the benefit derived from them, even as the Egyptians deify the Nile' (B 5)

That says it all: utility, the naturalist explanation, the comparative approach. Prodicus' theory, which has some-times been compared to Euhemerism (although he does not seem to have envisaged the possibility of men becoming gods), is certainly extremely bold and represents a great step forward in the direction of a radically scientific attitude. Is this at last true atheism, as some ancient authors (including Sextus Empiricus) have claimed? We cannot be certain. Else-where, Prodicus also speaks of the gods; and some modern scholars such as Dodds[12] have carefully distinguished Prodi-cus' doctrine from atheism, regarding the former simply as the expression of a mind of a very modern cast. The most remark-

---

[12] Commentary on *The Bacchae*, 274–85, where Tiresias (a diviner, no less!) declares that Demeter is a goddess, but so too is the earth, and Dionysus is a god, but so too is wine.

able feature of this text is certainly the way that the scientific spirit breaks through, gains in confidence, and is confirmed. It leaves scant room for religious preoccupations. All the same, it does not attack them directly.

The Sophists were to make many such statements—more and more as the years passed. We possess a fragment twenty-two lines long from a play entitled *Sisyphus*, which constitutes a striking example. Unfortunately, it is hard to say who wrote it, for when cited the lines are sometimes attributed to Critias, sometimes to Euripides. Strangely enough, almost all the tragic fragments ever attributed to Critias have also, at some time or other, been claimed for Euripides. That in itself testifies to the resemblance between the thinking of these contemporary writers, all of whom were so receptive to the new ideas and influence of the Sophists. For many years the opinion of Wilamowitz, who attributed this fragment to Critias, prevailed. Recently however, a careful study has made out a good case for attributing it to Euripides.[13]

From the point of view adopted by the present work, the authorship of these lines makes quite a difference. Critias is a well-known figure. He was Plato's uncle and one of the most intrepid of the thirty oligarchs who seized power in Athens in 404; but he was also a Sophist, at least so the tradition of antiquity would have us believe. Even if he did not receive any payment for his lectures, he lived as an intellectual, writing treatises on constitutions, taking part in philosophical debates, and helping to spread the Sophists' ideas. On the other hand Euripides, though influenced by the Sophists, clearly remained an outsider. Is the text truly attributable to a Sophist or not? Should it be considered evidence of their doctrines or merely of their influence?

Whatever the truth may be, the choice between these two names is in itself significant for, as it turns out, this, the most outspoken of all the texts hostile to religion that we shall be examining, is also the one connected in the most marginal fashion with the Sophists' circle, and certainly no more than distantly with the earliest great masters: either the author

[13] A. Dihle, 'Das Satyrspiel "Sisyphes"', *Hermes*, 105 (1977), 28–42.

was an Athenian who had listened to the Sophists, namely Euripides; or else he was a man who, although he is sometimes called a Sophist, was another Athenian, one decidedly inclined to practical action and highly ambitious—in short, a man who was no longer a Sophist in the strict sense of the term. As the Sophists' doctrines spread to a wider audience, beyond the inner circle of the masters themselves, they tended to adopt a harder line, as abundant testimony shows. If the fragment from the *Sisyphus* is included here among the works of the true Sophists, it is therefore only with reservations and to avoid any accusation of watering down the Sophists' thought.

We know, at any rate, that the passage comes from a satirical drama of the late fifth century. It conveys the thoughts of a character remarkably unencumbered with moral scruples (rather like Euripides' Cyclops), but who expresses himself in a somewhat dogmatic fashion. He begins—like so many others of this period—by describing the progress of human life since its disorderly beginnings. He points out that initially there were no rewards for the good and no punishments for the wicked. Then men set up laws, so that justice should reign. But those laws had no effect upon actions performed in secret with no witnesses. So then

a wise and clever (*sophos*) man invented fear [of the gods] for mortals, that there might be some means of frightening the wicked, even if they do anything or think or say it in secret. Hence he introduced the Divine [religion] saying that there is a god flourishing with immortal life, hearing and seeing with his mind . . .

In truth, though, it was no more than a handy invention, for he was 'covering up the truth with a false theory'. Now men became fearful of all natural phenomena. But their fear put a stop to their disorders.

In this text, the existence of the gods really is accounted an invention and a lie. There can be no doubt about the full implications of these lies. At first sight, the point at issue might seem to be solely the justice of the gods and whether or not they are concerned to punish the wicked. It is quite true that the text tackles this idea forthrightly and concludes that the notion of divine justice is a baseless myth. In this respect the *Sisyphus* is in line with a well-attested tendency of the day which did much to encourage religious doubts and which the Sophists played their part in spreading. People were tending to wonder whether the gods really existed, given that, as dispensers of justice, they made no impact upon human life. Another fragment by a Sophist of the same period, Thrasymachus, noted that the gods did nothing to help justice to prevail:

The gods do not see human affairs; otherwise they would not have overlooked the greatest of all blessings among mankind, Justice— for we see mankind not using this virtue. (B 8)

Divine justice had always been problematic, and the Sophists were certainly not inclined to let the matter drop. Half a century later, Plato was to refer to this attitude, noting in *The Laws* (10. 888 c) that a belief does remain 'not indeed with many, but still with some—the notion, namely, that the gods exist, but pay no heed to human affairs'. The problem was to be resuscitated by Plutarch and was later to pervade the whole of Western thought.

However, the short text from the *Sisyphus* did not limit itself to that degree of incredulity. For this author, the gods themselves are a fabrication, a myth designed to frighten the wicked. The last two lines of the fragment dispel all doubt on this score; they run as follows: 'Thus, I think, for the first time did someone persuade mortals to believe in a race of deities (*daimonōn*)'.

This is completely different from the scientific view adopted by Prodicus. For Prodicus, the starting-point was the spontaneous feelings that exist in human beings; and his explanation, with various modifications, was to remain a feature of all materialist philosophies.[14] He had pointed out the natural awe that human beings feel, faced with everything that is useful to life. The Epicureans (following

---

[14] These doctrines should, of course, be distinguished from those of certain ancient writers on 'physics', who believed more or less divine forces to be at work in nature (the Whirlwind, the Ether, Strife, Love . . .); these forces could be regarded as new gods, at least that is the attitude of Aristophanes, who suggests that Socrates invented his new deities, the 'Clouds'. In the eyes of the public, all forms of impiety seemed much the same.

Democritus, who was a contemporary of Prodicus) were to emphasize the natural fears that those same human beings feel when faced with phenomena that they do not understand. All these philosophers were trying to account for certain spontaneous tendencies that human beings could be seen to possess. The author of the *Sisyphus*, in contrast, suggests that these same human beings were artificially inspired with fears by one of their own number. This individual invented the lies which writers such as Lucretius were later to try to refute in order to set mens' minds at rest. In the *Sisyphus*, the anger of the gods is represented as a fable invented by a clever politician.[15]

After Protagoras' agnostic reservations, a rapid evolution thus took place. A few bold statements sufficed to convert an ability to produce lucid definitions into a veritable free-thinking spirit. Man, the measure of all things, became the sole inventor of the false notion of the transcendent.

It is all too easy to see how it was that the new line of thought was upsetting to the public; and the emotional response that it provoked was itself instrumental in distorting peoples' perceptions. The domain of religion which was affected by these theories was so closely tied up with the citizens' traditions and beliefs that it proved impossible for them to understand and respect the subtle differences of degree that are so important in philosophical thought. In the context of the scandal that broke, people did not take the trouble to look into details or enter into fine distinctions. The sense of scandal and shock was the more understandable since, if belief in the gods foundered, one of the essential bases upon which morality and respect for the laws rested might well be swept away with it.

Justice

When laws were sanctioned by the gods and implemented their will, they had a clear and solid basis. Even without

---

[15] Theories as bold as this have seldom been formulated in such a forthright fashion. W. K. C. Guthrie (*The Sophists* (Cambridge, 1971), 244) considers that only Polybius and the German thinkers of the eighteenth century are at all comparable; and even they lacked the uncompromising force of the earlier thinkers.

the sanction of the gods, it might just be possible to preserve some idea of a cosmic equilibrium that was reflected
in human justice. But how could anyone know of such an
absolute justice? Where was it to be found? If man was the
measure of all things, the only justice was his justice, that is
to say, his particular idea of justice, as expressed in his laws.
In that case there was no difference between justice and
legality. And legality varied according to place and time. So
now justice itself had become unstable and relative, without
any solid basis. Justice too was about to go by the board, like
everything else.

It should be noticed that this collapse was also related to
another side to the current critical trend. Here, the starting-
point was not theoretical analysis but a new concrete
awareness of diversity. Herodotus was one of Protagoras'
contemporaries. In his ethnological enquiries, he had recently revealed the wide variety of human customs. He had
even expounded upon the subject in some of the little tales
that he told. The conclusion that he drew from his discoveries
was that one should always display tolerance. In book 3 (38),
he suggests that if one collected together all the finest rules
of life and all the finest laws and offered them to the human
race, each individual would choose those of his own society.
Then he cites as examples customs held to be monstrous by
the Greeks but which were practised in other parts of the
world: eating the body of one's father, for instance, as certain
Indians did.

The recognition of the diversity of human customs might
lead one to consider them all as equally vain and without
foundation. It was the kind of subject that intrigued the
Sophists. Hippias in his turn appears to have carried out
some ethnological research and written on the names of
different peoples. More certainly, the short treatise known as
Double Arguments demonstrates clearly that this variety in
value-judgements could serve as a marvellous argument for
relativists, and that the latter did not hesitate to make full
use of Herodotus. Setting out to demonstrate the relativity
of the notions of beautiful and ugly, the author cites a whole
string of customs, both Greek and barbarian, all of which
were severely condemned by other peoples. The Spartans

considered it correct for girls to strip to practise gymnastics, while the Ionians considered it most unbecoming. The Thessalians thought it fine to tame horses and slaughter oxen; the Sicilians found such practices degrading... and so on. The text lists the customs of many different peoples: the Macedonians, the Thracians, the Massagetæ, the Persians, the Lydians, the Egyptians... It reads like a passage from Herodotus, especially where it declares that if one collected together all the rules of life devised by men so that each could choose those that suited him, every single custom would find favour in some quarter or other; none would be rejected. At 2.18, this treatise in effect summarizes Herodotus' text at 3.38.[16] In *Double Arguments*, however, the purpose of the author is no longer to preach tolerance. It is to show that there are no such things as objective beauty or ugliness, any more than objective justice or injustice. It is a thesis that frequently recurs in the writing of the Sophists, on the borderline between philosophical relativism and anthropology.

Strangely enough, Protagoras, who is so often the one to set the ball rolling, seems to have been remarkably reticent in this area. He does not appear ever to have attacked the concept of justice. He certainly recognized that each city had its own legality and its own laws. But this does not seem to have prompted him to construct any critique of the principle involved. At all events, no such work has come down to us. In fact, in his *Protagoras*, Plato himself has Protagoras recount a myth which celebrates the role of 'shame and justice' that Zeus allots to men in order that harmony and the creative ties of friendship should reign in their cities. One gets the impression that, in this domain at least, the all-out attacks began after Protagoras. Those attacks needed more than the notion of man being the measure of all things as their stimulus. They only started up once a clear distinction had been made between nature and human rules, between *phusis* and *nomos*.

The history of the opposition between *phusis* and *nomos* illuminates one important aspect of the intellectual upheaval

---

[16] And both authors prefigure Voltaire.

of the fifth century. It has been studied in detail by
F. Heinimann[17] and there is no need to go back over the same
ground. However, it is essential to realize that this opposition
is one that is established in the works of nearly all the
Sophists, where, however, it is not necessarily treated in a
destructive and negative fashion. Indeed, in some instances,
it plays a purely constructive role, helping to free people from
over-constricting traditional frameworks. As used by two of
the Sophists, Hippias and Antiphon, the theme produces
precisely such a liberating effect.

Hippias was a man of many activities and interests. In
Plato's *Protagoras*, however, his chief role is to draw attention
to the distinction between nature and human law. He firmly
declares that 'the law, despot of mankind, often constrains us
against nature' (337 D). In other words, there exists on the one
hand the domain of nature, on the other the artificial rules
which are imposed by human beings and which run contrary
to the state of nature. The point is made in the clearest
possible terms, the distinction established beyond dispute.

But everything depended upon the use to which the distinction would be put. In the *Protagoras*, from which we have
cited it, Hippias' statement is in no way revolutionary. Quite
the reverse: what he says is that all those present, who hail
from many different cities but share a common love of philosophy, are 'kinsmen and intimates and fellow-citizens by
nature, not by law' (337 D). Here, Hippias is simply pleading
for good understanding between people of goodwill, whatever
their origins may be.

It is only just possible to detect in passing that, over and
above its conciliatory purpose, the statement, which is an
extremely general one, might have other applications or be
used to cast a certain discredit upon a number of social
distinctions. Fifth-century literature sometimes repeats it in
connection with slaves or bastards, whose status is founded
upon pure convention (in contrast to nature) and constitutes
no more than a 'word' (in contrast to something real).

Clearly, the distinction might also be applied to the laws

---

[17] *Nomos und Physis: Herkunft und Bedeutung einer Antithese im griechischen
Denken des 5. Jahrhunderts* (Basle, 1945).

and rules of justice in general. Hippias himself undoubtedly gave it that meaning: in Xenophon's *Memorabilia* (4. 4. 14 ff.) he is represented as recognizing that human laws, which change so easily, cannot really be taken seriously. The prospect that opens up is alarming . . . But Hippias himself was disinclined to pursue that path. According to this same passage in the *Memorabilia*, alongside these variable and uncertain laws he believed in the existence of the famous unwritten laws, laws which were valid in all countries and which, whether divine or natural, depended upon no written legal text of any kind.

Not until more uncompromising Sophists appeared upon the scene would the opposition between human law and nature put the notion of justice in any real jeopardy. Moreover, we should remember that, even when such figures did arise, the opposition, even as represented by the boldest of them, sometimes retained a positive and—one might even say—humanist aspect. The Sophist Antiphon provides us with striking evidence of that in a fragment which affirms the natural fraternity of all men, whether noble or base, Greek or barbarian:

We are all by nature born the same in every way, both barbarians and Greeks . . . in none of these things is any one of us distinguished as barbarian or Greek. We all breathe into the air through mouth and nostrils . . . (fr. B 44 B, col. 2)

In making such a declaration, Antiphon was, to be sure, not advocating that those categories be abolished in practice. He was simply analysing and distinguishing what stems from nature and what from convention. All the same, in the Greece of the city states, a Greece still proud of its victory over the barbarians, it was an astonishingly bold statement to make. It was the first time that the thesis of a brotherhood of man had ever been put forward.

Some may find it movingly significant that this bold statement should have been made by one of the few Sophists who was actually a citizen of Athens, the city that was so convinced of its own superiority. On the other hand, it was by no means by chance that this line of thought, inspired by a sense of the relativity of human customs and the wide diversity of the world, emerged in the cosmopolitan circles of the Sophists. For these wandering professors who hailed from every corner of Greece and who had freed themselves from the bonds of social convention were bound to look beyond the limited framework of the city state, in their triumphs as in their rejections. That is by no means the least of their contributions to our culture.

Meanwhile, however, there were other ways of using the opposition between law and nature and, although its liberating and positive aspects could open up new perspectives such as those described above, it is not hard to imagine the eminently destructive force that it might assume when applied—as it was by Antiphon himself, among others—not to social or national distinctions, but to human laws and justice.

Neither Protagoras nor Hippias had really opened fire. But Thrasymachus and Antiphon certainly made up for their reticence—a fact which again suggests that there was a certain break in continuity between Protagoras and the later Sophists. After him the Sophistic critique seems to gather rapid momentum.

It is hard to say which, of Thrasymachus and Antiphon, was the elder. They were contemporaries, but Thrasymachus may have been slightly younger. The only reason for our considering him first, rather than Antiphon, is that his work is less well known to us. The only surviving fragment of his of any substantial length comes from a political speech and is concerned neither with laws and justice nor with the opposition between nature and human conventions. The only evidence of his doctrines on these matters is constituted by the words that Plato puts in his mouth in book 1 of *The Republic*; and, given that Plato was out to refute Thrasymachus, it seems reasonable to suppose that he exaggerated the inflexibility of his thinking, presenting it without much sympathy. But the role that is attributed to him here at least shows that Thrasymachus played an important part in the debate.

Thrasymachus' thesis according to *The Republic* is simple and forthright. He bursts rudely into the discussion. He ridicules all that the other participants have said and goes on to

declare that justice is neither more nor less than 'the advantage of the stronger' (338 c). What can he mean? Socrates
seems surprised and says that he cannot respond until 'I first
understand your meaning, for I don't yet apprehend it'. We
too are surprised, no doubt. But Thrasymachus' thesis turns
out to be neither as mad nor as radical as it seems at first
sight.

Thrasymachus may well have loved justice, regretting that
it was so badly served in human life. Hermias credits him
with a reflection which has already been cited above, in
connection with the gods. He is supposed to have said:

The gods do not see human affairs: otherwise they would not have
overlooked the greatest of all blessings among mankind, Justice—
for we see mankind not using this virtue.

'The greatest of all blessings' is clearly a term of praise. But
the speaker's regret and bitterness are not the only things to
strike us. Note too the detached tone of an observer that he
adopts: 'we see mankind'.

However, it is not of that justice that Thrasymachus speaks
in *The Republic*, rather of the justice that stems from some
political decision, taken at a particular moment, in a particular city. Other thinkers had already noted the extent
to which this type of justice could vary. But in relation to
the other texts that have come down to us on this subject,
Thrasymachus' originality lies in having posed the question:
who in fact takes the decisions? Who makes the laws? The
answer is, obviously, those who possess the authority or
power to do so, that is to say, those who govern, Equally
obviously, their decisions serve their own interests. That
is exactly what justice, as defined by the law, seems to
Thrasymachus to be: 'the advantage of the stronger'.

It is a conclusion that applies equally well to the people, an
oligarchy, or a tyrant. All of them set up laws which serve
their own interests. It is a political observation which somewhat resembles the advice that Aristotle was to give for the
preservation of different kinds of regimes. But, according
to Plato's representation of the discussion, Thrasymachus
follows it up with a more general analysis which is loaded
with further implications. Some scholars have even suggested

that Plato's interpretation of it is unfair and exaggerated, but
it cannot be dismissed a priori just because it seems to take a
far bolder line than is suggested by any other source of
evidence. Thrasymachus' purported analysis declares that
legislators are concerned for their own interest. It points out
that all those who are in charge of either a herd of animals or
a group of human beings are inspired by a similar goal. How
could it be otherwise? Everybody knows perfectly well that
justice is a rotten business in which nobody ever gets his just
deserts.

That is the gist of Plato's version of Thrasymachus' ideas.
And there can be no doubt that the step that Thrasymachus
is represented as taking has serious implications. Justice,
whatever its form, now becomes a trap from which no good
can come. For it is not from justice but from injustice that all
profit comes. Carried to extremes, it procures for the tyrant a
prosperity that no longer attracts a word of criticism. Nobody
would dare to criticize it or even wish to, for in the last
analysis anything that is said against injustice is prompted
by one sole fear, not that of committing it, but the fear of
being subjected to it. When injustice knows no bounds it is
something that is stronger, freer and more dominating than
justice ever is (344 A–C).

Even allowing for Plato's possible exaggerations, there can
be no doubt that this was a perfectly coherent thesis with a
dauntingly destructive potential. In its basic pessimism, it is
in tune with the more timid text cited by Hermias; and in its
insistence that all human beings pursue their own interests
and nothing but them, it is in line with a constantly recurring
theme of Sophistic thought.

In the realistic world, utility and advantage are always to
the fore. Even in the business of rhetoric, the probability is
always that each and every one pursues his own interests.
All the psychology, both individual and collective, which
underpins rhetorical arguments is centred upon this one
idea. It provides the basis of justification for the actions that
are recommended—even heroic ones. The orators use it to
explain, quite naturally, the political options open to any
individual. *A fortiori*, the same idea applies with force to
cities: a city's interests are the concern of all its citizens and it

makes no secret about pursuing them above all else. As is well known, that is one of the themes of Thucydides' analyses. Clearly, in this respect, Thrasymachus is well in tune with the spirit of the time.

But Thrasymachus is not content simply to adopt a pessimistic moral line and turn his back on idealism. In an even bolder and no doubt more personal move, he goes on to produce a radical condemnation of that idealism. For him—still according to *The Republic* (348 C–D)—justice is a 'most noble naïvety', whereas injustice is the mark of a knowing mind (for it is on the side of *euboulia*, he claims, using the word which from this point on was to denote the eminently practical kind of wisdom encouraged by the new ideas). Protagoras would never have said such a thing. Nobody would, before Thrasymachus and his friends came upon the scene. It is not hard to see why, for Plato, every defence of justice now involved refuting these particular ideas and attacking this particular thinker.

We are bound to recognize that; and it is important to admit it openly. Yet a few qualifications are called for. Truly, we must take care. Even supposing that Thrasymachus' thought was in no way distorted by Plato, it should be interpreted with caution and circumspection. We must be alert to the dangers of forcing or distorting his meaning.

One of those dangers stems from our modern tendency to detect statements of personal 'commitment' on all sides. That is a very real danger when it comes to interpreting the Sophists and these fragments of their writing which reach us out of context. Saying that justice 'does not pay' is simply a statement of fact. Even declaring it to be misjudged and naïve to opt for it is still no more than a statement of fact. Nothing could be more risky than to conclude from such statements of fact that the author is 'for' this or 'against' that.

But, in the case of Thrasymachus, there is one circumstance which renders the risk even greater. In another dialogue, the *Gorgias*, Plato introduced another figure—Callicles—to represent quite similar ideas, and there is perhaps a danger of confusion here. Like Thrasymachus, Callicles dismisses the idea of justice as a mere convention. He too declares it to have been invented arbitrarily, in order to defend particular interests. But he is moved by a much stronger spirit of revolt than Thrasymachus.

First, we should note one important difference. Thrasymachus said that the rules of justice were fixed by those who govern, that is to say, the stronger. Callicles, for his part, says that they were fixed by a coalition of the weak, as a means of safeguarding themselves against the strong: which is virtually the opposite. The reason for the contradiction is that Callicles is an individualist. He detests having to obey rules. He detests the Athenian democracy in which he lives. With ardent longing, he imagines a superman who could trample underfoot all these written laws which run contrary to nature: the law of nature would then be able to shine forth in all its brilliance.[18] This is a case of egoistical ambition rebelling against the the law, rejecting it in the name of force. It suggests a bestial society, in which each individual's place is decided by its individual strength: in fact, the kind of society of the days before laws existed.[19]

But above all, as is clear from the last of those words of his, Callicles declares the triumph of the stronger to be just and in accordance with nature. He recognizes a natural law which is opposed to human law. Whereas Thrasymachus simply acknowledged the difference between the two, Callicles slips justice over to the side of natural law.

We shall be returning to Callicles, who in some respects has more in common with some of the other Sophists than he does with Thrasymachus. We shall have to try to discover who he was and why he should have been the one to express views that are so much more radical than the rest. Meanwhile, though, the contrast between the two should help us to see Thrasymachus' extraordinarily bold declaration in its true perspective, recognizing the extent to which it belongs to the context of a purely theoretical and analytical line of thinking. To make an absolute distinction between justice

---

[18] On Callicles, see the discussion at the end of Ch. 5.

[19] 'Bestial' is the epithet commonly applied to life at the beginning of time, before men came together in social groups. The word is used in a dozen or so texts which describe the life of those days; see J. de Romilly, 'Thucydide et l'idée de progrès au Ve siècle', *Annales de l'École normale supérieure de Pise* (1966), 143–91, esp. 146–8.

and interest and to say that justice does those who practise it
no good is almost tantamount to advising against it. Almost,
but not quite.[20] That is a step which Callicles takes but
Thrasymachus—even as portrayed by Plato, who was bent on
placing his thought in an unsympathetic light—does not.

We can see what an alarming influence such ideas could
acquire if they were even slightly distorted. But the difference introduced by such a distortion also reveals that, with
their meaning left undistorted, it was perfectly possible for
the Sophists' analyses to combine other doctrines of a far less
subversive and amoral nature, doctrines which we shall try
to elucidate in due course. It is, at any rate, only fair to
recognize that Thrasymachus' analyses by no means exclude
such a possibility.

His impatient onslaught in *The Republic* was as sharp a
blow against the old morality as was ever delivered in the
context of an ethical discussion. However, it reflects the
critical rigour of a Sophist's daring mind more than it represents a statement of personal, practical commitment. That is
why, so far, the present work has not been concerned to
discover how this analysis fitted in with other fragments
with a less destructive air. That is a general problem of
interpretation to which we shall have to turn our attention by
referring to several Sophists, especially those authors whose
texts have been better preserved. One is Antiphon, in whose
hands the critique of justice was strengthened and further
developed, and in his case we do possess some fragments that
run to several pages. Their discovery caused great excitement.

The fragments of Antiphon were recovered on papyrus and
published in 1915.[21] We can tell, from definite correspon-
dences, that they belonged to his treatise *On Truth*. The title

[20] He defends the wisdom of injustice only in the case of those who practise
it to a supreme degree, subjugating whole cities and peoples (cf. 348 D: 'those
who at least'): minor transgressions are not worth bothering about, but
possibly these do not serve the interests of those guilty of them, for their
perpetrators run the risk of being found out! (ibid.: 'if they escape').

[21] To the edition here mentioned must be added a fragment published in
1984. See now: Corpus dei Papyri filosofici greci e Latini, 1. 1*. 1989,
Florence, pp. 176 ff.

in itself suggests that this meditation on justice put forward some of Antiphon's major ideas. It was a title that had also been used by Protagoras and, it is believed, by Antisthenes. In itself, it seems to announce a manifesto on certain fundamental points in the philosophical critique. In the three extracts that we possess, the thinking presses further forward than in any other treatise on justice.

Unfortunately, however, even the existence of a preserved text, such a rare godsend, is not enough to clarify the situation. Interpreters are by no means in general agreement. It is unnecessary to enter into the details of the discussion but, once again, we are obliged to track down the meaning by concentrating on the detailed implications of the precious yet controversial words.

The first fragment (B 44) takes off with a definition of justice about which there is nothing particularly surprising, given the intellectual atmosphere of the day. The very first words declare that justice means not trangressing any of the legal rules recognized by the city to which one belongs. The positivist nature of the definition implies recognition of the variation in human laws that we have already encountered.

At this point, however, certain difficulties arise. Some interpreters believe that Antiphon cited that definition purely to demonstrate its consequences, but did not identify himself with it. There are two sets of reasons to account for that belief. In the first place, one of the other newly discovered fragments, the third, offers a different definition: here, justice is defined as not infringing the rights of other people; and the fragment then proceeds to demonstrate the contradictions that follow upon this definition. It seems reasonable to suppose that the first fragment followed a similar pattern, also starting off with a definition which was no more than provisional. After all, the fragment begins at a random point which just happens to be at the top of the rediscovered page. We have no inkling of what came before or served as an introduction to the definition which has come down to us. But now we come to the second reason for this—to put it mildly—hypothetical interpretation. Some of the scholars who have resorted to it have done so quite simply because they are shocked by the consequences that Antiphon drew from his definition. They cannot bring themselves to attribute such revolutionary theses to a man who, in other respects, seems generous and concerned for the general good.

Surely this is bad methodology. The fact is that all the rest of the text follows perfectly logically from the definition with which it starts, and is justified by it. It is all of a piece with the definition. Besides, the argument is also too forceful to be one introduced merely incidentally. As it stands, the fragment is unmistakably a coherent whole. We should therefore do better to try to accommodate the two difficulties mentioned above, namely: first, how to account for the fact that a different definition is produced later on; second—and above all—how it is that a generous man, concerned for the general good, could possibly have defended the ideas that he does. Clearly, though, our first duty is to read the text as it stands.

It makes startling reading, for the famous opposition between nature and the law, or convention, could not be applied to the idea of justice in a more radical fashion. Antiphon makes a clear distinction between two separate orders: on the one hand, the order of nature, which has always existed everywhere and in which every living creature pursues its material satisfaction; on the other, that of justice, which is superimposed upon it and contradicts it.

In Plato's *Republic*, Thrasymachus said that justice ran counter to our interests. The same idea now surfaces in Antiphon, but in an infinitely more radical, more elaborated, and more systematic form. Having defined justice as obedience to the legal rules, the text goes on as follows:

A man therefore can best conduct himself in harmony with justice if, in the company of witnesses, he upholds the laws and when alone, without witnesses, he upholds the edicts of nature. For what belongs to the laws is an addition and what belongs to nature implies necessity; what belongs to the laws is reached through agreement, not by natural growth, whereas what belongs to nature is not a matter of agreement, but is natural. So, if the man who transgresses the legal code evades those who have agreed to these edicts, he avoids both disgrace and penalty; otherwise not. But if a man violates, against possibility, one of nature's arrangements, even if he evades all men's detection, the ill is no less, and even if all can see him, it is no greater; for he is not hurt on account of an opinion, but because of truth. (Translation adapted by J. de Romilly)

It would be hard to imagine a more positive distinction between the two orders, or to produce a more rigorous analysis of the contrast between the two systems. What exactly is meant by what belongs to nature is perhaps not quite clear. However, the following passages promptly explain, demonstrating not (simply) the difference between the two domains but indeed the opposition—or you could even say state of war (*polemiōs*)—that exists between them:

For there is legislation about the eyes, what they must see and what not; and about the ears, what they must hear and what not; and about the tongue, what it must speak and what not; and about the hands, what they must do and what not; and about the feet, where they must go and where not; and about the mind, what it must desire and what not. Now the law's prohibitions are in no way more agreeable and more akin to nature than the law's injunctions. For what belongs to nature is life and death, life being the result of what is profitable, death of what is unprofitable. (Translation adapted by J. de Romilly)

The fragment winds up with some ideas about pleasure and suffering, which are even more explicit.

The two domains or systems (of law and nature) are thus fundamentally different. Antiphon says as much forcefully and insistently. However—and it is important to be quite clear about this—that is as far as he ever goes.

He does not refer to any natural laws. In contrast to the idealists, he never speaks of natural justice, based upon the order of the world. On the other hand, nor—in contrast here to Callicles—does he speak of any 'laws of nature' that spell triumph for the stronger. Not only does he make no such pronouncements but, in this respect, the reserve that distinguishes what he does say is most remarkable. He never uses the words 'laws' or 'rules' in connection with nature. Instead, he refers, rather oddly, to nature's 'arrangements'; and, to express whatever it is that nature impels us towards, he falls back on an almost untranslatable neuter:[22] what

---

[22] The exact translation of the text involves great difficulties. Exactitude has been the aim here, not elegance.

'belongs to nature'. 'What belongs to nature' comprises the tendencies that prompt living creatures to survive, prosper, and enjoy themselves. These operate independently of any human decree. They are 'free', whereas laws are 'chains upon nature'.[23] But we should not presume to draw the conclusion that the latter should, on that account, be shaken or cast off, for Antiphon himself does not.

Of course this is not to say that nature imposes no constraints. For example, it is true that fire always burns, that sharp implements wound, that we cannot live without air, food, and drink. That is why Antiphon speaks of cases in which 'one violates nature, against possibility'; and he openly admits that there is a price to be paid for disregarding those constraints. But the limits that he defines are just as natural as desires and pleasures, as universal as feelings and as life itself. It is not a matter of rights, let alone of models. The rigour of the analysis is not distorted by any use of metaphor.

What might distort it in the eyes of the reader is, rather, the heavy emphasis of the text. Thus, to underline the contrast between justice and interest, in the next column (5) Antiphon cites the example of those who push their respect for their parents to the point of repaying evil with good. Such people exist; and they are idealists. However, they are obviously acting against their own interests.

Similarly, the text points out that the law cannot protect those who respect it for the very good reason that, in practice, it only intervenes after the event. It can do nothing to prevent people from being attacked. It only comes into play when the damage is done, and is not concerned to discover who started it all. It would be madness to count upon it.

Then again, reminding the reader that justice presupposes that a person does no harm to those who have done him none, he points out that any citizen who testifies against another is harming someone who has done nothing to him. Having already noted the weaknesses of the law, Antiphon now draws attention to its contradictions.

---

[23] The opposition between a universal natural state and a precarious human artefact reappears in a fragment relating to matter and form, in which an opposition is set up between wood and a bed (DK B 15).

He seems to be going even further than the defence of his thesis demands. Too far, parhaps. His definition of the two domains (of human law and nature) was perfectly clear, almost a statement of the obvious. But now the line of argument (which we unfortunately do not possess in its entirety) seems to be alluding either to a justice that is altogether wider than that encompassed by the law, or to the weaknesses that characterize that law, or to the contradictions that are inherent in it. He makes use of whatever comes to hand.

But we should not look a gift-horse in the mouth. We should not complain because everything is grist to Antiphon's mill if it helps to prove that laws are artificial and opposed to one's interests. For he would only be at fault if, somewhere along the line, he had changed his definitions[24] or switched to a different thesis. He has not. Despite the gaps in the exposition of the argument and the uncertainties that remain, he never swerves from the path he has set himself, never adopts a different tack. His thesis remains unchanged: to obey justice is to run counter to one's own interests.

That is the point to which he always returns. His line of thought seems blindingly clear. It makes one wonder how on earth it can have given rise to so many conflicting interpretations and misunderstandings. But the very existence of all those conflicting interpretations and misunderstandings serves to warn us of the dangers that constantly beset those who seek to interpret the thought of the Sophists. For the trouble is that it is all too easy to distort it to suit oneself.

Where Antiphon is concerned, the risk of doing so is even greater than in the case of Thrasymachus, where we have detected two factors that make for misunderstanding: the existence of Callicles, and the fact that there is so little hard evidence to go on. Where Antiphon is concerned the same two factors are reinforced.

Callicles takes over from Antiphon quite as much as he does from Thrasymachus. Furthermore, from what little we know of these lost texts, he seems to have adopted a position closer

[24] Not to harm those who do you no harm is, of course, a traditional definition of justice; but it simply reflects the transitive use of the verb *adikein* (to harm somebody); and Antiphon is here playing upon the two meanings of that verb: 'to harm somebody' and 'to commit an injustice'.

to Antiphon than to Thrasymachus, since, like the former, he takes as his starting-point the opposition between law and nature. 'For the most part', Callicles remarks, 'these two—nature and convention—are opposed to each other' (*Gorgias*, 482 E). Because he then proceeds to draw a rebellious moral from that observation, it was not long before the two men's thought was being assimilated and Callicles' moral philosophy was being ascribed also to Antiphon. Yet a closer examination shows that, on the contrary, the two differ on at least one essential point. Antiphon is, throughout, purely objective. Callicles, in contrast, is openly partisan. In his view there exists a 'law of nature' by virtue of which the strong predominate over the weak, and the rules that men have invented are designed to maintain respect for the strong. So, good for those who reject all that hypocritical mumbo-jumbo! Good for those who know how to seize an advantage for themselves! What is theoretical analysis in Antiphon's writing becomes advice, choice, and practical decision in Callicles' declarations. The thought of the two men seems very close, but to confuse the two would be a serious injustice, however tempting it may be to do so at first sight.

The trouble is that it is all too easy to slip from the one into the other; and the temptation to do so is all the greater because it is so difficult to be objective—especially in times of crisis such as fifth-century Athens, and in times marked by committed thinking such as our own. Yet surely it should be possible to stop short at the idea that there is a difference between nature and the law and that they run contrary to one another. Antiphon at no point says any more than that. Why must people insist on reading a personal commitment into what is in truth analysis pure and simple? That is what critics constantly do. Some, noting that Antiphon claims that justice runs counter to our interest, proceed without hesitation to assume him to be 'hostile' to the law of the city, declaring that he rejects it, and is an 'upholder' of nature. When he says that it is not to a man's advantage to respect the law when no witnesses are present, those same scholars interpret him as meaning that, in those circumstances, one 'should' not respect it. It would be pointless to name the authors of such misinterpretations. They include some of the most respected

thinkers from many different countries. But what grounds do
they have for their assertions? To say that a line of behaviour
is disadvantageous does not necessarily imply hostility towards it. There are surely many reasons for defending justice
which are not based on the immediate and personal interests
of the individual. The classical scholars of today would
appear to be more devious, and more spellbound by practical
advantages, than the Sophists themselves were. Or perhaps
we should take it that Socrates' famous paradox according to
which 'the best' coincides with 'the most advantageous' by
now seems self-evident to all . . . Yet in truth we all know
what a strange, bold, and isolated paradox that was. The fact
of the matter is that it is perfectly possible to love justice
without confusing it with self-interest. Thinking along the
lines described above has all too often led to Antiphon, like
Thrasymachus, being forced into the mould of amoralism—a
distortion of the utmost gravity.

Another, equally grave distortion operates in reverse, tending to whitewash the Sophists and rescue them from the
slightest taint of amoralism. Why should it be felt important to do so? Why all these efforts? The reason is that in a
number of cases—as we have suggested in passing in relation
to Thrasymachus—we possess slight but incontrovertible
evidence of quite a different side to their personalities and
thought. Alongside the critical fragments of the Sophists, we
find words, sentences, even whole pages which reflect a most
responsible moral position.

We have seen how Thrasymachus saps the very foundations
of human laws, painting a picture of a world guided by self-
interest. Elsewhere, however, he calls justice the greatest of
all human blessings. And yet elsewhere, in the only fragment
by him that we possess, which appears to be part of a political
debate, he seems to recognize the importance of harmony
within the city and points to the merits of a good political
regime: so he must believe that what is good has a role to play
in politics. Faced with this, certain scholars minimize the
meaning of what we read in *The Republic*. They suggest that
Plato somewhat exaggerated the situation and that, while his
evidence may be valid for the early part of Thrasymachus'
intervention, it cannot be considered so later, when the

Sophist's remarks become more radical. These should be regarded more as an interpolation on the part of Plato himself. Plato may indeed be misrepresenting Thrasymachus; but there can be no doubt that Thrasymachus is equally ill served by scholars who set out to reconcile the intentions of one text with those of another by dint of favouring certain remarks and ignoring others.

In the case of Thrasymachus it is no easy task to reconcile the various fragments and testimonies. Where Antiphon is concerned it is even harder. With Thrasymachus, it is the absence of texts that makes it difficult. With Antiphon, the problem is their presence. Once again there is a clash of evidence. The author of those daunting fragments *On Truth* is also the author of a treatise entitled *On Concord*, a few fragments of which survive: it was clearly the work of a man concerned with morality. In it, Antiphon speaks of friendship, of the temptations amid which one triumphs over oneself, and of courage.[25] What is to be done? Various solutions have been adopted. For some, the answer lies in interpretations, for others in a selection of the sources to be followed.

Those who place their faith in interpretation, for example, claim—without a scrap of evidence from the text—that the definition of justice that is given is not the one that Antiphon himself adopted, and that, on the contrary, the allusion to people who do more than they need implies a deep attachment to justice on his part. In short, they read into these purely objective and descriptive fragments all kinds of innuendoes with moral implications.

Alternatively—and these are desperate measures indeed—one begins to pick and choose, distinguishing a number of different Antiphons. There is, admittedly, a precedent for doing so. It has become customary to draw a distinction between Antiphon the orator (the orator of the *Tetralogies*, which were so important to rhetoric) and Antiphon the Sophist (the author of several treatises, including *On Truth* and *On Concord*). That is an ancient distinction which goes back to the third century AD at least, possibly to the first—not that it is necessarily justified on that account. The differences

---

[25] See below, pp. 183–4.

of genre and style between the two sets of texts do not constitute sufficient evidence, for there are other explanations
that could account for them. The mention of 'the Sophist' in
some of our sources of evidence is of equally little significance,
for that title is tacked on to many names even when there is
no question of distinguishing between two people with the
same name.[26] In this respect, what *is* perhaps surprising is
that nobody should have taken the trouble to guard against
any such confusion in the case of a figure as famous as
Antiphon the orator (whose praises are eloquently sung by
Thucydides). None the less, it has become customary to
make the distinction: people tend in passing to express vague
doubts about the distinction between the Antiphons, then
prudently rally to what appears to be 'the majority opinion'.

Of course, as we have already recognized, there may indeed
have been two Antiphons. But the reasons that are generally
adduced for claiming that there were spotlight the very misunderstanding that we are at present attempting to dispel. It
is such a serious one that it is worth pausing for a moment to
think about this custom of distinguishing between two—or
perhaps even three—different Antiphons.

The argument runs as follows: the orator was (as we know
from Thucydides) a determined supporter of oligarchy, and
paid with his life for his ideas; the ideas that the Sophist
expresses could hardly be more democratic. So it cannot
possibly be the same man speaking. Oh dear, oh dear...
The text that expresses these terribly 'democratic' ideas is
none other than the one in which the author shows that
the distinction between people of noble origin and people
of humble origin stems purely from human conventions.
Once again, what we have here is simply an incontrovertible
statement of fact. Yet some people insist that it must mean
that the author is *for* this or *against* that...[27]

Similarly, some scholars argue that the orator shows

---

[26] The term 'Sophist' could either be used to denote the subject's profession
or to suggest his fame. In some cases it might even reflect the user's own
attitude to the doctrines in question. The expression 'Antiphon, the Sophist'
appears as early as Xenophon's *Memorabilia*.
[27] On the basis of this remark, he has sometimes even been described as a
'left-winger'.

respect for the laws while the Sophist is 'against' them. Oh dear, here we go again . . . In truth, he is not 'against' them. It is perfectly possible to respect a convention while at the same time recognizing it to be precisely that, if it seems a useful one.

As if all this were not enough, just because the fragments of *On Truth* are revolutionary while *On Concord* expresses the views of a man concerned with morality, soon the suggestion is made that these two treatises must also be by different authors. Some scholars (such as Nestle) believe *On Concord* to be by 'the orator'. (At least he spares us the prospect of *three* different Antiphons.) But then there is also an Antiphon who is credited with a number of tragedies and a work on the interpretation of dreams . . . You could go on discovering new Antiphons for as long as you pleased on the basis of this biased and distorted interpretation of the fragments.

To be sure, the fragments are revolutionary. To be sure, they deal the concept of justice a heavy blow. But, as in so many other Sophistic texts, the blow is dealt on a purely philosophical level. These texts never fall into the spirit of exhortation and proselytism that it is so tempting and so mistaken to ascribe to them.

In truth, herein lies the great misunderstanding which has always dogged the Sophists and which, even in their own lifetimes, dictated the form of their influence. These great teachers declared that there was no truth other than variable individual impressions, that it was not known whether the gods existed, and that justice was purely a convention which it was not in one's interest to obey. Even at the time, the Athenians listening to them could hardly fail to become scornful of the ideas and values that they analysed, and to act accordingly. The present work tries throughout to assess every piece of evidence and every surviving word left by the Sophists, seeking to define the limits of their thought and to reveal the diamond-hard neutrality of their analyses. It was a necessary precaution, for their doctrines tend towards a slippery slope where there is a constant danger of slipping too far. Even passing from Protagoras to Hippias and Critias, the slope grows steeper. Moving on to the practical interpretations of the 'uninitiated' a veritable chasm suddenly opens up. The Sophists' followers took over their doctrines, adding to them and simplifying and vulgarizing them.

That is why it is essential to get back to them in their original form, or at least to a point before they began to be distorted. When we do so and examine the fragments themselves, we discover that there was all the time another possible slope to follow, leading in a direction that is, moreover, clearly indicated by a series of landmarks. Now a whole new system of thought comes into view and in it the fragments from the Sophists' critical attacks on traditional thought, which we have been examining so far, complement those other fragments which have only been mentioned as sources of embarrassment, but which none the less exist: the fragments in which these Sophists whom we have seen so bent on destruction instead speak as responsible moral philosophers.

The phenomenon that has come to light in connection with Antiphon is a general one. It affected even the earliest Sophists, Gorgias and Protagoras. They too elaborated positive, constructive doctrines, as did all the Sophists who came after them.[28] All of them defended moral values and virtues. All did so starting from the *tabula rasa* described above. It was on this basis that they all set out to reconstruct a new morality, with different foundations, a morality centred upon man alone. Rather than water down or diminish one aspect or another of their thinking, we should aim to understand how it was that the destruction of all notions of transcendency in the event led them to reconstruction: the combination of the negative and the positive aspects of Sophistic thought is undoubtedly its most original feature; and that double impulse produced a way of proceeding which was to prove crucial to the history of ideas.

On the basis of one and the same critical attack upon tradition, intellectually radical but unconcerned to draw practical conclusions, two opposite tendencies developed. The one is reflected not in philosophical texts but in the literary works of the period: it leads to a total rejection of

---

[28] On Xenophon's contradictory testimony, see above, p. 27.

values. The other, in contrast, finds expression in the Sophists' own fragments and it opens up totally different perspectives, establishing man in a society created for him and by him.

Let us now examine the two tendencies separately. The wide disparity between them is an indication of how difficult it is and always has been—even in fifth-century Athens—for a new line of thinking to be understood both as a whole and in its detailed elaboration.

5

The Dangers of the *Tabula Rasa*: Immoralism

IN the last quarter of the fifth century BC, a grave crisis developed, in the course of which all kinds of people exploited the Sophistic critique to justify resolutely immoralist points of view. So much is established beyond doubt by the testimony of the various contemporary writers: Euripides, Thucydides, Aristophanes, and, a little later, Plato.

The crisis was clearly not solely due to the influence of the Sophists. Many other circumstances contributed towards it, in the first place the war. Every year Attica was invaded. It was a pattern which continued until 421. Then, after a few years' respite, it found itself under partial occupation by enemy forces. Each year the death-toll rose. People's faith in the justice of the gods began to waver as they noticed that, in human society, it was the strong who triumphed. Such long, widespread wars are never conducive to the maintenance of moral values. As Thucydides remarked, 'war . . . is a rough schoolmaster and creates in most people a temper that matches their condition' (3. 82. 2).

The war was compounded by other evils, with even more disastrous effects. First there was the plague, with its endless train of sudden, agonizing deaths. Thucydides himself described its effects upon the morals of the citizens:

The plague first introduced into the city a greater lawlessness. For where men hitherto practised concealment, pretending that they were not acting purely after their pleasure, they now showed a more careless daring. They saw how sudden was the change of fortune in the case both of those who were prosperous and suddenly died, and of those who before had nothing but in a moment were in possession of the property of others. And so they resolved to get out of life the pleasures which could be had speedily and would satisfy their lusts, regarding their bodies and their wealth alike as transitory... The pleasure of the moment and whatever was in any way conducive to it came to be regarded as at once honourable and expedient. No fear of gods or law of men restrained them. (2.53)

One cannot in good faith discount such clear testimony on the part of a contemporary witness.

After the plague came the horrors of civil war. The first civil wars broke out outside Athens itself, in the cities which both Athens and Sparta claimed as their allies or vassals. Athens would support the democrats, Sparta the oligarchs. Already in the early years of the war Thucydides was pointing to the moral effects of this scourge, which was later to fall upon Athens itself. He devotes a long and brilliant analysis to it, describing its attendant evils, which stem from human nature itself but are certainly aggravated by war and civil war. In circumstances such as these, moral values are spurned and good qualities regarded as faults:

Reckless audacity came to be regarded as courageous loyalty to party, prudent hesitation as specious cowardice, moderation as a cloak for unmanly weakness, and to be clever in everything was to do naught in anything. Frantic impulsiveness was accounted a true man's part, but caution in deliberation a specious pretext for shirking. (3.82.4–5)

It becomes impossible to control human passions:

For there was no assurance binding enough, no oath terrible enough to reconcile men; but always, if they were stronger, since they accounted all security hopeless, they were rather disposed to take precautions against being wronged than able to trust others. (3.83.2)

Thucydides' analyses confirm both the gravity of the moral crisis and the clear link between it and the war, with all the latter's terrible side-effects.

We should also remember that Athens was defending her empire in this war, and that the propaganda put out by her enemies harped ceaselessly upon the unjust and tyrannical dominion that she exercised throughout Greece. Even in Athens itself, this propaganda sometimes found sympathetic ears. Many had been shocked at Athens using her allies' money to build monuments for herself; many were indignant at seeing those allies humiliated; and, if we are to believe Thucydides, even those in Athens who defended the empire did so in the name of security but acknowledged that, from the point of view of justice, it was totally indefensible. Thucydides' Pericles certainly recognized as much:

> From this empire, however, it is too late for you even to withdraw ... for by this time the empire you hold is tyranny, which it may seem wrong to have assumed, but which certainly it is dangerous to let go. (2. 63. 2)

The Athenians who took part in the Melian dialogue (in book 6) were to find harsher words still to describe power founded solely upon brute force. There can be no doubt that a city driven to acknowledge such facts provided a dangerous model for individuals.

Thucydides notes the progress of selfish ambition in the course of the war. A man such as Alcibiades, whose life was punctuated by scandals and who moved from one camp to another without scruple, producing cynical justifications for his behaviour, is a good example: Athens' ambitions as a city seem to have released the private ambitions of her citizens.

That connection is confirmed by a passing remark of Plato's. Presenting the ambitious Callicles as the very incarnation of the immoralism of the day, he has him appeal in self-justification not only to animals, creatures that lack laws, but also to war and conquest:

> Nature herself proclaims the fact that it is right for the better to have advantage of the worse, and the abler of the feebler. It is obvious that this is so ... not only in the animal world but in the states and races, collectively, of men[1]—that right has been decided to consist in the sway and advantage of the stronger over the weaker. For by what manner of right did Xerxes march against Greece, or his father against Scythia? Or take the countless other cases of the sort that one might mention ... (*Gorgias*, 483 D–E)

---

[1] The example of animals is invoked by Strepsiades' son, in *The Clouds*, to justify his beating his father: 'Look at the game-cocks, look at all the animal creation, / Do *they* not beat their parents?' (1427–8).

The example of Athens was one of those 'other cases of the sort'.

It seems so obvious to explain the moral crisis by the war, the civil war, and imperialism that one might even consider the same explanation to account for Sophistic thought itself. Arriving at precisely the moment when the old values were giving way on all sides, before the pressure of social and intellectual evolution, the Sophists might themselves have been affected by the common experience, by what people were saying, and by the general trend of public opinion.

The idea should not be dismissed, for there is assuredly some foundation for it. An intellectual revolution such as that launched by the Sophists is not achieved without a deep measure of coincidence between external circumstances and the tendencies that they foster. Nevertheless, as many indications show, the role played by the Sophists was itself crucially influential.

In the first place, contemporaries themselves considered it to be so, and said as much repeatedly. As we have noted, in *The Clouds* it is from studying under the new teachers that Strepsiades' son learns how to justify injustice. And those new teachers clearly included others besides the Sophists we have been considering, since Aristophanes makes Socrates their spokesman; but this is a Socrates who is an atheistic and devious master of rhetoric—a Sophistic Socrates. Besides, the double arguments here, the one strong, the other weak, refer us directly to Protagoras, and Prodicus himself is also named. If the young man has become impious, if he shows no respect for the laws and ends up by beating his own father, the fault must be laid at the door of all these thinkers. Aristophanes, furthermore, suggests that the language that they use is extremely obscure, implying that, to his mind, they must certainly be professional philosophers—not necessarily philosophers in the Platonic or Aristotelian sense of the word, but men with specialist intellectual skills. Aristophanes' play even shows precisely how it is that it ever occurs to such a simple fellow to place himself in the hands of men skilled in what would appear to be a somewhat esoteric form of meditation.

As for Plato, he is even more specific. He repeatedly points to the moral dangers involved in the teaching of rhetoric and what is claimed to be political skill, and apportions blame to Protagoras, Gorgias, and Thrasymachus. His attacks cannot be dismissed simply as discussions between philosophers. Plato never argues with such determination against other philosophers such as Heraclitus, Democritus, Empedocles, or Diogenes of Apollonia. He clearly reserves his most serious criticisms for those he considers responsible for the current moral crisis and the rejection of all notions of transcendency.

It is no surprise to find the picture expanding from a handful of specialists to include a wider public. Those specialists were, after all, also lecturers and skilled performers in public debate. As we have seen, Thucydides credits Cleon with a revealing reproach to the Athenians. He accuses them of behaving more like an audience assembled to hear Sophists lecturing than like citizens engaged upon the deliberation of public matters (3. 38. 7).[2] All the testimony converges: it points the finger at philosophers in general and the Sophists in particular.

Another reliable indication is the very tone that even authors who are not philosophers—historians and dramatists, for example—adopt to describe the crisis-ridden world in which they live. Whoever the writer, the tone remains the same: invariably, it is abstract and theoretical, almost too theoretical. The choice of vocabulary, the distinctions that are drawn, the very allusions are all directly inspired by the philosophical investigations and well-known formulas of the fashionable thinkers of the day. The similarity between all these texts and the very abstraction that characterizes them would be impossible to explain if they were merely concerned to describe concrete experience. Between that experience and the lesson that these writers proceed to draw from it there is a missing link: namely, the sudden, revelatory impact made by the Sophists' articulate and authoritative thought.

The history of ideas suggests that the situation is a common one. Latent feelings exist, seeking expression. When the right means of expression or the right doctrine appears, those

---

[2] He is supposed to have made this remark in 427, the very year of Gorgias' arrival in Athens.

feelings are formulated and thereby acquire increased force. In the absence of particular material or political circumstances, the influence of thinkers might remain relatively limited; conversely, however, without the thinkers the situation itself would not evolve in such a clear-cut or radical manner. Through their thinking, their analyses, and the meaning or new emphasis that they give to words, thinkers too have a hand in the creation of history.

Of course, though society used those ideas, it also modified them. It made use of the Sophists' thought to the extent that it suited the moment. People seized upon the statements that they had heard bandied about and the theses whose boldness had brought them to the public eye. From them, they extracted excuses, rules of action, and practical consequences. The 'philosophers' had provided society with an exoneration.

It is thus fair to say that the moral crisis owed much to the Sophists and to the use to which their theses were put. In their concern for practical action, they provided ambitious men with means and arguments, and it may well have seemed as though they had deliberately set out to do so. But the true meaning of their analyses was exaggerated and distorted.[3] It is assuredly not the only time in history that thinkers have been overtaken and left behind by their followers, and that their ideas have been distorted by a superficially informed public opinion chiefly concerned with practical daily life. However, the case of the Sophists is especially remarkable.

It is accordingly well worth trying to see how the Sophists' many-sided critique of traditional ideas was taken over lock, stock, and barrel, and subsequently developed outside philosophical circles. The testimony of Athenian writers on this point is both eloquent and convincing. Not only do these writers reveal the existence of a crisis in the various fields at which the Sophists' critique was directed; through their very choice of words and arguments they furthermore show how

---

[3] It is often thought that, because the Sophists' teaching was directed towards practical achievement, all their analyses also were. However, that is to disregard both the highly theoretical nature of these analyses and also the specific remarks on record which suggest that the Sophists were far less inclined to 'immoralism' than those who made use of their work.

far the Sophists' influence was responsible for that crisis and also how much their thought had, in the course of events, been distorted and over-simplified.

All this is clear from the testimony of three great writers of the period, Aristophanes, Euripides, and Thucydides. But alongside these well-known authors, we should also take account of a figure who is otherwise unknown and who wrote nothing, but whose abrasive tone and very existence provide evidence of a startling kind. We have already come across him several times: Callicles, the man to whom Plato allotted such an important role in the *Gorgias*, despite the fact that he was himself neither a Sophist nor a philosopher nor a well-known politician. He seems to embody an extreme and alarming form of the immoralism which the young Athenians of the day, intoxicated by the negative side to the Sophists' thinking, were currently embracing.

Public opinion and the non-philosophical writers could hardly be expected to echo the Sophists' critiques on ontology and truth. But the new ideas concerning the gods and justice were to unleash a storm. That it truly seemed a storm is clear from the known facts. The last decades of the fifth century suddenly produced an increasing spate of signs of impiety and openly avowed atheism.

We have already noted the phenomenon of prosecutions for impiety. Charges were pressed against Anaxagoras, Pericles' friends, and others too, including a number of philosophers. It is hard to be certain of every case, for the evidence at our disposal is sometimes suspect and invariably imprecise. However, one recent work mentions the names of eighteen people who were charged, nine of them during the period in which we are interested.[4] We know that the definition of impiety given at the beginning of the war was aimed at thinkers 'who taught doctrines relating to celestial matters'.[5] Even on the threshold of the fourth century, one of the unjust yet revealing charges brought against Socrates was that he

[4] W. Fahr, in a work published in 1969 and entitled *Theous nomizein*, in which he studies this Greek expression. This was the period in which it passed from the religious domain into that of general beliefs.
[5] This is in an official text, quoted in Ch. 4.

had refused to accept the city gods (although he was not, strictly speaking, tried for impiety).

Clearly much unease was felt, and it tended to turn against the doctrines of the thinkers. The term 'philosopher' began to take on overtones of 'free thinking'—as it was to later, in eighteenth-century France. Certainly Plato, in his *Apology*, writing of the criticisms levelled against 'those who occupy themselves with philosophy' immediately mentions the accusation of not believing in the gods (23 D).

The general anxiety and the trials were simply Athens' blind and erratic response to certain signs which were becoming increasingly common. There were a number of serious scandals. The most famous involved the mutilation of the Hermae and a parody of the Mysteries. These two startling manifestations of impiety both came to light in 415, at the moment when the Sicilian expedition was being prepared, the one scandal leading to the discovery of the other. The reaction to the trail of mutilated religious statues across the city and a parody of the Mysteries being enacted in a private house was one of shock. Given that Alcibiades found himself compromised, this twofold profanation led to serious political consequences. That is one reason why we know of the incident, another being that the speech in defence of Andocides, who was involved in the affair, has been preserved. But in any case, these were blatant, seemingly provocative acts of impiety. Another affair of a similar nature attracted less attention but is nevertheless mentioned in a number of literary texts (Aristophanes' *The Frogs* and *Ecclesiazusae*, among others). It involved the desecration of the statues of Mecate, for which a certain Cinesias was held responsible. In this case, it definitely was more an act of provocation than of atheism.

There was also the case, probably at roughly the same period, of a man about whom not a great deal is known but who was notorious for his impiety: Diagoras of Melos, known as 'the atheist'.[6] Several acts of impiety are ascribed to him,

[6] Some people believe him to have belonged to an earlier period. However, the date of the decree published against him seems to have been 415 (unless it was 433): see L. Woodbury's meticulous analysis, 'The Date and Atheism of Diagoras of Melos', *Phoenix*, 19, (1965), 178–211.

in particular against the Mysteries of Eleusis; and he was duly solemnly condemned. He is said to have justified his refusal to believe in the gods by drawing attention to the evasiveness of divine justice (a ploy which brings Thrasymachus to mind). Apparently his impiety was so notorious that to say 'Socrates the Melian' was another way of calling Socrates an atheist. Aristophanes does so in *The Clouds* and that is precisely the explanation that the scholiasts give.

As well as the trials for impiety, tradition has recorded lists of named atheists. The same work about the trials also lists fourteen names, eight from the period in which we are interested. They include Protagoras, Prodicus, and Critias, which shows that the Sophists must have seemed confused in this wave of atheism and were themselves regarded as atheists. Cicero, however, correctly points out that a distinction should be made between Protagoras' agnosticism and true atheism, and he goes on to compare the Sophist with two acknowledged atheists: Diagoras, mentioned above, and Theodorus of Cyrene.[7] He even makes the point three times over in *De Natura Deorum*. The provocative sensationalism evoked by the name Diagoras certainly does have a very different ring from the lucid and rigorous analyses produced by the Sophists. Following their analyses, however, the fire that they may have sparked off blazed up and gained ground on all sides. Small wonder, then, that by the fourth century atheism had become such an important phenomenon that, in *The Laws* (908 B–C), Plato distinguishes several different forms of it, of varying degrees of gravity. It would not have occurred to anyone to do such a thing in Pericles' day.

The facts noted above suffice to show how swiftly irreligion gained ground during the Peloponnesian War, that is to say, during the period of the Sophists' activities. But they do not demonstrate that this was due to the Sophists' influence, and the few indications that do suggest such a link are by no means conclusive. The picture changes, however, when we consult, not the factual evidence marking the progress of atheism, but the texts in which it is reflected. The evidence provided here makes it possible to pursue the analysis further.

---

[7] His dates are somewhat later.

The literary texts which, for their part, are neither suspect
nor ambiguous provide much clearer testimony of both the
increase in atheism and its direct connection with the new
philosophies. In Aristophanes' *Clouds*, scorn for the gods
is a major element. Socrates declares the clouds to be the
only deities. What about Zeus, Strepsiades wants to know.
What Zeus? Zeus does not even exist (366–7). Strepsiades
immediately passes this information on to his son, who has
just called upon the name of Zeus:

> Olympian Zeus! You blockhead, you,
> Come to *your* age, and yet believe in Zeus!

Strepsiades dismisses such beliefs as archaic and explains at
length that they are completely out of date. In truth, in invok-
ing the Vortex as a deity that has replaced Zeus, Strepsiades
(like Socrates before him) is closer to philosophers such as
Empedocles and Diogenes of Apollonia than he is to the
Sophists. He is prompted to replace Zeus by the clouds by
what he has learned from the controversial teaching about
celestial matters. The fact remains, however, that responsibility is said to lie with thinkers and teachers and the source
of irreligion is represented as being philosophical. What is
more, Aristophanes refuses to drop the subject. He repeatedly
returns to his diatribes against irreligion, neatly reversing the
earlier situation. When the young man is initiated into the
new ideas and sets to beating his own father, he throws in his
face, by way of excuse, the principles expounded at the
beginning of the play: 'Look there! "Paternal Zeus!" What
an old fool . . . There is no Zeus'. Zeus, who used to stand as
the guarantor of virtue (and in whom Strepsiades, incensed
at being beaten, is beginning to believe again), is now, for
thinkers as depicted by Aristophanes, no more than an
example and a precedent to be cited in one's own defence
when one is caught in the act of adultery (1070 ff.).[8]

Aristophanes' denunciation of irreligion is brilliant and
powerful; and at every turn it is associated with the theories

---

[8] These excuses, which put one in mind of Gorgias' *Helen*, were also to be
used in Euripides: see, in connection with Helen, *Tr.* 987 ff. and esp. the
speech of the Nurse in the *Hipp.* 451–9. The expressions used are so close to
those of *The Clouds* that either a common source or a direct allusion seems
extremely likely.

of the philosophers and the practice of the rhetoricians, in other words the Sophists. Furthermore, the peremptory tone of all these teachers, caricatured by means of repetition, is made to seem typically erudite. Simple folk believe in Zeus spontaneously; it takes a philosopher to teach them that their belief is no more than an outdated fad.

However, this aggressive atheism, applied to practical life with the assumption that it is as easy to change one's beliefs as it is to change one's fashions or money, seems a very distorted caricature of the epistemological or anthropological analyses of the real Sophists. Zeus is rejected. People no longer even know who he is; and they make the most of the situation to do exactly as they wish, lacking all respect for everything. If the theories of the philosophers do lurk in the background, they are given a totally distorted look.

Nor is this simply because *The Clouds* is a comedy. Euripides and Thucydides also record this increase of irreligion. Both ascribe the same intellectual inspiration to it, and both betray the fact that these same changes of tone and emphasis took place. Euripides often speaks of the gods. His characters, between them, express virtually every possible attitude towards them. But the general trend of his critique is extremely revealing. Sometimes he simply carries on the tendency to purify religion which was already detectable before his day, and tends to internalize belief. But this by no means excludes a willing 'acceptance' of the divine.[9] There are no grounds for imputing atheism or even impiety to him.

Nevertheless, though the reservations that he expresses on the score of mythology are legitimate, they do stem from a mind already enlightened, a mind quite prepared to take liberties with religious traditions. His characters cannot bring themselves to believe in legends which they find shocking (*Ion*, 435–51, *Heracles*, 1341 ff., *Iphigenia in Tauris*, 391). What is more, their religion sometimes takes on a remarkably philosophical air. The most famous example is the prayer in *The Trojan Women*:

---

[9] On this inclination towards purification, see Ch. 4. The expression acceptance of the divine' is borrowed from the excellent study by F. Chapouthier: 'La Notion du divin depuis Homère jusqu'à Platon'. *Entretiens de la Fondation Hardt*, 1 (1954), 205–37.

O power, who mount the world, wheel where the world rides,
O mystery of man's knowledge, whosoever you be,
Zeus named, nature's necessity or mortal mind,
I call upon you.[10]

(884–7)

Sometimes a doubt about the nature of the gods creeps in. Characters refer to the gods, 'whatever those gods may be' (*Orestes*, 418), which is already going quite far. One of the lost plays contained a line which expressed serious doubts about Zeus: 'Zeus, whatever he might be, for all I know is what people say.' The remark is very much in the style of Protagoras and it must have shocked. The story goes that Euripides corrected the line, replacing it with one that was above criticism: 'Zeus, as the truth tells me.' Another isolated line of his is perhaps even closer to the spirit of Protagoras. This is fragment 795, in which the word 'know' occurs three times. It deplores the crazy pretension of anybody 'who boasts of knowing anything concerning the gods'.

These bold, isolated sallies are indications of the extent to which Euripides was imbued with the new spirit. Above all, though, his plays no longer reflect any belief in the justice of the gods. For religious faith, this was the severest of all blows. Another passage, also very philosophical in tone, says as much quite openly:

What is god, what is not god, what is between man and god? Who can say, however long he seeks to know, when he sees the gods incline first one way, then another, then change again with contradictory lurches and unexpected changes of fortune? (*Helen*, 1137–43; translation adapted by J. de Romilly)

All these lines reflect growing doubts and increasing reservations, and the tone is always didactic, calling the philosophers to mind. From time to time, Euripides even produces an idea worthy of Prodicus himself or of the *Sisyphus*. For

[10] Here again, the text contains a vague reference to the systems of philosophers who were not Sophists. However, the very number of suggestions offered implies an element of doubt even as regards the Sophists. In Euripides there is also an as it were internalization of religion and an attempt to make it more moral. It is clearly expressed by Theonoe in *Helen*, when she speaks of the sanctuary that exists in her heart (1002).

example, in *Iphigenia in Tauris* it is suggested that cruel men ascribe their own tendencies to the gods. As for the *Sisyphus* itself, if it truly is by Euripides, the evidence that it provides is startling. We have already seen how radical the speech is, yet it was written to be delivered in the theatre, in the very heart of Athens. There are moments when everything seems about to topple over, for instance when a character from a fragment of a lost tragedy entitled *Bellerophon* exclaims, 'They say that there are gods in the heavens. but there are none, none!' Impious declarations such as these, in a work presented publicly, with the city itself defraying the costs, suggest that free-thinking was spreading fast.

All this explains the reputation that Euripides soon acquired of not believing in the gods, and spreading impiety through his works. In Aristophanes' *Thesmophoriazusae*, a woman complains that she has been ruined by Euripides, for she used to earn her living making wreaths to crown the gods, but now Euripides has written in his plays that 'there are no gods' (451). In *The Frogs*, Aristophanes was to ascribe to Euripides a prayer to gods 'different from the others' (889) and have him invoke 'Aether'[11] . . . volubly rolling tongue, intelligent wit and critic nostrils keen'. In *The Clouds*, similarly, Socrates is said to worship the deities of Air and Language. One becomes somewhat confused amid all this mockery in which the laughs matter more than the strict truth. It makes for more fun, no doubt. But one thing is certain: in the eyes of the public, all these new philosophical ideas were so many blows dealt against the traditional beliefs.[12]

They were serious blows, too. Behind the jokes, we sense a premonition of Socrates' trial. All these examples drawn from Euripides show well enough how easy it was to go further than the agnosticism pure and simple of the philosophers. Certain isolated remarks, like those in the *Bellerophon* and

[11] *The Clouds* (264 ff.): 'O Master and King, holding earth in your swing, O measureless infinite Air, / And thou glowing Aether, and Clouds . . . '. See also 'Tongue', at l. 424. The Ether, together with a citation from Euripides, also appears in Ar., *Th.* 272.

[12] A line from *The Clouds* (248) is frequently compared. It states that Zeus does not 'pass for current coin' here; the Greeks used the same word for currency and custom. It is related to *nomos*, law.

certain hasty judgements such as that passed on Euripides in the *Thesmophoriazusae* to the effect that he has persuaded people that 'there are no gods' suggest a far bolder and more deliberately negative attitude than any of the Sophists' analyses. If the extract from the *Sisyphus* is indeed by Euripides, it confirms what other passages from his works indicate clearly enough: namely, that when religious doubt spread to the public it became more uninhibited and took on quite a different tone. Critical reflection was replaced by open revolt.

The evidence from Thucydides is less richly varied, but the little that we discover there is every bit as revealing. The very fact that so little is said about the gods is in itself significant: by now history has become the business of human beings; the gods have nothing to do with it. The oracles are not what they were in Herodotus. Here, they are made to vary to suit the circumstances, as Thucydides himself explains in connection with the oracles on the plague and the variants between 'pestilence' and 'famine' (2. 54). For the most part, people admit to no fear of the gods; if Thucydides does mention it, it is usually to note that it is disappearing. Above all, the only time that his characters embark on a systematic analysis relating to the order of the universe and divine justice, they express themselves in a manner that is astonishingly close to the agnosticism of some of the Sophists and also to the ideas about the law of the stronger that were so often put forward by others. In the Melian dialogue, the representatives of this small island hope for salvation from the gods since they are a god-fearing people threatened by unjust aggression. But the Athenians reply that their city's project of conquest is in no way at odds with what people believe about the gods or what they desire in their mutual relationships:

For of the gods we hold the belief, and of men we know, that by a necessity of their nature, wherever they have power, they always rule. (5. 105. 2)

Those lines sum it all up: uncertainty about the gods, of whom we know nothing except through 'opinion'; the idea that opinions about the gods are inspired by the habitual behaviour of human beings; and, finally, the triumph of the strong, which is ratified by 'nature'. It is easy to see that the style is not at all suited to national delegates supposed to be discussing a political matter. It is too abstract, too meticulous, too much like the language of the philosophers not to be a reflection of it. What is more, Thucydides chooses to use such language in the very passage where he carries his historical analysis further than at any other point in his entire work.

However, in this case the terms themselves do not reflect the exaggeration that we detected when the philosophers' language was transposed to other works of literature. Yet even here a comparison is revealing. The actual terms may not differ from those used by the philosophers, but there is still a difference: it lies in the circumstances, the context, the intention. These are not theoretical reflections on human knowledge or lack of knowledge about the gods, but excuses proffered by unscrupulous conquerors in the midst of their activities. Scepticism regarding divine justice has opened the door to violence and amoralism. This text, seemingly so in tune with the Sophists, thus illustrates better than any other the way in which the meaning and effects of philosophical thinking can change when translated into action. I have repeatedly deplored the tendency to declare the Sophists to be 'for' or 'against' such or such a principle. However, people engaged in action—not only conquerors and men of ambition or greed, but also ordinary people, concerned simply to survive—clearly are, for their part, motivated by desires which oblige them to be either 'for' or 'against'.

An examination of the various types of evidence thus clearly reveals a definite sequence of events: the Sophists had disseminated ideas from which it was possible for anyone to extract a justification or argument in favour of a practical course of action. They had provided the words and opened up the way—only to be left far behind by those who then rushed forward. The change of register led on to a hardening of attitudes that nothing could arrest. The situation was extremely grave, for religious beliefs were a priori the only true guarantor of justice.

As we have seen, however, the Sophists' critique of justice proceeded by way of a basic distinction between nature and law. In a quite remarkable fashion which testifies to the importance of the role played by the philosophers, that intrinsically abstract distinction reappears in many of the texts of the day, even the least philosophical, leaving its mark there like a powder trail.

This is not the place to log the spread of the fashion, for other scholars have collected and commented on a host of examples. But one of the signs that the distinction truly was all the rage is the large number of cases in which the two terms are associated for no very good reason, seemingly as a kind of stylistic obligation.

In practice, the opposition between law and nature was not always used to downgrade law.[13] Nevertheless, it did constitute a splendid tool for those who were intent upon doing so and, in the texts of the period, it is repeatedly used by those in revolt against tradition.

In *The Clouds*, Strepsiades' son does not go quite so far, but he is at pains to draw attention to the arbitrary nature of the laws that are used to define right and wrong. He maintains that it was a man who declared it to be wrong to beat one's father, so another man can say the opposite. Arguing against human laws which are purely a matter of convention, he invokes the natural behaviour of cockerels and other animals. The line of argument is directly inspired by the Sophistic method and is a caricature of it. What is more, the same idea reappears, in a similar form, in *The Birds*, in which we are reminded that beating one's father is perfectly acceptable among the birds despite the fact that among human beings it would be wrong in the eyes of the law (755–9, 1345–8). The many variations in human law, as opposed to the natural order, constitute a justificatory argument which the philosophers have made available to people of evil intent. The excuses that the latter produce are full of themes that were currently fashionable just as, nowadays, the notion of 'complexes' often provides a ready-made exoneration.

Henceforward the clash between law and nature provides both sides with their key arguments in matters of morality. The unjust speech in *The Clouds* makes a proud stand against

---

[13] See below, p. 195, in relation to a text from *Hec.*

the *laws* (1040) and advises the young man to 'follow *nature*' (1078). The same contrast is drawn both by Thucydides and Euripides and, for both, the opposition between the two terms helps to explain the antagonism that exists between human desires and what is good. Thucydides mentions it as a disillusioned observation of fact. Euripides and his characters often use it as a more or less brazen excuse.

In Thucydides' *History*, book 3 alone contains a whole string of examples. The first is Diodorus' speech recommending that leniency be shown towards the rebels of Mytilene because it is impossible to prevent such mistakes:

All men are by *nature* prone to err, both in private and in public life, and there is no *law* that will prevent them. (3.45.3)

It is just as well to face facts:

In a word, it is impossible, and a mark of extreme simplicity, for anyone to imagine that, when human *nature* is whole-heartedly bent on any undertaking, it can be diverted from it by rigorous *laws* or by any other terror. (3.45.7)

Next comes the analysis on the disorders that attend civil wars. Here, Thucydides speaks of evils 'which will always happen while human *nature* is the same' (3.82.2). The evils take the form of disrespect for the law, for men enter into associations 'not . . . for the public good in conformity with the prescribed *laws*, but for selfish aggrandisement' (3.82.2 and 6). Then the last paragraph of this analysis (a paragraph whose authenticity has been questioned but which does no more than echo the sentiments expressed in general by Thucydides) declares that the city has been seriously undermined by this crisis:

Human *nature*, now triumphant over the *laws*, and accustomed even in spite of the *laws* to do wrong, took delight in showing that it was stronger than justice. (3.84.2)

Finally, in Euripides, the opposition crops up all over the place to make now one point, now another; and startling claims are sometimes based upon it. One character declares: 'For my part, I say that, in a critical situation, there is no reason to respect the *law* any more than necessity' (fr. 433). Another says: 'I possess Judgement, but *nature* forces me' (fr. 840). In a third passage, the two terms are used as a pair: '*Nature* decreed it—nature, which has no concern for *laws*' (fr. 920).

Texts such as these clearly demonstrate the impact of this idea which (as Plato specifically points out) was originally a favourite theme of Hippias, but was then taken up by a number of other Sophists. It entered into common parlance and current morality. In the process, however, both its meaning and its implications changed. In theoretical analysis, the opposition between law and nature had been a helpful intellectual tool. In the last of the texts cited above it became a weapon of amoralism. To say that the laws are a convention,[14] set up in opposition to nature, may imply the idea of a useful, healthy, and profitable convention. But the literary texts express only revolt against them. Whenever conventions are mentioned, it is with a view to pointing out how easy it is to reject them. On looking into the matter, it soon becomes apparent that not only is the opposition now used for a different purpose, but the concept of the term 'nature' has itself changed.

What kind of 'nature' do these non-philosophical texts have in mind? Except in the caricature of an argument produced by young Pheidippides, it is certainly not the nature to which the Sophists referred: that was an abstract, universal order which encompassed all that exists; and the clashes in which it was opposed to the human order were purely theoretical. The literary texts, in contrast, refer almost invariably to *human* nature, *our* nature; and the clashes to which this gives rise are psychological conflicts between different inclinations, desires, and interests. These conflicts take place within ourselves, and their outcome determines our actions. Either we do, or we do not, obey this 'nature'. Once again, it serves as an excuse. Under the cover provided by seemingly identical ideas and words, the shift is emphatic and obvious.

[14] Whether attacking or defending the laws, people now frequently described them as 'the laws that now obtain' (*kathestōtes*): the very word suggests relativity.

That in itself suggests that, in these texts, the critique of justice was to acquire a place of particular importance. All the rest—the gods, nature, and law, even truth—led up to the central problem of justice.

Justice was the golden rule in the Greek moral system. As the texts already cited show clearly enough, morality was going through a crisis. Not only were people increasingly flouting the idea of justice but, to justify their behaviour, they had no hesitation in making use of the ideas that had recently become fashionable. A single detail suffices to establish the point. At the beginning of *The Republic*, Glaucon declares that he is already familiar with the critique of justice as currently purveyed 'by Thrasymachus and countless others' (358 c).

It is consequently unnecessary to refer to all the existing sources of evidence or to all the arguments that could be said to reflect the influence of Sophist doctrines. Instead, let us concentrate upon particular passages from Thucydides and Euripides which prompt certain revealing comparisons.

Thucydides' point of departure is clearly that the determining factor is force, and the law is seldom heeded. That is probably also his own personal opinion for, almost without exception, the historical explanations that he gives are based upon motives of self-interest: upon fear, the desire to be safe, the desire for power. There is nothing surprising in that. Thucydides writes of the relations between one city and another and of war—a domain in which justice and the law were irrelevant except as a somewhat vague notion of certain human rights. The relations between one state and another were dictated by might rather than by right. He makes a number of forthright and arresting statements on the subject of States, most of them designed to justify Athenian imperialism.

It is remarkable to find ambassadors producing excuses of such a philosophical nature. They never claim that their intentions were pure or that they were provoked, or use any of the familiar justifications that are usually put forward. Instead, they point to the order of the world and the normal relations that obtain between might and right. For example, in book 1 they put their case before the Assembly of Sparta as follows:

Thus there is nothing remarkable or inconsistent with human nature in what we also have done, just because we accepted an empire when it was offered to us and then, yielding to the strongest motives—honour, fear and self-interest—declined to give it up. Nor, again, are we the first who have entered upon such a course, but it has ever been an established rule that the weaker is kept down by the stronger. (1.76.2)

In their next breath the delegates even speak of reasons of justice 'which no-one, when opportunity offered of securing something by main strength, ever yet put before force and abstained from taking advantage', and soon they are claiming to deserve praise because, while 'yielding to the instinct of human nature to rule over others', they have shown more justice than their strength warranted. The doctrine is absolute, uncompromising, and cynical, but it is presented in abstract, universal terms, taking on the air of a general philosophy of action.

There is a comparison with Thrasymachus to be made here; and it reveals some significant differences. Thrasymachus certainly held, as though self-evident, that 'men do not practise justice'. But the idea of a world completely dictated by relations of force is far more startling; and, used to justify practical action, it acquires a daunting power.

It is true that in certain respects Thucydides stops short of confronting some of the problems that Thrasymachus raised. Thrasymachus was concerned with justice in the cities. He sought out its origin and in every case found this in the rules promulgated by the government in power, that is to say, by those who were strongest. In contrast, Thucydides' Athenians look no further than the facts. What concerns them is knowing the practical circumstances in which attention is paid to justice. And they observe, quite simply, that such cases are relatively rare for, as they point out:

You know as well as we know that what is just is arrived at in human arguments only when the necessity on both sides is equal, and that the powerful exact what they can, while the weak yield what they must. (5.89)

But even if this description aims for no more than concrete objectivity, there is an all-encompassing, universal aspect to it, as is shown by the fact that even Athens' adversaries sometimes accept it. A Syracusan thus admits:

That the Athenians entertain these designs of aggrandisement is quite pardonable; and I have no word of blame for those who wish to rule, but only for those who are too ready to submit; for it is an instinct of man's nature to rule those who yield, but to guard against those who are ready to attack. (4.61.5)

In both its actions and its reactions, human behaviour is dictated by forces none of which, apparently, have anything to do with justice.

It is only fair to insert that 'apparently', for Thucydides does mention some cases in which certain men are passionately committed to justice. He even suggests that, in the longer term, if justice could rally sympathy, love of it might turn out to be the most advantageous attitude.[15] But the remarks that he puts into the mouths of his Athenians show clearly that, in the field of practical action, the Sophists' teaching was producing devastating effects.

It goes without saying that individuals applied just the same maxims to their own private affairs, as is proved by the rising tide of private ambition. We have already noted Alcibiades' disorderly behaviour. Thucydides tells us that his most noticeable fault, the one which aroused the anxiety and hostility of so many Athenians, was his tendency to ignore rules and laws, his *paranomia*. Thucydides refers to it at 6.15.4 and again at 6.28.2, relating how Alcibiades' enemies (themselves ambitious and jealous men) wound up their attack against him by 'citing as further proofs other instances of his undemocratic lawlessness of conduct' (6.28.2).

Thucydides' picture of unscrupulous ambition leads straight on to Euripides. His plays may not contain such overt statements as those formulated by Thucydides and his ambassadors, but he does sometimes set on stage characters who are quite ready to express their scorn for the laws. One is his Cyclops, who, in what was probably an early play, was already producing blasphemies which included the following remark: 'As for those who set up laws to enhance human life, they can go hang!'

---

[15] See the texts in Ch. 6.

In more serious vein too, Euripides has at least one character launch into a passionate defence of injustice. Characteristically enough, the context is once again a struggle for power. This time, however, the protagonist is a royal prince, Eteocles, one of the two sons of Oedipus, who does not hesitate to engage in battle with his own brother and tear his country asunder in order to be the sole heir to an undivided patrimony. He would do anything, he says, to possess 'sovereignty, the greatest of all deities'; and that 'anything' includes injustice, as he himself admits, assuming full responsibility for the consequences:

> When it comes to violating justice, it is fine
> To do so for the sake of sovereignty
> Piety applies to other situations.
>
> (*Phoenician Women*, 524–5)

His view could hardly be more extreme or his words more damning, more cynical. Eteocles is ambitious and unscrupulous. Perhaps he represents all the other ambitious, unscrupulous men who were then fermenting civil war in Athens. He certainly wastes no time on philosophy and theory. His words are not even backed by any coherent system of thought, for he assumes that an exception will be made for him in his quest for power, without considering that one exception may open the door to a host of others. Eteocles could not care less: he is set on his goal and has heard plenty of people criticizing justice and shrugging it off. That is why he dares to behave as he does.

Eteocles bears excellent witness to the moral crisis through which Athens was passing and the Athenians' current tendency to do nothing without calling into question justice, power, and equality, along with other general concepts. However, the connection between Eteocles and the Sophists might seem somewhat slender and the case of this ambitious prince somewhat inconclusive were it not for the fact that he had a terrible twin, namely Callicles, a figure who, without Plato, would be unknown. It is Callicles who establishes the link between the two sets of testimony: on the one hand the philosophical analyses circulating under the names of the Sophists, on the other the professions of amoralism scattered through other works of the time. Callicles' words bind them into a single whole.

Who is this Callicles? He is known to us only through Plato's *Gorgias*. Plato gives him no introduction and tells us nothing about him, except that he is Gorgias' host. Yet his role in the dialogue is of the first importance, as is clear even in material terms. Socrates' conversation with Gorgias takes up twelve pages (in the traditional pagination); over the next twenty pages he is engaged in discussion with Polos, a fervent young admirer of Gorgias. Then Callicles abruptly takes over, to be Socrates' sole interlocutor throughout the remaining forty-five pages of the dialogue. But it is not just a matter of the space devoted to him. The discussion with Gorgias did no more than sketch in the problem of rhetoric; the argument with Polos revealed its moral implications; the great confrontation between Callicles and Socrates probes deep into the question of justice and the very ends of human life.

The importance of the various subjects of debate seems ill-assorted with the respective interlocutors selected, each one less qualified than the last. It is an intriguing puzzle; and the further we look into it, the more baffling it becomes. Plato tells us nothing of Callicles here, and never mentions him anywhere else. The ancient tradition has thrown up nothing about him. This total blank has led some scholars to believe that he is a pure figment of Plato's imagination.

Of course, he may have existed without our knowing anything about him. He may have been someone quite obscure. But to give a position of such prominence to an unknown or to invent him from scratch comes to much the same thing. Whatever the truth may be, for us he exists purely by virtue of the role that Plato gives him, namely to play the most ardent and most abrasive of all the defenders of amoralism without, however, himself being a Sophist.

Surely, that is the whole point: Callicles is not a Sophist. He is a rich man who spends time in their company but does not himself teach: he is far too ambitious for that. He has studied under a number of teachers, in the company of other young men whose names Plato mentions (487 c). But he has felt no inclination to carry the pursuit of knowledge too far;

and—as we know—he proclaims extreme contempt for those who continue to philosophize once their youth is over:

When I see an elderly man still going on with philosophy, and not getting rid of it, that is the gentleman, Socrates, whom I think in need of a whipping. (485 D)

No Sophist could have said such a thing. Callicles thus presents a perfect picture of the practical and secular uses to which teaching (which he himself saw no point in pursuing) can be put.

This too is thought-provoking, for it is the only instance of an unknown being given a major role in Plato's dialogues. If our thesis so far is correct, one can see that Plato may have been obliged, for once, to resort to such an exceptional device. He needed just such an unknown figure to be able to criticize all the dangers that the Sophists' theses presented to those who distorted them to further their own passions and ambitions. He was out to show that rhetoric implied amoralism. But unless he grievously distorted the situation, he could not in all conscience represent any of the true Sophists as defending amoralism. What he needed was a young man of ambition, schooled in the procedures of Sophistic debate, but concerned solely with practical success. He needed a quintessential interpretation of the Sophists' critiques and an extreme example of revolt against the moral values. Only thus could he denounce what he considered to be hidden behind rhetoric and all that the new teaching implied for those who sought practical norms of action in it.

This may have the appearance of an a priori reconstruction. But in the light of it every detail in the text begins to make sense and bear our thesis out. In our analyses so far we have noted a number of aspects to this problem. Now is the moment to consider their telling combination.

Callicles enters upon the scene with brash arrogance, as does the Sophist Thrasymachus, in *The Republic*. The first idea that he tosses out is that it is necessary to distinguish between two totally opposed domains, namely nature and law. At this point he sounds like the Sophist Antiphon. He declares, 'For the most part these two, nature and convention, are opposed to each other.' The same applies to justice: 'For

by nature eveything is uglier that is more evil, such as suffering wrong; doing it is uglier only by convention' (483 A).

The notion of ugliness in itself implies admiration for the
strong. Callicles extols the man strong enough to trample
underfoot all these arbitrary laws and impose his own rule.
Thrasymachus too had celebrated the injustice of the superman and had declared injustice to be 'more beautiful, more
free, more dominating'.

At this point we are still close to the real Sophists. But
we must beware, for in no time they are overtaken and left
behind. In the first place, this arbitrary definition of the
law is no longer that of the Sophists. Callicles is not concerned about the law varying according to governments. In
his opinion, it is not the strong who make the laws, but the
weak. Callicles is ambitious and impatient and cannot bear to
see superior people being pushed around by the 'majority'.
He loathes the obscure majority. The reason why his interpretation of the law is different is because it is not objectively
anthropological, but passionately and personally committed.
It is in line with the amoralism of the literary texts but goes
beyond it.

All this is nothing, however, compared to Callicles' next distortion of the Sophists' true doctrines. Having distinguished
between two contrary orders and principles of action, he goes
on to apportion 'law' and 'justice' to the order of nature,
which decrees that the strong shall triumph over the weak.
He thus gives nature a normative value: 'Nature, in my
opinion, herself proclaims the fact that it is right for the
better to have advantage of the worse, and the abler of the
feebler.' Citing the examples of animals, warriors, and military conquerors, he declares that it is they who 'follow
nature—the nature of right—in acting thus; yes, on my soul,
and follow the law of nature!' (483 D).

None of the known Sophists had ever argued in favour of
the law of the strongest, the law according to nature. But
Callicles does so, revelling in the shock that his words impart.
This is the way to make it possible for a superman to triumph,
a superman who will dare to trample underfoot all these
artificial laws: the superman, 'our slave, rises in revolt and
shows himself our master, and there dawns the full light of
natural justice' (484 A).

Callicles uses the 'law of nature' to convert a theoretical analysis into a rule of life. Antiphon had simply observed that it is not to one's advantage to obey the law unless witnesses are present. Callicles makes such disobedience a new rule, a new law ... The danger was always inherent in the Sophists' analyses; this was always the next step, which might or might not be taken. Callicles, for his part, takes it, more boldly than any other amoralist of the day.

The same ideas, or implications, resurface repeatedly in the discussion into which the ungracious, tetchy Callicles is drawn by Socrates. Socrates besieges him with questions, re-establishing the moral values at every turn. Who exactly are these 'powerful people' whose praises Callicles sings? Surely, the crowd is more powerful than individuals; and the crowd favours the equality of justice. And who exactly are 'the best people'? Surely, not just the strong; must they not also be intelligent, courageous, skilful politicians? No, says Callicles, they must have many desires and be able to satisfy them. But what desires? Should certain distinctions not be drawn? Little by little, pushed from rejection into agreement, and forced to abandon his arguments, Callicles falls silent, but not before two opposed models have been set up, the one centred upon the good, the other upon pleasure.

They reveal the fundamental nature of the choices that are implied by Callicles' attitude and by his determination to derive practical rules of action from the analyses of the Sophists. Meanwhile, what also becomes clear is that both ways of life are reflected in politics.

That should come as no surprise. There is, after all, a political term for the law of the strongest, namely tyranny. The idea of it lurks behind all the declarations of those who claim to defy the law, and sometimes it rises to the surface. Thrasymachus himself, at the end of the speech ascribed to him in Plato's *Republic*, cited tyranny as an example of perfect injustice (344 A). As he saw it, injustice of such pro-portions was beyond blame or punishment: it became the envy of all. The literary texts were quick to reflect a similar view. According to Thucydides, Athens' empire, founded on force, was called a 'tyranny'. And when Euripides' Eteocles claims to accept injustice when it is a matter of winning 'sovereignty', the Greek word used again means 'tyranny'.

The ambitious Alcibiades was similarly accused of coveting tyranny, and Callicles, who is merely a demagogue in a democracy, openly admits that he wishes he were more than just that, and were in a position to reject the law entirely. Small wonder, then, that the advantages and disadvantages of the tyrant were so much discussed in *The Republic*. Small wonder, equally, that—as Aristophanes testifies—the Athenian democracy of the period lived in fear of tyrannical plots. Behind the rhetoric aimed to promote success could be sensed the ideology of the regime that it so much dreaded.

That is assuredly why the debate between Socrates and Callicles, in the *Gorgias*, closes with an evocation of the two opposed political regimes, followed by a myth about the punishment meted out in the underworld to the tyrant whom some consider such an object of envy. The discussion thus comes full circle, returning to the problem of rhetoric which was its starting-point. But thanks to the part played by Callicles, the problem has been expanded into a choice between two ways of life, two political systems, two moralities.

Callicles' role in Plato's dialogue thus becomes clear. Had the Sophists had nothing to do with the current amoralism, Plato would not have needed to start the discussion with Gorgias or to ascribe to his Callicles ideas so closely associated with their doctrines. The very fact that Callicles is sometimes mistakenly described as one of the Sophists in itself testifies to the connection that Plato subtly conveys. Conversely, however, if the Sophists had themselves been immoralists, Plato would not have needed to create his Callicles. The very existence of this figure testifies to the strength of the current of ideas that was sweeping so many along.

It stemmed from the theses of the Sophists and, fuelled by the vocabulary and statements of these teachers, it grew in strength. But, at the same time, it falsified those ideas and distorted their meaning. It switched courses, took a different turn and swept along in a new direction.

There is certainly a line of continuity between the prudent old teachers and the impatient, arrogant young men who followed them; and it is not easy to see exactly at what point the break came. Certainly, though, somewhere along the way a break occurred. The Sophists' theses were first exaggerated, then distorted by the Athenians of the day. The war, with all its trials and tribulations, encouraged the latter to seize upon the new ideas set before them and convert them into weapons and justifications.

As a result of that blatant and presumptuous exploitation, it was soon forgotten that, in their original form, the Sophists' doctrines might have opened on to different perspectives. The passions of those filled with ambition obscured everything but the element of immoralism, blotting out the constructive aspect which, in the work of the original Sophists, coexisted with the critical aspects.

Now—as was announced earlier—we must work our way back up the slippery slope and start out again from the initial philosophical texts, to discover what could be reconstructed on the basis of the *tabula rasa*. It was to be not immoralism, but a new kind of morality.

6

Reconstruction on the Basis of the *Tabula Rasa*

WE possess only brief fragments of Protagoras' writing, the interpretation of which is frequently problematic. However, Plato fortunately has this Sophist make a long speech in the dialogue that bears his name, and all the details suggest it to be an extremely faithful imitation of Protagoras himself, his style and his line of reasoning included. Even were that not so, it would be absurd to suppose that Plato would go to these lengths to put into the mouth of such a well-known figure ideas which did not belong to him.

This text, with the myth to which the greater part of it is devoted, puts forward a theory which constitutes an extremely solid defence of justice: it shows that man's well-being depends utterly upon certain moral values, for it is these that make it possible for him to live in society. This is an idea which gives entirely new meaning to the thought of the Sophists. What can no longer be justified by reference to the gods or the absolute is once again given validity, although now this is derived from human life, even from the self-interest of human beings.

We are nevertheless bound to recognize that, in the myth, these values still appear to be linked to the gods and the gifts that they bestow, for it is those gifts that make it possible for human beings to live as a society. That fact—to which we shall be returning[1]—indicates that Protagoras' contemporaries cannot have considered him an atheist in either word or deed. All the same, we should not overestimate its significance. What we have here is, after all, just a myth, that is to say, a figurative form of expression within a traditional

---

[1] See Ch. 4.

framework, upon which the speaker embroiders freely in order to convey particular ideas. Protagoras was at liberty to use either a myth or a reasoned speech, a *logos*, and chose the form of myth which, he explained, gave greater pleasure (319 c). But clearly, that pleasure stemmed partly from a measure of invention. So the important point is not the poetical mythical packaging, with the figures of Zeus, Prometheus, and Epimetheus, but what happens to the human race and why it happens.

That is borne out by the fact that the myth of the origins and progress of the human race was at the time a theme much in vogue, used by many different authors. Aeschylus' *Prometheus Bound* tells how men originally lived 'in disorder and confusion' with neither skills nor knowledge, until the day when Prometheus presented them with all the arts that make for civilization. Sophocles' *Antigone* evokes the same series of inventions, attributing them to men themselves but adding in conclusion that, unless used for good ends, they are worthless. In *The Suppliant Maidens*, Euripides also addresses himself to this theme, evoking the 'confused and bestial' life of the early days (201), then describing all the inventions which followed, and praising 'whichever of the gods' it was to whom men were indebted. Similar pictures are painted in the treatise *On Ancient Medicine* (3), in the famous text from the *Sisyphus* cited above for its suggestion that the gods are a human invention, and also in a passage in Diodorus Siculus (1. 8), which some eminent scholars have attributed to Democritus (although today that hypothesis is questioned).[2] Finally, the theme also appears in Archelaus, the disciple of Anaxagoras and teacher of Socrates, who analyses how human beings set themselves apart from the animals at the beginning of time. The fifth century as a whole seems full of wonder at all that redounds to the glory of the human race, which started out with so little.

The theme was long to retain its popularity: five centuries

---

[2] This attribution was for many years generally accepted but is now considered doubtful. A number of names have been suggested as the source for the text. They include Leucippus, Posidonius, and even Protagoras himself.

later Lucretius treated it at considerable length in book 5 of his poem *De Rerum Natura*. This was a familiar framework, then, in which an analysis could be accommodated in a more or less fictional form. But—as a large number of texts testify—the theme also prompted fundamental reflection on the beginnings and evolution of the human race. Furthermore, it seems to have been of particular importance to Protagoras, to judge by the title of one of his treatises which has not come down to us: *On the Original Condition of Mankind*.

It is, of course, crucial to note the nature of the inventions that all these authors choose to emphasize. Minor details vary from one author to another, but the originality of Protagoras' version is startling when compared to the rest. His is the only one in which the evolution of the human race does not depend solely on the arts and skills. It introduces two successive stages in the progress of human beings. First come the arts and skills given by Prometheus, then political expertise bestowed by Zeus.

The two separate initiatives are necessary because the arts and skills are not enough to correct the confusion and bestiality of the beginning of time. In fact, they leave human beings in danger of total extinction, for they are obliged to struggle against not only the animals but also others of their own kind. Protagoras (still according to Plato) expounds his theme with eloquence: because men have no cities, they are destroyed by wild animals:

Although their skill in handiwork was sufficient aid in respect of food, in their warfare with the beasts it was defective; for as yet they had no civic art [the art of politics], which includes the art of war. So they sought to band themselves together and secure their lives by founding cities. Now, as often as they were banded together they did wrong to one another [*adikein*] through the lack of civic art, and thus they began to be scattered again and to perish. (*Protagoras*, 322 B)

The originality of human beings certainly lay in their coming together to form cities, obliged to do so by their vulnerability. But, for other authors, the principle of congregation appeared to pose no problems. Sophocles had spoken of 'the aspirations from which cities are born' (*Antigone*, 354); Isocrates was to describe men yielding to the persuasion to unite. Thanks to this 'we have come together and founded cities and made laws' (*Nicocles*, 6 = *Antidosis*, 254); even Plato, in *The Republic*, was to paint a picture of men coming together in cities in order to satisfy their needs, since it was impossible for them to do so as isolated individuals. But those groups could only be formed and survive on one condition; and Protagoras was the only one to spot it. He alone made out two separate stages in human evolution, first that of the arts and skills, then that of the political skills, whose role was essential and decisive.

The originality of Protagoras, compared to the other texts that tell of the birth of human societies, lies entirely in the special role that he assigns to political virtues. Of course, Protagoras might be said to be simply justifying his own role in the city of Athens; he himself acknowledged that his speech was designed to do so. But the fact that his practical role complemented his doctrines does nothing to invalidate the latter, for the analysis is original, coherent, and specific.

Protagoras explains the importance of political virtues perfectly clearly:

So Zeus, fearing that our race was in danger of utter destruction, sent Hermes to bring respect (*aidōs*)[3] and right (*dikē*) among men to the end that there should be regulation of cities and friendly ties to draw them together. (322 B)

What is more, Zeus makes sure that these sentiments are bestowed upon one and all, 'for cities cannot be formed if only a few have a share of these, as of other arts' (322 D). Men incapable of harbouring them would have to be put to death: that corollary underlines the importance of political virtues to the survival of the group as a whole.

Thus, we now find justice, the very justice no longer sanctioned by the gods, firmly implanted in human life, which it alone has the power to preserve. It is the guarantor of social life, which is the only form of life possible for human beings. Indirectly, justice is the most essential of all human posses-

---

[3] The word 'respect' is, of course, inadequate. The Greek term, which has no exact equivalent in French or English, denotes all the kinds of consideration that may be shown for others when one is mindful of all that is their due.

sions, although that is something all too easily forgotten.

Now we can see how very important the laws, which ensured the cohesion of the State, were to Protagoras and how it was that this agnostic was chosen as the legislator for the new town of Thurii, the Panhellenic colony which Pericles set up as a model town. It was justice that made it possible for groups and, consequently, individuals to survive. It is important to remember that, in those days, people were convinced that the well-being of individuals stemmed from the well-being of the State. Thucydides has his Pericles declare as much, as does Sophocles his Creon. But Protagoras is not content simply to make an unsubstantiated statement of principle: his very analysis of the development of human life establishes clearly that, outside organized groups, no survival is possible.

Every human being needs other people, needs to belong, with them, to a united and coherent group.[4] Such associations presuppose a respect for others and a recognition of mutual rights. Our own self-interest is served by justice. The principle could be said to imply a kind of contract according to which each individual links himself with the others in the group in order to derive the advantages that stem from such a pact. Protagoras does not specifically set out the idea in that form, but the seed of what was, centuries later, to be known as 'the social contract' is clearly detectable in his thinking.

It was just a seed, but it does seem to have been germinating on all sides, in fifth-century Athens. There has been much discussion about how far the term 'social contract' is applicable to the doctrines of this period. Some scholars hold that (in certain texts, at least) the idea is not presented as describing an event taking place in a chronological sequence. Others consider that (in certain texts, at least) the moral obligation to obey the law did not emerge clearly enough. But these are minor quibbles. It would be foolish to expect to find doctrines formulated in the fifth century BC as rigorously as they were to be in later ages. Nevertheless, the important point is that, by and large, the idea did already exist. It was forcefully

---

[4] On the fact that every group of human beings depends upon its members respecting justice between them, see p. 174.

expressed by many writers, among them the Sophists. In one form or another, it had already taken a hold on all sides.

The trouble is that it crops up in discussions of widely diverse kinds; and if we are to avoid misunderstandings and seize upon the full implications of Protagoras' thought, it is important to pinpoint the different ways in which it could be interpreted. Some of the Sophists' texts use the idea of a contract or agreement to show that the law has no absolute foundation. That is certainly one of the possible forms that the idea can take. Similarly, one can hold that the law is essential, for it stems from an agreement upon which our survival depends and which is therefore important: this was Protagoras' own view. But on the other hand, one could say that the law is of no importance since it is no more than a convention.[5] That was the argument of those who sought to show up the artificial and arbitrary nature of written laws. What better way to make that point than by emphasizing that human beings themselves deliberately laid the foundations for those laws? Authors such as these also spoke of 'agreements' and 'conventions'.

Hippias was one who did so. In Xenophon's *Memorabilia* (4. 4. 13), he defines justice as 'covenants (*sunthemenoi*) made by the citizens whereby they have enacted what ought to be done and what ought to be avoided'.

Antiphon was another who opposed law and nature declaring: 'the edicts of the laws are arrived at by consent (*homologēthenta*), not by natural growth, whereas those of nature are not a matter of consent'. In the lines that follow, the word is used again in connection with 'those who have agreed to these edicts', as if this was a specific act, performed at a particular juncture and thereafter repeated for each generation.

A third was Lycophron, a slightly later Sophist, who appears to have been a disciple of Gorgias. All we know of him is what is briefly reported by Aristotle, but the evidence is

---

[5] We should, however, recognize that those who are intent upon denigrating the law stress not so much its conventional character, but rather the arbitrary nature of the power which imposed it. That arbitrariness elicits responses like that of the young man in *The Clouds* (ll. 1421–4): in his view, what one man has set up another may knock down.

explicit, for Aristotle tells us that Lycophron called the law an agreement (*sunthēkē*), and said that it was justified as 'a guarantor of mutual justice' (fr. 3). He went on to remark that it did not have the power to make men good and just, thereby drawing a radical distinction between the social contract and morality.

These authors, or rather these texts (a more suitable term to use, as we shall see) did not adopt quite the same line as Protagoras. But at least they show that the idea of a 'convention', 'agreement', or 'contract' was familiar to the Sophists and constituted one of the fashionable themes of the day.

Could the same be said of the justification of justice that Protagoras believed it provided? Or did this remain an isolated idea? That is an even more important question.

Protagoras was certainly not the only thinker to produce a justification of justice. It is now time to discover the other side to the thinking of the day. As we shall see, the justification of justice which Protagoras offered was remarkably influential and, on the basis of new arguments founded upon self-interest, the defence of justice was taken up on all sides—not only by the Sophists themselves, but also by moral philosophers who were outside their movement or were trying to counter their critiques.

All these thinkers seem to have been determined to defend the law as the most beneficial of all human inventions. Some emphasized the existence of a contract, others did not. Some spoke of utility, others of commitment. But for all those who aimed to defend justice and thereby refute the negative tendencies of the time, the new ideas provided marvellous arguments. No longer guaranteed by the gods, the law was instead now assured by the true interests of human beings. Justice could thus be reconstructed.

This is the thesis expounded in a text probably written by a Sophist who is known as the Anonymus Iamblichi, because his speech is preserved in a long citation in Iamblichus' *Protrepticus*. Although the identity of this writer is not known, it is unanimously agreed that he must have been writing during the Peloponnesian War, and most scholars believe him to have been a Sophist, although some identify him as Democritus. As to which Sophist he might be, many names have been put forward, with a slight preference for either Hippias or Protagoras.[6] There is no need to dwell upon this problem, but the very uncertainty of the author's identity testifies to the current popularity of these ideas and the ease with which they were taken up and adapted by first one, then another writer, in a subtle exchange of views.

The text refers to many arguments on the subject of law and nature and to the view held by some that it is cowardly to obey the laws. But its purpose is to produce a firm defence of the law, a defence based on the necessity for human beings to live in societies:

If men were given such a nature that they were not able to live alone, but formed an association with one another under pressure of necessity, and found out our general way of life and the skills related to it, and cannot associate and live with one another without observance of law (for this would be even worse than living alone), we can conclude, then, that because of these necessities Law and Justice are kings among men, and that they must never suffer any change, for they answer a strong need, rooted in nature.[7] (Iamblichus, *Protrepticus*, 6. 2)

The two stages of progress which Plato's Protagoras distinguished are detectable here, but without the mythological wrapping, for in between the evocations of isolation and civilization there is at least a hint of the disaster that would befall any group not ruled by law. Outdoing the text of the *Protagoras* in audacity, the author even establishes a link between law and nature, arguing that the social links imposed by law are themselves based upon nature. Furthermore, as in the *Protagoras*, the justification is designed to defend not only the law and legality, but justice itself. The author repeatedly uses the terms in conjunction: what the human

---

[6] Protagoras: K. Töpfer (1907); a disciple of Protagoras and Democritus: A. T. Cole (1961); Hippias: Untersteiner (1943; 1944); and already, hypothetically, H. Gomperz (1912); Democritus: Cataudella (1932; 1950). But others also suggested have included Prodicus, Critias, Antiphon, Antisthenes, Theramenes, and others too.
[7] *phusei*.

group needs is a spirit of unity and equity. United, such a group is all-powerful.

Next, the author counters the dream of the superman as evoked by Callicles in the *Gorgias*.

If there should be anyone who had from the beginning of his life a nature such as we shall describe; if he should he invulnerable, not subject to disease, free from emotion, extraordinary, and hard as adamant in body and soul, perhaps someone might believe that the power based on consideration of one's own advantage would be sufficient for such a man, on the grounds that a man of that type is invulnerable even if he does not submit to the law. The man who believes this is wrong. If there should be such a man, as in fact there could not be, such a man would be preserved if he placed himself on the side of the laws and what is just, strengthening these and using his strength to support these and what confirms them, but otherwise he could not endure. For it would appear that all men would be in a state of hostility to a man formed of such a nature, and because of their own observance of law and their numbers, they would surpass such a man in skill or force and they would get the better of him. Accordingly, it appears that power itself, the real power, is preserved by law and justice. (*Protrepticus*, 6.2)

The text is remarkable for the way that it counters the individual strength of the superman, and no less so in that, precisely on that account, it lays a greater emphasis than Protagoras' myth did upon the self-interest of each and every individual, not simply upon that of human beings in general. The group links are a natural necessity, allowing no latitude to rebels, however strong. In the *Protagoras*, Zeus said that it would be necessary to put to death those who were devoid of a sense of justice. The Anonymus Iamblichi declares that such people would inevitably disappear.

He goes on to give a direct description of the advantages of justice in daily life. At this point he is no longer concerned with the origin of laws, but with respect for them and the way to maintain them in life as presently lived. The law respected and maintained is presented as the source of all the good things in life: mutual trust, the right use of chance and time, the absence of anxiety, tranquil sleep, a minimum of wars, and many other advantages. Disrespect for the laws, in contrast, brings in its train all the converse evils and, on top of them, tyranny, which comes into being when the law is no longer respected and no longer protects the mass of the population. So long as it is respected, it is impossible for anyone to become a tyrant.

This defence, which, without advocating a contract, limits itself (like Protagoras) to suggesting the need for an agreement, is both clear and firm. It even represents an advance on Protagoras, in that it is concerned with real cities, presenting the part played by laws and justice as every bit as indispensable in them now as it was at the beginning of time: it is essential for day-to-day survival and for the happiness of each and everyone.

The reason why the Anonymus Iamblichi has sometimes been identified with Democritus is partly that Democritus seems to have held similar views. This compatriot of Protagoras thus seems to take his place in the list of defenders of justice, alongside the Anonymus. Yet one is bound to hesitate, for one text (A 166) suggests that Democritus criticized the invention constituted by the law, declaring that the sage should liberate himself from it. But that text is no more than a summary and may well be as suspect as the summaries produced by critics of the present day who conclude that an author is 'against the law' simply because he opposes it to nature. Besides, Democritus may well have supposed the sage's freedom to be regulated by some internal model that was more demanding than the law. There is no way of knowing.[8] It is certain, however, that elsewhere he too praises the utility of the pact constituted by the law. He declares:

The laws would prevent each man from living according to his inclination unless individuals harmed each other; for envy creates the beginning of strife. (fr. B 245)

And his words seem to echo a definition of the law that appears in Antiphon: 'not to wrong anyone unless wronged oneself is just'. Also familiar is the condemnation of civil war, presented as a disastrous scourge: the *Protagoras* made the

---

[8] Yet that is what the fragment cited below suggests. The lack of context also gives rise to another certainty: Democritus recognizes that in nature dominion goes to the strongest (B 267); but, in the absence of any context, it is not possible to make out whether he approves of that fact or regrets it.

same point. In another fragment, Democritus states that the law is designed for the good of human beings but can only ensure it if they support its action for, he says, 'To those who obey it, it shows their own particular virtue' (fr. B 248). Here, we are reminded of the Anonymus Iamblichi's remarks on the benefits which stem from respect for the laws. Elsewhere, other fragments show the extent to which the lot of individuals depends on that of the State (fr. B 252), how harmful dissension is for all and sundry, how necessary concord for communal projects (frs. B 249, 250). It seems clear enough that Democritus, deeply influenced by the Sophistic discussions of the day, took up the defence of the law on the grounds of it being an eminently beneficial human convention. On this point, the views held by the two thinkers from Abdera were probably relatively close.

But this kind of thinking extended further afield, to quite different circles. In Plato's *Republic*, Glaucon sums up the doctrine (to which he himself does not subscribe) which holds that, 'according to nature', to suffer an injustice is an evil; and he explains how those who wish to avoid such subjection,

determine that it is for their profit to make a compact with one another (*sunthesthai*) neither to commit nor to suffer injustice, and that this is the beginning of legislation and of covenants between men (*sunthēkas*), and that they name the commandment of the law the lawful and the just . . . and that this is the genesis and essential nature of justice—a compromise between the best, which is to do wrong with impunity, and the worst, which is to be wronged and be impotent to get one's revenge. (359 A)

The text is inspired by the theories of the Sophists, and Glaucon asks Socrates to refute these ideas. But although he is scornful of this purely protective law, he nevertheless recognizes its utility, almost its necessity.

As for Socrates himself, it is certainly not the case that, anxious for an absolute justice which would be a good thing in itself, he totally dismissed all these ideas, regarding such a contract with scorn. All he did was alter the moral significance of that contract. For, in the last analysis, in the *Crito*, he refuses to leave Athens out of loyalty to its laws, explaining that a contract links him to those laws, a contract which he is bound to respect. He makes this quite clear: 'Ought a man to do what he has agreed to do, provided it is right, or may he violate his agreements?' (49 E). The laws are then made to speak for themselves, to make the point even clearer: 'Is this what was agreed between us?' They go on to point out that they have presided over Socrates' entire life with his tacit consent. For if a man chooses to remain in the city, then 'he has thereby entered into an agreement with us to do what we command' (51 E). The point is insistently made with a string of repetitions. The next page alone contains four forms of the word meaning 'to agree' (*homolegein*), three instances of the word 'agreement' (*homologia*), as well as a doubly emphatic tautology, 'agreements and undertakings' (52 D).

It is remarkable to see how each writer uses the theme in his own particular way, some emphasizing the role of self-interest, others that of morality, some dwelling upon the political, others upon the material aspects, each interpreting the meaning of a convention in his own particular fashion. But equally remarkable is the omnipresence of the idea itself, and the way that the Sophists' *tabula rasa* was forcing every author, whether Sophist or not, to adopt the notion of a contract as the basis upon which to reconstruct a defence of justice—a defence for which the new Sophistic spirit had suddenly created a need.

As a result of the wide impact of the new thinking, this idea of a contract soon came to be regarded as virtually self-evident. It appears repeatedly in the works of the most diverse thinkers in the fourth century, which produced a whole sheaf of similar texts on the topic. The fullest that we possess is the first speech *Against Aristogiton*, wrongly attributed to Demosthenes—if, that is, it truly was composed in the fourth century (there is some doubt on the matter). This speech defends the law at length, explaining that in nature everything is irregular and individual, whereas the law, which is the same for all and sundry, aims for what is just, fine, and useful (15). Observations of this kind were thus still referring to the opposition between law and nature; and the law was described as a 'convention' (*sunthēkē*, paras. 16 and 70). But the convention was regarded as good and healthy, infinitely superior to the anarchy that reigns in the order of nature.

Why should it not be? Isocrates, for his part, also celebrates, as a reason for human beings to be proud of themselves, the fact that they got together, used persuasion on one another, and then instituted laws for themselves. In fact, this must have been an idea to which he was strongly attached, since the text is repeated, appearing in two separate speeches (*Nicocles*, 6 = *Antidosis*, 254). Again it is a matter of a convention, but a fine and profitable one. As for Aristotle, he makes only one correction: he retains the idea of a useful association, but insists that virtue should be its goal. The idea had thus undergone considerable development and it was long to continue to do so. It reappears much later, in Lucretius, who writes:

Then also neighbours began to join friendship amongst themselves in their eagerness to do no hurt and suffer no violence . . . A good part, indeed most, kept the covenant (*foedera*) unblemished, or else the race of mankind would have been even then wholly destroyed, nor would birth and begetting have been able to prolong their posterity to the present day. (s. 1016–24)

The similarities between this text and the earliest ones in which the idea of a convention appeared is striking: his flights of civic moralizing aside, this Epicurean poet falls closely into line with the tradition established by Protagoras and the Anonymus Iamblichi, and probably also follows in the footsteps of Democritus, the atomist.

There thus exists a whole collection of texts in which common or connected attitudes and ideas appear. On closer examination it becomes apparent that each author produced his own particular interpretation; and some scholars ardently strive to establish the connections, similarities, and differences between them. But the dominant impression is one of a common tendency. In this rich corpus of works, the similarities that exist between the different authors indicate that one and all were determined to find in social unity a justification for law.

To these texts one might add all those which, more generally, draw upon the idea that strength lies in unity and that, consequently, the interest of individuals is served by the existence of collective rules which ensure the cohesion of the group. The idea surfaced briefly in the Anonymus Iamblichi. But in Thucydides it is also expressed by those giving warning to powers intent on imperialistic conquest, the prediction being that the weak, by banding together, will eventually prove the stronger. Isocrates follows in this line, explaining that this is why those hoping to preserve their own power and strength need to respect the opinions of the people. Opinion serves as an intermediary between justice (which wins sympathy) and strength (which stems from that sympathy when it is given public expression). The same notion of unity is also used by Socrates in the *Gorgias*, when he shows Callicles that the majority, as such, is stronger than his superman; and it is again spelled out clearly in *The Republic*, when Socrates—once again—explains that injustice prevents men from acting in concert and effectively:

Do you think that a city, an army, or bandits, or thieves, or any other group that attempted any action in common could accomplish anything if they wronged one another? (351 C)

Finally, the same idea is forcefully expressed by Demosthenes in his speech against Midias, where he explains that the reason why the citizens banded together was precisely so that, in their unity, they would be stronger than people such as Midias. Again, the texts vary from one author to another. However, they are in agreement at least to the extent that they all constitute versions of one and the same line of reasoning designed to defend, in the name of self-interest, the notion of a justice now stripped of other supports and guarantees. Both the series of arguments described above aimed to demonstrate the validity of justice, for such a demonstration now proved indispensable if legality was to be protected against the temptations of anarchy and tyranny[9] and the order of the city was to be preserved.

In *The Eumenides*, Aeschylus had made Athena responsible for that order, for it was she who transformed the erstwhile Erinyes into the Eumenides, protective deities, and thereby introduced into the city a salutary awe. Now Athena's role passed to human reason; and on every side thinkers strove to

[9] Cf. below, p. 217.

prove that the well-being of citizens depended upon the law.

The fact that so many efforts were directed to this end provides convincing confirmation of the importance that had come to be attached to the Sophists' critique and the new spirit that they had promoted. But that in itself poses a considerable problem. The arguments presented above are drawn indiscriminately from both those who opposed the Sophists (such as Socrates) and those who numbered among their ranks (it was, after all, Protagoras who had set the ball rolling). The question that thus arises is: who exactly was it who was attacking justice? And who was defending it? Perhaps the fact of the matter was that the famous attacks launched by the Sophists were not unanimous; or, alternatively, perhaps they did not represent the last word on the subject. If we are to understand the nature of this movement of thought, the answers to these questions are clearly crucial.

One possible—and perfectly valid and believable—explanation is that there were two kinds of Sophist: to put it simply, the good ones and the bad ones, on the one hand those determined to reconstruct a new kind of justice for which man himself was the measure, on the other the purely destructive critics who took delight in underlining its weaknesses. According to this hypothesis, the 'good' Sophists would be headed by Protagoras, the oldest of them, the most moderate, the closest to Socrates. After him, attitudes became increasingly critical. However, one cannot be too categorical, for at dates that are uncertain but certainly later than Protagoras, one comes across writers whose attitudes are every bit as moral as his: Prodicus is a case in point, even if his ideas on moral philosophy are only reflected in the apologue for Herakles: here Herakles, caught between Vice and Virtue, chooses the life of heroism which will lead him to true happiness. Another, as we have seen, is the Anonymus Iamblichi. By and large, however, one might hold that there were two different, more or less successive tendencies.

Perhaps, after all, it was simply a matter of different schools. There is absolutely no reason why these roving teachers, who hailed from a variety of cities and had received a variety of educations, should all have subscribed to the same doctrines either in politics or, as here, in the field of moral philosophy. They engaged in similar kinds of activity and shared similar enlightened views in tune with the spirit of the times. But that is not to say that they necessarily supported the same theses. On the contrary, they are likely to have welcomed confrontations, as philosophers and professors always have and always should.

If that is the case, the relationships between Protagoras, the Anonymus Iamblichi, Democritus, and Socrates may have been quite close and those between Protagoras and, for example, Antiphon considerably less so. We should accept that possibility and bear it in mind. Yet, if we look beyond the apparent clash of arguments and beyond these fragments without context that the polemics of the day have by chance preserved for us, we soon realize that the scene is much less confused than it seems and that the similarities between the various Sophists may well have been far more fundamental than is suggested by these particular fragments.

It transpires—and it can assuredly not be simply by chance--that all the Sophists who are known to us are reported to have produced constructive thinking as well as the critical analyses to which we have so far referred. In their constructive thought their sense of the social collectivity played an extremely important role. They undermined the traditional bases of morality but all, without exception, also adhered to a lucid and demanding moral philosophy of their own.

They must all have thought along somewhat similar lines to Protagoras, and this enabled them to give back with one hand what they had taken away with the other. Just as this contract which can be made to depreciate the law may also serve to defend it, so the essential character of the Sophists' thought may be to have destroyed everything only to rebuild it upon different foundations. Confirmation of that thesis emerges from a study of the very Sophists who would appear, on the face of it, to be those most suspect and least likely to rally to the defence of justice.

Let us set aside Protagoras, Prodicus, and the Anonymus Iamblichi, the three Sophists whose moral convictions have never been in any doubt, for we shall be returning to them later. Let us also set aside the obscure Lycophron, about whom virtually nothing is known. That leaves the three Sophists who adopted the most fiercely committed line against the law: Thrasymachus, Hippias, and Antiphon. There can be no doubt that even their thought included a positive side and that this was every bit as important as the negative element. Proof of this is provided both by the testimony of other writers and by the fragments of their own work that survive.

In Plato's *Republic*, Thrasymachus launches a vigorous attack against the law. The very fact that he does so shows that his ideas on the subject were well known. In Plato, it is he who defines the law as the interest of the stronger and who is of the opinion that justice is a nonsense compared to injustice, which makes far better sense. From a moral point of view, he looks like a dead loss who can only be considered a propagandist for unscrupulous selfishness.

But such a view would be mistaken. As we have seen,[10] Thrasymachus is no Callicles. And if we step back from Plato's representation of him in *The Republic*, we are bound to revise our opinion. Alongside the testimony of other writers relating to his rhetorical teaching, his own fragments include two texts which it would be wrong to pass over lightly. The first phrase to strike one is where he laments that the gods pay no heed to human affairs, 'otherwise they would not have overlooked the greatest of all blessings among mankind, Justice,—for we see mankind not using this virtue'. 'The greatest of all blessings among mankind': those are his very words. So what are we to believe? How can the justice which was such a foolish *naïveté* in *The Republic* be reconciled with this justice, which is such an extraordinary asset? Even if one attempts to explain away the anomaly by differences in tone or the man's bitterness, nothing can alter the fact that these are two completely different points of view. Surely, it would be better to try to reconcile them than to deny it; and the only way to reconcile these two conflicting judgements of one and the same man is to recognize that the two are linked by a bridging connection in the shape of the idea of collective

---

[10] Above, pp. 119–21.

interest. Justice may not be to the advantage of separate individuals, but for human beings who live as a community it may constitute a means of salvation and the greatest of blessings. That is certainly what Protagoras and the Anonymus Iamblichi maintained, as did many others at the time. Thrasymachus may have developed the same idea; or perhaps he accepted it as a self-evident truth recently revealed by others. At all events, as soon as the notion of a common interest is re-established in some form, the apparent contradiction is resolved as part of a coherent system.

We know from another of Thrasymachus' fragments that he was concerned about the common interest, indeed set great store by it. It is the only surviving fragment of his that is over a page long. It is an extract from a speech cited as a model of style, in which the author defends the ancestral constitution. To us, the ideas that he expresses are of far greater importance than the style on account of which the passage is cited. For here Thrasymachus praises the good old order (in which the young showed respect for the old) and deplores the mistakes that have since been made, for it is these that have introduced war instead of peace and strife instead of concord. At this point, Thrasymachus very likely had in mind the very evils that the Anonymus describes as resulting from an absence or disregard of law. The word used for concord, through which such evils can be avoided, is *homonoia*, and this was to remain a key term. Now if—as seems likely—the text dates from the civil disturbances of 411, this may constitute one of the very first authentically attested instances in which the term is used.[11] At all events, Thrasymachus' text seeks to establish that the argument put forward by the one side in the last analysis encompasses that put forward by the other,[12] and that the ancestral constitution is the one that is the most 'common' to all citizens, his point no doubt being that, in its moderation, it reconciles the interests of all

[11] See J. de Romilly, 'Le Mot *homonoia*: Vocabulaire et propagande', in *Mélanges Chantraine*, Études et Commentaires, vol. lxxix (Paris, Klincksieck).

[12] At first sight, this idea appears to be at odds with the practice of opposed arguments. But that contradiction is no more than apparent, for agreement (which is the essential point) depends upon each party picking up one particular aspect of his adversary's thought.

parties. The idea of a community of interests and of social unity thus comes over very strongly from this short text: the entire argument is based on the existence of concord within the group.

Admittedly, this text may have been composed to mark a particular occasion. But it is the only authentic text by Thrasymachus that we possess; and no other political speech dwells so insistently upon the role played by collective organization in the realization of man's well-being. The author may have believed that, for individuals, obedience to the laws was a priori unbeneficial. But he appears to have believed that it was a good thing for the city, upon which the fate of individuals depended. All the evidence that we possess, with the exception of Plato's, not only suggests but positively demands that the two beliefs be reconciled on the basis of a social contract.

Besides, Thrasymachus' bitterness when he points out the practical advantages of injustice, in *The Republic*, may well be prompted by the same irritation that is expressed at the beginning of the fragment on the city system and by the same desire to improve matters by political means. Seen in this light, Thrasymachus' thought as a whole becomes perfectly coherent, and the management of the city emerges as one of his major preoccupations.

This is surely the most convincing interpretation—all the more so since, if it is indeed correct, Thrasymachus falls remarkably closely into line with the other Sophists. The same demonstration could be applied to all of them; and Hippias is no exception. As we have seen, in Xenophon at least, Hippias produces an extremely relativist definition of the law, which he describes as a convention. In Plato's *Protagoras*, he calls the law not 'the queen of men' as Xenophon's quotation has it, but 'the tyrant of men', which is infinitely more critical. Yet in truth he was by no means hostile to the law. In the first place, even in the text of Xenophon's *Memorabilia*, Hippias recognized the existence of unwritten laws which are the same for all and which he seemed to associate with nature. Furthermore, although his work may give the general impression of a scholarly œuvre devoted to historical, ethnological, and scientific curiosities, we know that he also wrote a treatise entitled *Trojan Dialogue* or *Trōikos*, which took the form of an exhortation to virtue. In it, the old Nestor explains to the young Neoptolemus how a man of excellence should show his worth. We do not know what practical advice this lecture contained, but there can be no doubt that it represented the practice of virtue as leading to glory, just as did Prodicus' treatise in which the young Herakles opts for Virtue. Here, virtuous efforts were shown to result in other people's appreciation and in honour—in other words in the gratitude of the collective group. If Hippias subscribed to a similar ideal, he too justified the practice of virtue in terms of membership of a social group. That is no more than a hypothesis of course, but surely a homily on the subject of glory addressed to the son of Achilles must have developed along similar lines. In any event, whatever the *Trōikos* may actually have contained, it certainly was a moral lecture, and moral intentions would be incompatible with the scepticism and spirit of revolt that so often tends to be ascribed to the Sophists.

Furthermore, a fragment from another, unspecified, work by Hippias, which is cited by Plutarch, took a stand against libel (and in a manner sufficiently impressive to be cited at many centuries' remove). The fragment might be regarded as an attack on law or convention to the extent that, in it, Hippias deplores the silence of the law *vis-à-vis* libellers. But what he favours is a law that is stricter, and stronger measures of repression. He would like to see a greater respect for what is due to others; and he censures attitudes likely to undermine friendship, which is the noblest of bonds (B 17). In the *Protagoras*, friendship was similarly represented as a treasure that resulted from the moral gifts given men by Zeus, gifts which made it possible for human beings to survive (322 c). According—once again—to Plutarch, Hippias also took a stand against envy. In other words, he tended to attack whatever threatened to damage the unity of the collectivity, while—conversely—he advocated whatever virtues might help to maintain it.

We should also remember that Hippias delivered lectures at Olympia, addressing himself to the Greeks in general and, in all probability, advocating unity. That is another sign, also suggesting the importance of his thought in this field.

Now we can see why it is to Hippias that some scholars attribute the text of the Anonymus Iamblichi. Hippias expressed a respect for communal values equal to that expressed in the short text of the Anonymus. Both for Hippias and for the Anonymus, communal values were justified by the happy results that they produced within the group constituted by the city.

The evidence thus all converges. All the indications suggest that the same constructive impulse which informed the thought of Protagoras also inspired that of Hippias. This is the only possible explanation for the presence of the scattered traces of positive thinking which, taken together, are impossible to ignore. In truth, that is not a very surprising conclusion to arrive at in the case of a man who (in his intervention in the *Protagoras*) presented the familiar opposition between law and nature in such an optimistic and sympathetic fashion. It would, on the face of it, be more surprising to find it applying also to Antiphon.

Yet it does hold good equally for Antiphon and, in point of fact, even in his case that is not altogether unexpected for, alongside his treatise *On Truth*, we have already noted the existence of another actually entitled *On Concord*. As we have seen,[13] faced with this apparent contradiction, some scholars have gone so far as to attribute *On Concord* to a different Antiphon altogether. Seen in the perspective that has now opened up, however, everything makes sense and falls into place.

In the first place, the title *On Concord* is one also used by Thrasymachus. In itself it suggests an analysis whose nature we can by now guess. The treatise itself is unfortunately lost. However, such fragments from it as exist not only confirm but exceed our expectations. They reflect the thoughts of a moral philosopher, rather pessimistic and austere, but manifestly inspired by a desire for the good. Furthermore, it soon becomes apparent that what these brief passages urge is more than mere observance of the law, considerably more. The

---

[13] Cf. pp. 128–30.

very word 'concord', which appears in the title, seems to take on a far wider meaning.

The foremost concern is clearly for unity within the city: that was the original application of the word 'concord' and remained the sense in which it continued to be used. Some of the fragments certainly confirm that their author valued everything likely to promote a community spirit among human beings. Fragment B 61 declares forthrightly: 'Nothing is worse for mankind than anarchy.' That is how Antiphon justifies the demand of obedience from children: it is designed to train them for their life as adults. The opposite of the anarchy that Antiphon dreads is clearly a harmony between citizens which is founded upon respect for the existing order.

Antiphon lays great emphasis upon friendship. He speaks of the bond represented by new friendships and the even closer one constituted by relationships of long standing (fr. B 64). He censures those who confuse true friendship with the flattery of sycophants (fr. B 65). He is thus fully aware of what membership of a group of human beings involves. He also observes that, between those who spend most of their time together, a measure of assimilation is inevitable (fr. B 62).[14]

All this confirms that in Antiphon's thought there is a positive side comparable to that which exists in the other Sophists and based on the same ideas. Almost certainly, then, the absolute separation between nature and law by no means implies a preference for nature in his case any more than in theirs. *On Truth* quite rightly declared that it was not in the interests of an individual to obey justice. But we do not know whether the same went for the interests of a collective group. Here too, a healthy kind of convention may have been regarded as a basis for reconstruction. The fragments of *On Concord* certainly suggest as much.

Remarkably enough, however, Antiphon does not appear to

[14] This assimilation is important, for it makes it possible for human values gradually to shape a new concept of nature. *On Truth* declares that in nature there is nothing to distinguish a Greek from a barbarian. But (especially in the case of Antiphon, if one accepts him to be the author of *On Concord*, which attributes such an important role to education), it is perfectly possible to recognize that distinct, homogeneous groups of human beings do come to be formed: nature does not have the last word in the history of the human race.

have been satisfied with this initial notion of 'concord'. Many of his extant fragments are concerned with wisdom of a far more internal nature. It was probably this aspect of his thought that attracted the philosophers in love with wisdom who cited him. Iamblichus, who also preserved the text of the Anonymus for us, commented upon this tendency in Antiphon's thought, observing that 'concord' had at first united towns, homes, and men, but that it also included an individual's agreement within himself, the kind of harmony that results from a soul obeying reason alone, instead of allowing itself to be tugged in conflicting directions (B 44).

Surprisingly, we seem to have come full circle. First, the virtues lost their guarantees; next, they were brought back out of purely political considerations; and soon politics, in their turn, provided a model for ethics; and so, from the city, they were returned to the soul. The reversal, here no more than sketched in, would have delighted Plato, even if the virtues involved are not quite those that he had in mind.

Antiphon follows the very same logic which drives the other Sophists to base everything upon man and whatever promotes his interest. He recommends a discipline capable of ensuring internal peace and banishing misery, or *alupia*.[15] It involves the avoidance of fears and hopes, passions and sensual commitments: the ideal of an Epicurean sage. But there is nothing cold about this wisdom: it can only be acquired by overcoming one's temptations (B 59).

This moral training is certainly directed towards the well-being of the individual. And it is clearly a far cry from injustice and the violent actions that always accompany the fear of vengeance or punishment. In his quest for internal peace of this kind, Antiphon turns out to be the most moralistic of all the Sophists and, in this domain of ethics, possibly the closest of all of them to Socrates.

Is that why Plato, who has so much to say about the other Sophists, never mentioned him? Or was it perhaps because this brilliant and many-sided man wrote tragedies in collaboration with Dionysius of Syracuse? Whatever the reason, in Plato's dialogues, the man who said that it was not in an

---

[15] Cf. below, p. 208.

individual's interest to respect justice when no witnesses
were present is never included among those accused of under-
mining justice.[16]

In a way, when one compares the scant remains of these
two works, *On Truth* and *On Concord*, one does see how it is
that some scholars have been tempted to regard them as the
works of two different authors. Nevertheless, the comparison
also suits the interpretation suggested here. And it is so much
finer to think that the two aspects, at first sight so contradictory, in reality complement each other in the inner movement
of Antiphon's thought, coming together there in a dazzling
unity which serves to promote a lucid notion of virtue, newly
reconstructed by and for man.

If we accept that interpretation, the whole of Sophistic
thought may have been directed towards combining its two
aspects—the one negative, the other positive—in order to
establish the bases for a moral philosophy which could be
justified in human and rational terms.

In a sense, then, the movement of Sophistic thought seems to
be finally returning to the very kind of morality that some
have believed it to be rejecting. But, thus expressed, that
conclusion would be doubly incorrect. In the first place, the
distinction that we have been at pains to draw between the
two contrary tendencies is a purely artificial ploy adopted in
the interests of clarity. For, at the time, these authors were
engaged in simultaneously re-creating with one hand what
they were knocking down with the other. Only those in a
hurry or motivated by ambition could possibly have retained but one aspect of the Sophists' thought, without
taking any account of its counterpart, which was part and
parcel of it.

What then, it might be wondered, was the point of drawing
that distinction? This brings us to the second risk of misinter-
pretation. The fact is that by changing the fundamental bases
of their moral philosophy, the Sophists changed everything.

---

[16] However, in *Mem.* 1. 6, Xenophon presents him as an interlocutor of
Socrates. But he only has him express surprise at the fact that Socrates lives
so poorly, receives no fees, and takes no part in political life: similar
astonishment would be likely to be felt by any Sophist.

The moral conclusions that they drew were unchanged; but instead of stemming from the gods or from absolute values, these were now reconstructed on the basis of a positivist analysis of the problems posed by human life and society. They thus acquired a new significance. This was not simply a return to the old values: it truly involved a new creative effort the strength of which lay in the fundamental combination of a negative critique and a positive reconstruction.

The reader will now appreciate why I did not think it fair to put the Sophists' various theses down to any opportunistic preoccupations, as is sometimes done. Had their motives been purely opportunistic, the purpose of their critical analyses would simply have been to provide weapons for the young men of ambition who expected this service of them. Conversely, their theories favouring legality might be interpreted as a mere ploy to curry favour with the Athenian democracy which had taken them in and to reassure it. But precious little justification can be adduced for such suspicions, even if we acknowledge the risks that the Sophists ran by concerning themselves with practical matters, and also the dangers inherent in their attracting disciples and exposing their teaching to the possibility of distortion. The circumstances of their position may indeed seem to encourage an unfavourable interpretation, and perhaps—who knows?—it is not groundless. They simply indicate how dangerous it is for any thinker to be brought into contact with practical matters or to have disciples who may practise distortion and suggest unfavourable interpretations. Perhaps opportunistic motives did influence some of the Sophists... But overall, it is fundamentally at odds with the orientation of their analyses and the rigorous coherence which welds together their two lines of argumentation.

In the combination of those two lines of argumentation, every word testifies to a lucid humanism. The Sophists were determined to accept neither the transcendental nor absolute truths nor divine agents of justice. But that did not prevent them from elaborating a moral philosophy which was founded upon reason and committed to the well-being of human beings. The two sides of the Sophists' thought are complementary, forming a single whole. What is good for human beings comes along, with abundant proof to support it, to take the place of 'the good' pure and simple.

But could it really fill that place? Perhaps not. We should not be misled by the series of texts that we have considered. Admirable though they are, they should not blind us to certain limitations which the Sophists' moral philosophy could hardly hope to overcome. Antiphon put his finger on the problem when he introduced the case of the individual who behaves unjustly in the absence of witnesses—in other words, with neither witness nor fear of witness, and without risking sanctions or punishment of any kind. In *The Republic*, Glaucon makes the same point more explicitly when he imagines the case of an invisible man, or one who possesses Gyges' ring, which has the power to render him invisible whenever he wishes. In such conditions the argument of self-interest carries no weight.

Plato takes this as his point of departure in *The Republic*, in which he seeks a different answer, one which involves more than harmony between the various components of the city, or between the various parts of the soul (although his description certainly starts with the idea of the soul). What is at stake here is an absolute justice and an equally absolute good. As opposed to the thinking of the Sophists, the corner-stone of Socrates' thought is the idea that an unjust action harms the one who commits it, damaging his soul, and nothing could be worse than this. And it is interesting to note that, in the face of this fundamental problem, Greek thought was to adopt the path indicated by Socrates—helped along by the progress that had been made in psychological analysis and in describing the conflicts that affect the soul.

That line of thought is more or less hinted at in *On Concord*, where the ideal of internal serenity is expounded. But by and large it lies outside and beyond the thinking of the Sophists. It was practical life within the city that almost invariably mattered above all else to the strictly rational Sophists and that interested them the most. Once they had demolished all the fundamentally suspect traditional values, thereby creating a *tabula rasa*, this was to be the key to their reconstruction of a moral philosophy based solely on human reason.

Even this was an enormously ambitious project—a fact that has in general received insufficient recognition, for a number of understandable reasons. The first has to do with the nature of our information on the Sophists. These short fragments, many of one or two lines only, are cited by some as arguments to support the Sophists' critique of traditional values, by others as arguments in their defence. By definition, they only ever reflect one side of the Sophists' thought. The temptation to emphasize one aspect at the expense of the other is consequently all the greater. Fortunately, Protagoras' myth comes to our aid. Though only a second-hand account of his thought, it is at least a coherent text and one which provides a key to the interpretation of many scraps of evidence which seem to be contradictory only because they reach us without a context. Thanks to this key, we can at last perceive a whole series of echoes, convergences, and suggestions, which enable us finally to reconcile the two aspects—the positive and the negative—which the thought of all the known Sophists without exception expresses without the slightest ambiguity.

One further point confirms the above remarks. The Sophists' reconstructive efforts, which we have been studying in connection with the idea of justice, are just as noticeable where other beliefs are concerned—beliefs which they initially rejected on the grounds of their a priori nature.

The coherence of the Sophists' movement of reconstruction is significant. Once launched, it was strong enough to reconstruct the entire spectrum of values and virtues for the benefit of human beings.

7

Recovering the Virtues

WHEREVER the blast of the Sophists' destructive analysis struck, there is also evidence of an effort of reconstruction. Except in the field of ontology, which does not impinge greatly upon peoples' lives, their analyses produced positive factors to compensate for the negative side of every theme tackled.

Truth and Utility

Protagoras had sapped the foundations of truth by declaring man to be the measure of all things and by rejecting all but subjective appearances, each of which was as valid as any other. As we have already noted, however, there were limits to that relativism of his, for it was subject to qualifications. In the *Theaetetus*, they are expressed by Socrates at the point where he presents his defence of Protagoras.[1]

His corrective principle is simple: it is, quite simply, to replace the notion of truth with the purely practical idea of utility. This was the first of the Sophists' salvage operations, and it was certainly effective. Even if there is no truth, there are, on the other hand, certain judgements and tastes which are more useful than others: wisdom and discernment are thus rehabilitated ('I do not by any means say that wisdom and the wise man do not exist', *Theaetetus*, 116 D).

What is meant by wisdom, here? Where theoretical definitions may be confusing, a concrete example is clear: it is provided by the doctor. A patient finds certain foods bitter. This judgement is certainly true for him, and is irrefutable. But through his remedies, a doctor can reverse the patient's impression, so that the very same foods seem to him good and

---

[1] *Th.*, 166 A; see Ch. 3.

become so. The same applies where value-judgements are concerned. Here too certain judgements can be corrected so as to become more satisfactory. Qualitative differentiation is thus reintroduced in the guise of a difference in utility. Utility takes over from truth.

There can be no doubt that what is at stake is indeed utility. The text mentions the patient's 'improved disposition'. But soon it employs the word *chrēstos*, meaning 'good, useful'; and further on, at 172, the word used is *sumpheron*, or 'beneficial'.[2] The judgements of any one individual may thus be as true as those of any other; but not all judgements produce equally useful results.

Already one cannot help admiring the salvage operation, which now bases upon practice, and proceeds to consecrate to the service of mankind, what was earlier rejected on metaphysical grounds: namely, the idea that some opinions are better than others. Furthermore, one cannot but be impressed by the fact that this doctrine produced by a teacher of rhetoric depends upon the possibility of convincing others and getting them to change their minds: the Sophist's thinking is at one with his professional activities. Better still, the concrete case that the text now likens to that of the doctor is that of the teacher who inculcates better attitudes in his pupils. He is clearly a Sophist, for the text explicitly states that the doctor produces these turn-abouts through his remedies, the Sophist through his lectures.

But those lectures are not addressed solely to his pupils. In next to no time the focus shifts from the individual to the city, in truth the essential target here. It is first and foremost the opinions of the city that need to be modified and corrected. The Sophist's aim is to be useful to the city. All this is directly in line with Protagoras' myth. In the task of moral reconstruction, the city is still the linchpin.

The examples of the doctor and the teacher lead directly on to the subject of the collective group. In a similar fashion:

the wise and good orators make the good, instead of the evil, seem to be right to their States. For I claim that whatever seems right and

---

[2] In the case of the patient, the text refers to 'useful and healthy sensations' (*Tht.* 167 c). It is a notion which could also be applied to the State: the health of a State depends upon *dikē* and *aidōs*; and here health is defined as concord.

honourable to a State is really right and honourable to it so long as it believes it to be so; but the wise man causes the good, instead of that which is evil to them in each instance, to be and seem right and honourable. (*Theaetetus*, 167 D)[3]

All the uncertainties into which the Sophists' analyses had plunged men as individuals are now repaired by an enlightened desire for the common interest—all of which, incidentally, is quite enough to explain and justify Protagoras' role as a legislator.

In conclusion, this passage reverts to the example of politics, reminding the reader that whatever is beautiful or ugly, just or unjust, pious or impious for a particular city is precisely what that city decides should be so. No one opinion is more valid than any other in this domain. But when it comes to the useful or harmful effects that the city's own decrees have upon it, differences matter and mistakes are possible. What is at stake is the city, the group, what is decided 'in common'. On this level utility is important, to advocate one course rather than another makes sense, advice is welcome, and political expertise is useful.

It now becomes easier to see why Protagoras defined his art as the art of politics (as Plato tells us he did). He not only taught a man how to succeed in politics but also how to give useful advice. We remember his earlier words:

If he applies to me [a man] will learn that learning consists of good judgement in his own affairs, showing best how to order his own home; and how to become most capable of dealing with public affairs, both in speech and in action. (*Protagoras*, 319 A)

We can also appreciate the enthusiasm with which the Sophists and their contemporaries seized upon the science of politics, founded by them upon experience and perspicacity. The new expertise that they mastered is exemplified in its purest form in the analyses of Thucydides, where he presents side by side the different opinions of various statesmen in order to identify a useful political strategy that has a chance of success.

Interesting though it would be to examine how the art of

---

[3] Plato must have enjoyed going on to suggest that this justified the large fees which the Sophists received.

politics was applied, let us concentrate upon the principle behind it. It rested upon the possibility of making a clean sweep of the notion of Truth at a metaphysical level while still, at the level of collective life in the city, seeking to influence people by persuading them to adopt better decisions— that is to say, decisions of a kind to promote the common good. Cities had been invented to bring about that common good. It now became the goal to which all human activities should be directed, a goal which slipped into the place vacated by Truth, now toppled from its throne.

The Gods and Utility

Where piety and the gods are concerned, the picture is not quite so clear. Even here, though, a few clues emerge. They are as fragile as the cigarette ash that the detective in a classic thriller eagerly collects, but, like that ash, they become meaningful when related to other facts.

Protagoras had forthrightly declared that he could know nothing of the gods—neither whether or not they existed, nor what form they might take if they did. Even leaving aside Thrasymachus (who, for his part, remarked that the gods were obviously concerned neither with human beings nor with justice), a number of alarming theories about religion were circulating. Prodicus was explaining that the sun, the moon, the rivers, and the springs used to be regarded as gods on account of their usefulness; and the *Sisyphus* declared that the gods were some clever person's invention, designed to keep human beings in order. Collected together, these ideas (which we have examined in an earlier chapter) left scant room for faith and certainly reflected the religious crisis that was taking place.

Yet, as we have seen, in this area too, those views expressed by the Sophists call for qualification and adjustment. Most of the Sophists mentioned could in no sense be considered atheists: they themselves frequently go so far as to refer to the gods specifically. We should recognize that it was not just those entirely above suspicion, such as Hippias, who did so: Protagoras introduces them into his myth; and Prodicus also speaks of them, in his moral apologue for Herakles poised between Vice and Virtue. According to Xenophon, he even suggested that one of the purposes of virtue is to win the goodwill of the gods. It is hard to believe that these well-known men, whose ideas were on everybody's lips, really—all of them—hoped to deceive people. On the other hand, it is perfectly reasonable to suppose that the contradiction between their destructive analyses and these unexceptional orthodox statements of theirs is no more than an apparent one which is easily explained by the limited nature of the sources at our disposal.

After all, there is no reason why the Protagoras who declared that there is no Truth and that nothing can be known of the gods should not at the same time respect the gods of the city in which he was living, just as he respected its laws, considering them to constitute the indispensable links that bound citizens together. He would certainly not have been the only writer to use the words 'gods' and 'divine' loosely to denote all that is best and most worthy of respect in human life. A mixture of agnosticism and a desire for the well-being of human beings might well lead to his using such words in that fashion. That is probably how it was that he described these links as a gift from the gods, declaring that men 'shared in the lot of the gods' since they set themselves apart from the animals through their piety, their language, and all the inventions of civilization. Using the word 'divine' could well simply be a way of exalting mankind. If one accepts such an explanation, his humanism fits in perfectly legitimately with a very real respect for what the gods in the widest possible and also the purest sense, represented. And, once again, all this does not seem far removed from the somewhat free but decidedly fervent religion of his contemporary Euripides.

A similar view can be taken of Prodicus. He certainly suggested an anthropological explanation for the religious cults. But, as the reader will have noted, that explanation was founded upon utility: the extant summaries of his doctrine repeatedly use the words *ōphelein* and *ōpheleian*; for, according to him, men loved whatever helped them to live. Remarkably enough, he, like Hesiod, was thinking not of the city, but of agriculture. His idea of an agricultural religion, so to speak, was to find considerable favour among modern scholars. Some (e.g. Nestle) have even imagined it to be an essential aspect of his thought and the subject of the whole of his treatise known as the *Seasons* or *Hours*. In any event, his thought was dominated by the idea of utility, and this established a link between him and Protagoras. But there is nothing to suggest that Prodicus rejected religious practice, just because he had an explanation for it. Furthermore, his preoccupation with agriculture by no means ruled out concern for the human group. It is surely no mere chance that he chose Herakles as the hero of his apologue, the very hero whom Euripides calls 'the benefactor of Greece'.

His philosophy seems to have been dictated by a concern for utility, human life, and human societies; and his pronouncements upon the gods should be restored to that context. So it is fair enough to say that he no longer accepts belief in the gods on the old, traditional bases, but brings to religious matters a new attitude that is more scientific, relativist, and critical. At the same time, however, even with that humanist perspective of his, he certainly still seems to have reserved a place for the gods.[4]

At the extreme limit, perhaps the *Sisyphus* itself, with all its positivism and all its theories about the opportunism of belief in divine justice, was simply—in its own way—saying 'if the gods did not exist, we should have to invent them'. And, given the value set upon order in the State and peace amongst men, this too constituted an encouragement for piety.

To return to the subject of Protagoras and Prodicus, it would, of course, be gratifying if there were a text which definitely explained the connection that I am striving to establish between the two aspects of their thought. It would be reassuring not to have to make do with these two separate fragments between which we ourselves of the twentieth century are obliged to build a bridge. Now, it so happens that the fifth-century texts do include a passage which appears to suggest just such a connection. However, the author was not himself a Sophist and the text's meaning remains extremely obscure. It consists of a few lines from Euripides' *Hecuba*

---

[4] See also *Mem.* 2. 1. 28.

which have long intrigued the critics. Desiring to obtain justice from Agamemnon, the old queen calls upon the gods and the law:

> I am a slave, I know,
> and slaves are weak. But the gods are strong, and over them
> there stands some absolute, some moral order
> or principle of law more final still.
> Upon this moral law the world depends;
> through it the gods exist; by it we live,
> defining good and evil. Apply that law
> to me. For if you flout it now, and those
> who murder in cold blood or defy the gods
> go unpunished, then human justice withers,
> corrupted at its source.

(799–809)

These are pious sentiments and, to that extent at least, traditionalist ones. By 'the law' we should no doubt understand those famous unwritten laws and the basic, generally accepted notion of justice. Yet the idea of order expressed in this passage is curious, and the relationship between the law and the gods is somewhat unexpected. The old orthodox view would have been that the gods order us to believe in justice, whereas in Hecuba's religion it is justice that leads us to believe in the gods. In orthodox belief it is the gods who ratify justice through their sovereign will. But, according to Hecuba's religion, the gods are themselves subject to the law, which is above them and dominates them with its superior power (*kratōn*). Whatever the precise meaning of the text may be, it was, at this period, clearly possible to make a fully convinced and optimistic profession of piety despite the fact that the idea now started not from the Gods but from human beings, moving in the opposite direction. It was upon the behaviour of men themselves that belief in the gods was founded.

Perhaps that new orientation helps to explain how it was that, each in his own way, all the Sophists managed to find in the human order new reasons for piety, reasons of a more pragmatic nature and more centred upon mankind than hitherto, but no less real on that account. *A fortiori*, they assumed a similar attitude when it came to the tutelary deities and national cults which were more or less indissociable from the human groups which adopted them.

We should remember that the gods of ancient Greece were very closely linked with particular cities, provinces, or even local groups. Special cults were devoted to them in particular sanctuaries or particular towns. They bore the names of these places, and protected their devotees and their religious sites as if committed to them by some kind of pact. What was involved was thus not so much an inner religion or faith in a particular dogma, but rather a group's relationship with its protector. The festivals devoted to local French patron saints in the French provinces perhaps reflect a similar atmosphere: even today, plenty of people take part in such festivals perfectly sincerely even if they do not believe in the miracles of the past which they are supposed to commemorate. In the same way, the piety of fifth-century Athenians did not necessarily reflect a religious faith in our twentieth-century sense of the expression: for them, the gods were to some extent identified with the city. That being so, it is easier to see how it was that, even without religious faith, the Sophists still allowed the gods a role to play. It does not seem unreasonable to suppose that they accepted them in the same spirit as they accepted other decisions made by the city—all of them open to question and variable yet, at the same time, all legitimate and beneficial.

City Education

In the religious domain, the details of the reconciliation effected between the two aspects of the Sophists' thought remains, perforce, somewhat hypothetical. However, as soon as we turn to the field of human behaviour, the role played by the city in the restoration of values emerges clearly as being of major importance.

The city contributed in various ways to the basic education of individuals and also to the diffusion and defence of values. The evidence is not abundant; nevertheless, it reveals two aspects of the city's role to which Protagoras certainly drew attention.

The first way in which the city made its influence felt was covert but effective. In Plato's dialogue which bears his name, Protagoras explains how individuals absorb certain ideas without which no city can continue to exist. Nothing could be of more crucial importance. What is indispensable to the city is not 'the joiner's or smith's or potter's art, rather justice and temperance and holiness—in short, what I may put together and call a man's virtue' (*Protagoras*, 324 E–325 A). But who inculcates these virtues? From their earliest childhood people acquire them, without realizing it, and they continue to do so throughout their lives. There follows a long passage which starts by describing the child at the stage where he begins to talk, when

the nurse, the mother, the tutor, and the father himself strive hard that the child may excel, and as each act and word occurs they teach and impress upon him that this is just, and that unjust, one thing noble, another base, one holy, another unholy, and that he is to do this, and not do that. (325 D)

Then comes the time for school, with advice from the teacher and the reading of texts and works in which

they meet with many admonitions, many descriptions and praises and eulogies of good men in times past, that the boy in envy may imitate them and yearn to become even as they. (326 A)

Next, there are lessons devoted to the cithara and fine lyric works which teach the child harmony and rhythm, both of which are essential to human life; and these are complemented by physical training. Finally, the city itself takes a hand, obliging young people to learn the laws. Just as a teacher gives children a model to copy when learning to write, it offers them a code of behaviour to emulate, insisting that it be observed and imposing sanctions upon actions that contravene it. It thus sets the seal upon a great endeavour 'both private and public, for the sake of virtue' (326 C). Virtues are thus acquired both for the sake of the city and thanks to it.

This remarkable text expresses ideas which are both new and profound. Their novelty does not stem from the originality of any particular perception or programme (although it is, in passing, worth reflecting on the value of certain ideas which these days are all too frequently underestimated: such as the role played by literature in moral and civic education). The novelty stems from the clear recognition of the means by which this anonymous education is quietly effected. Particularly striking is Protagoras' keen sense of the moral effects of a particular environment, the way in which it moulds the mind and the emotions of every individual who belongs to it.

A comparison will serve to underline the importance of that idea and the force with which it is transmitted by Protagoras, for it is an idea that is certainly to be found elsewhere. It appears in Plato to the extent that he recognizes the traditional education (albeit with modifications). However, he limits it to lessons in the strict sense of the word and does not credit them with the power to disseminate justice.[5] It also appears (thereby confirming the authenticity of Plato's testimony) in the short treatise known as *Double Arguments* which in every respect so fundamentally reflects the thought of Protagoras, but is so much dryer and more limited than anything we hear about the great Sophist himself. The *Double Arguments* treatise takes up Protagoras' idea of an education which proceeds imperceptibly, first through the father and mother, then simply through the child's contact with the day-to-day realities of life. But whereas Protagoras speaks of the teaching of values and justice, the author of the *Double Arguments* speaks only of language: a Greek child brought up in Persia would speak Persian, although it would be impossible to say who taught him the words... Expressed thus, the idea is perfectly sound but somewhat obvious and not particularly striking. In the form in which Protagoras expressed it, it was far more profound.

The idea is also to be found outside the specialists' debates,[6] in particular in Thucydides. In two instances, the one in

[5] Protagoras, in harmony with Athenian democracy, recognizes an element of justice in each individual citizen. Plato, the partisan of order, sees justice in a healthy ordering of the various classes, in which each should fulfil its own allotted role.

[6] In Pl., *Ap.*, Meletus, Socrates' accuser, is presented as arguing that the laws and judges, even all Athenians, act as masters of virtue in relation to the young.

connection with Sparta, the other with Athens, whose respective moral characters he so strikingly contrasts, he uses expressions suggestive of the kind of progressive integration that Protagoras describes. In the funeral speech delivered by Pericles, he shows how Athens' greatness itself fosters a love of the particular virtues which characterize it and which are responsible for the city's pre-eminence. Then, in the speech of Archidamus, the King of Sparta (1. 84), he shows how Sparta too has elaborated its own particular form of wisdom and virtue with which it inculcates the citizens of each succeeding generation. It is all a matter of upbringing; and he twice uses the same word for the two cities when speaking of this kind of upbringing or education. The influence of Protagoras is detectable both in the idea of different sets of virtues which may vary from one place to another and in that of the role that the city plays in education. The texts of both authors display the same relativism and a similar deep sense of the common good. In Thucydides, however, there are no more than fleeting hints, whereas in Protagoras' speech in Plato the thesis is fully and systematically developed and is stated with force.

It is clear that Protagoras' words imply a real commitment to these values, whose form may vary but whose utility to the social group is beyond doubt. He describes them as 'justice, temperance, and holiness' (325 A). What is more, he also recognizes and extols other virtues, indeed all virtues, when he recalls those of 'the ancient heroes'. That is no doubt partly because, directly or indirectly, their sacrifices ensured the well-being of the city and the spread of its influence. But they achieved even more than that. Just as harmony and rhythm encourage a good balance and co-ordination with others, the models that the ancient heroes provide foster a total commitment to the common good. To serve the city and through the city, all the virtues are thus re-created on a new basis.

In a way, then, Protagoras could be said to justify the moral exhortations produced by Prodicus and Hippias. He supplies that bridging link that we were seeking, the link that makes it possible to reconcile the critique of values at a metaphysical level with their reintroduction at the level of human utility.

He makes everything fall into place, revealing the novel element in this humanism, which is at once systematic and productive.

However, this 'ongoing education', effected through lessons and examples, also—as we have seen—held a place for sanctions. For Protagoras, the idea of an education directed towards the city and effected by it went hand in hand with a theory relating to the educative role of punishment. The originality and force of his theory remains striking even today.

It, too, is expounded at the beginning of the *Protagoras*, at the point where the Sophist seeks to prove that virtue may be learned. The existence of punishments is significant, for their purpose is clearly to provide a warning for the future:

No one punishes a wrongdoer from the mere contemplation or on account of his wrongdoing, unless one takes unreasoning vengeance like a wild beast. But he who undertakes to punish with reason does not avenge himself for the past offence, since he cannot make what was done as though it had not come to pass; he looks rather to the future, and aims at preventing that particular person and others who see him punished from doing wrong again. (324 B)

This theory of punishment as a warning for the future was not altogether new. In Aeschylus' tragedies it is linked with divine justice. Divine justice is a 'beneficent violence', which encourages the guilty to reflect and allows wisdom to enter their hearts despite themselves. Similarly, the fear of punishment operates for the good of the city, thanks to the healthy sanctions imposed by the court of the Areopagus for, as Athena points out in *The Eumenides*, 'What man who fears nothing at all is ever righteous?' (699). As soon as justice thus took the place of vengeance, Greek thought in general adopted the new orientation, regarding punishments as incentives to do better. A quarter of a century after the *Oresteia*, however, the idea acquired a far greater emphasis: it was now applied specifically to the human punishments inflicted by human justice.

At this point we are in for a surprise. For Plato credits both Protagoras and Socrates with this same theory, despite the fact that he is usually at pains to set these two thinkers in opposition. On this issue they are at one. In the *Gorgias* (and—what is more—right at the end of the dialogue, where the tone becomes loftier, as it considers the myths of the beyond), Socrates himself takes over the idea formulated elsewhere by Protagoras. He expounds it with a measured emphasis:

It is fitting that everyone under punishment rightly inflicted on him by another should either be made better and profit thereby, or serve as an example to the rest, that others seeing the sufferings he endures may in fear amend themselves. (525 B)

The text goes on to distinguish between those whose faults are curable and those who are incurable. In the case of the latter, punishment serves solely as an example to others, producing the effect of a kind of bogyman set up as a warning in the prisons of Hades.

It is truly fascinating to compare the two texts. The resemblance between them proves conclusively that in truth the gap between the Sophist and the philosopher is not nearly as deep as the emphatic contrast drawn between certain of their doctrines might suggest. On this particular point, there was agreement between these two men, both respectful of the laws of Athens, both concerned with teaching and with virtue. Plato would not have attributed this doctrine to Protagoras if the Sophist had not in fact defended it. So we must believe that he did so and that, as soon as they turned their attention to the practicalities of life within the city, Socrates, and Plato after him, quite naturally fell into line with the thought of a master who was clearly by no means as immoralistic as has sometimes been believed. Even if the influence had been in the opposite direction, or if Protagoras and Socrates had both got the idea from a common source, the agreement between them would remain no less significant.

In truth, this instance of agreement between them is not so very exceptional. Plato, like Protagoras, describes the birth of cities in a realistic fashion, presenting justice as a condition of their stability. The existence of such agreement is altogether compatible with the deferential tone that Plato invariably adopts towards Protagoras. It is also compatible with a piece of evidence which astonishes most critics, who are accustomed to establish a radical distinction between the 'goodies' and the 'baddies'. The testimony, which comes from Aristoxenus and is transmitted by two sources, states that Plato's *Republic* was to be found, virtually in its entirety, in Protagoras' *Antilogies*. As strictly factual information, the statement is clearly either mistaken or a deliberate fabrication. But from the point of view of similarity, convergences, and agreements on points of principle, the idea that Protagoras had paved the way in the domain of political analysis contains a large measure of truth. All the positive side of Protagoras' thinking may well have influenced Plato or, to put it the other way round, the practical side of Plato's thought must surely have owed much to Protagoras.

However, while the similarity between the two shows up links which it is worth bearing in mind, the differences are equally fascinating. For, however close these two texts on punishment may seem, they are not identical. In the first place, when Socrates speaks of punishment, he is thinking mainly of punishments inflicted in the beyond; his analysis forms an accompaniment to his myth of the underworld. Protagoras, in contrast, is concerned solely with the city and punishments devised by human beings.

Similarly, Socrates makes considerable use of the image of sickness. He wants punishment to make people better, to cure them if they are curable: his main concern is the state of the guilty person's soul. Protagoras, on the other hand, is purely concerned to avoid future wrongdoing. His attention is focused upon the state of the city, which wrongdoing could poison and divide. He makes it quite clear that he is describing the current type of behaviour which prevails, in particular, in Athens. He is concerned neither with the gods nor with individuals. He is thinking solely of the civic justice which serves to defend the city laws.

Finally, Socrates, for his part, draws distinctions between different crimes and different cases—and some critics applaud him for doing so on the grounds that this presupposes a more meticulous analysis. He proceeds in the same fashion as the Plato of *The Laws*. In book 9 of this work, Plato sketches out an entire system of penal justice, distinguishing between damage done and injustice, and establishing special categories for involuntary crimes, murders committed in anger, with or without premeditation, etc. His work constitutes a valuable piece of research and marks an interesting stage in the history of moral and legal ideas. Protagoras in contrast— in this passage at least—seeks to make no distinctions. He concentrates solely upon one idea, which appears to have been essential to both his thought and his life, namely the idea of an education which continues through every stage of human life. He discovers it at work as much in penal justice as in political life or in ordinary daily life; and it is a matter that appears to be of essential importance for all human beings. As he sees it, the ongoing educative role of the city is the very thing that sustains it and that justifies all the measures taken to ensure its cohesion—whether they be aimed at repression or simply encouragement.

Taking as his starting-point the eminently Greek idea of man as a citizen, Protagoras thus drew from his thinking on the subject of the city a justification for the moral virtues, founding it upon the common interest. Just at the moment when the virtues' other foundations suddenly proved so fragile, he discovered within the civic group new reasons for honouring and practising them.

The Advocacy of the Moral Virtues

The example of Protagoras shows how humanist and rational thinking contrived to find in collective life a new justification for many moral values. A number of other Sophists produced no less closely reasoned arguments also designed to encourage the practice of all kinds of virtues.[7]

This is an important point. It accounts for the fact that, even in the eyes of the public, the Sophists sometimes passed for teachers of virtue. In the dialogue which bears his name, Meno wonders where to turn in order to acquire

the wisdom and virtue whereby men keep their house or their city in good order, and honour their parents, and know when to welcome

---

[7] The text in which Xenophon appears to take the opposite view is cited and discussed towards the end of Chapter 1. Applied to the early great masters it would clearly be flagrantly unjust.

and when to speed citizens and strangers as befits a good man
(*Meno*, 91 A)

and Socrates immediately suggests he should consult the
Sophists. The suggestion is not at all well received by Anytus,
and can hardly have been serious in the first place. All the
same, the wording of the beginning of the sentence is very
reminiscent of the definition that Protagoras gives of his art
in the *Protagoras*. On the other hand, it then proceeds to list
some of the most traditional and conformist of the virtues—
hardly those usually associated with the Sophists. The list
even ends with good manners. In a light-hearted fashion this
assortment of virtues suggests that, even as a group, the
Sophists were not considered to have totally broken away: it
was perfectly possible to teach their new art and at the same
time remain a respectable teacher of virtue.

There can be no doubt of that. We know of several Sophists
who played just such a role. For reasons similar to those of
Protagoras, they even wrote in defence not simply of justice
but of all kinds of virtues and values for which they were the
self-declared advocates. Prodicus was one, the Anonymus
Iamblichi another, and both left exhortations which leave no
room for misunderstanding, reflecting as they do similar
moral views to those which, in Chapter 6, we detected in
Antiphon, in connection with the theme of concord.

These two speeches appear to be of a more traditional
nature, but they certainly show how far the Sophists really
were from being amoralists; in fact both texts go so far as to
lay considerable emphasis on the importance of effort. In
Prodicus' apologue on Herakles at his point of decision, one of
the two women who address him praises the life that is the
pleasantest and easiest (Memorabilia, 2.1.23). The other,
identified as Virtue, opens her plea with the idea that it is, on
the contrary, important to make an effort, 'for of all things
good and fair, the gods give nothing to man without toil and
effort' (28). To achieve anything, it is necessary to undergo
some form of training, involving effort and sweat. The word
'sweat' directly calls to mind Hesiod's words in praise of
work: 'Before merit, the gods have placed sweat.' That very
fact is an indication of the extent to which the new teachers

often deliberately associated themselves with the moral traditions of the past. Prodicus was certainly not the only one to do so. The Anonymus Iamblichi also starts off by declaring that, in whatever domain, in order to be successful, one must be a 'lover of effort'. Nor should it be forgotten that Antiphon also makes the point that joys do not come of themselves. Speaking of athletic triumphs, intellectual success, and many other kinds of pleasure, he notes: 'Honours, prizes, delights, which God has given to men, depend necessarily on great toils and exertions' (B 49). We should also remember that Thucydides and Euripides, the two writers who were disciples of the Sophists, both emphasized that the Athenian achievement (indeed, achievement in general) was the fruit of many trials and efforts. They exalted action in preference to a soft life of leisure; in fact Thucydides put those very sentiments into the mouth of another friend of the Sophists, Pericles himself.

The efforts of which these writers speak were to be directed towards practical action and the acquisition of some form of excellence or *aretē*. Neither Prodicus nor the Anonymus Iamblichi specify what kind of *aretē*, but leave the choice open. However, the general nature of the expressions that both use shows that they were prepared to accept all kinds. Prodicus mentions 'good and beautiful' things, then goes on to speak of helping one's friends, or one's town, or Greece in general, of distinguishing oneself in warfare, and of strengthening one's body. The form of action seems much less important than the principle involved, which is to aim for quality and the greater well-being of human beings. Thus—Virtue suggests—the most enjoyable spectacle of all is the contemplation of a fine piece of work (or a fine action) for which one is oneself responsible. The ideal is certainly a positive one, but, equally certainly, it is no more than vaguely defined. In similar vein, the Anonymus speaks of wisdom, courage, or virtue (*aretē* in the widest possible sense), either in general or concentrating on one particular aspect. Subsequently, he becomes more specific, discoursing at some length upon two virtues in particular: the first, the refusal to become a slave to money; the second, the refusal to be miserly with one's own life. The first is precisely the virtue for which Thucydides

praises Pericles; the second, the one for which Pericles praises
the Athenians who died for their country. The ideal here is
thus both loftier and more specific than that of Prodicus. But
the Anonymus only defines general sets of conditions, making
no attempt to classify different forms of excellence or virtue.

Allowing for this qualification, it seems that both Prodicus
and the Anonymus prefer to leave the choice of merits to individuals, as if they were anxious to recognize the legitimacy
of individual decisions here, just as Protagoras recognized the
equal legitimacy and value of all opinions, whatever they
might be. On the other hand, for both these Sophists the goal
to which efforts should be directed is quite clear. For both it
is, in fact, twofold.

The essential aim, especially for Prodicus, is to win the
respect and goodwill of others in return for certain services
rendered. In other words, here again the human group constitutes the ultimate justification. Prodicus thus acknowledges a
kind of reward for good actions. The emphasis of the text of
the *Memorabilia* is quite touching in its naïvety. The various
virtues mentioned are only excellent to the extent that they
elicit appreciation:

If you want the favour of the gods, you must worship the gods; if you
desire the love of friends, you must do good to your friends; if you
covet honour from a city, you must aid that city; if you are fain to
win the admiration of all Greece for virtue, you must strive to do
good to Greece. (2. 1. 28)

The examples that follow, which include working the land
and warfare, also stem from the idea of just deserts, although
they are no longer concerned with the human group. However, the importance of the latter is soon reaffirmed. Virtue
shows that her rival is rejected and despised, whereas she
herself is in contact with the gods and with men of worth;
no fine project, whether human or divine, can be achieved
without her: ' I am first in honour among the gods and among
men that are akin to me,' she declares, and goes on to speak of
her good relations with craftsmen, masters, and servants
alike, in works pertaining to both peace and war. Finally, in
words which put one in mind of Protagoras, she proclaims
herself to be 'the best of partners in friendship' (2. 1. 33).

The point is made by the accumulation and repetition of words such as 'praise', 'honours', 'appreciation', followed by 'honours' again, and, finally, 'memory', through which the esteem of other human beings is prolonged even beyond death.

That last idea brings us back to Thucydides' Pericles. For though Athens' empire may have been won by dint of many trials and tribulations, its glory will last for ever. And for Pericles, that was the supreme reward:

The memory of this greatness, even if we should now at last give way a little—for it is the nature of all things to decay as well as grow—will be left to posterity for ever. (*History*, 2. 64. 3)

As in Prodicus, human efforts are rewarded by being remembered.

There is thus a somewhat grandiose aspect to the aspirations that Prodicus' Virtue proposes. Furthermore, it is not insignificant that the figure to whom she addresses her words is Herakles, the most glorious of all heroes. However, since the heroic age, moral ideals have lowered their sights. In daily life, fame and glory have become less important than feelings of respect, affection, and unity. If one helps other people one is appreciated and, in return, helped by them. This is now the way that people express their opinions. It also seems yet another sign of the importance now ascribed to human relations within the city. Protagoras is not far away. In Prodicus' philosophy, the need for good social relations restores the importance of all virtues involving generosity, helpfulness, courage, and so on.

The emphasis of the justification of human virtues produced by the Anonymus Iamblichi is slightly different, but his thinking clearly follows much the same general lines. He too is concerned about other people and the unity of the group. Thus, having declared that one should direct one's virtues towards all that is 'fine, beautiful, and in conformity with the laws', he goes on to explain that the highest virtue of all is making oneself 'useful to the greatest number of people'. The only way of doing that is to adhere to the laws and justice: 'that is what founds and maintains the cities of mankind'. As in Protagoras' conception of justice, the ideal of being of service and help to others (once again that ideal of utility) is developed within the context of unity between citizens. Also as in Prodicus, the existence of the links which bind people together leads on to the notion of a lasting memorial. Paragraph 5. 6 speaks of virtue as a means of glory (or good reputation). On the subject of the primary objective for all human efforts, the two texts are thus in close agreement.

However, the time has come for us to recognize that this, so to speak, extended ideal of everyone within the group or city acting in such a way as to be of mutual service to his fellows is not the only one in play. Each individual likewise will enjoy for himself the happy results of such behaviour. Prodicus' apologue does not dwell upon this second aspect. It is, however, briefly suggested in the passage which describes an individual's greatest joy as the contemplation of a fine achievement or a good action for which he or she is responsible (31). Winning the praise of others was an external motive; in contrast, contemplation of one's own good works lays more emphasis upon the enjoyment of a good conscience. This leads on to an idea that we have already detected in Antiphon: the notion of an internal felicity and peace of mind which are in themselves advantages and are consequently worth striving for.

Now, this is the clearly expressed message conveyed by the whole of the last section of the Anonymus' text. The author describes the advantages which stem from respect for the laws. The first to be mentioned are those connected with good relations and concord between human beings. But then he moves on to the personal peace of mind that is engendered by such concord: spared the troubles and anxieties that attend altercations, people find themselves liberated. They can sleep easy, without fears or misery, and awake without anxiety, confident that their efforts will be rewarded with success.

A euphoric picture, to be sure, but one which will have a familiar air to the reader. The word meaning 'without misery' (*alupos*) reminds us that (according to the *Lives of Ten Orators*, which is ascribed to Plutarch) Antiphon had developed 'an art of banishing misery'. We are told that he even ran a kind of clinic where he treated misery very much as a doctor treats physical maladies. And the reason why this same Antiphon condemns personal emotions and links is that they tend to bring misery in their wake: marriage, for instance, doubles our pains. The quest for a state 'free from misery' thus seems to refer directly back to Antiphon. As for the idea of slumber free from all fears, this too has a familiar ring. It also appears, in more or less similar form, in Prodicus' apologue, where work is said to produce more enjoyable sleep. It is no hardship to awaken from the sleep that follows upon hard work.

There is an interesting coincidence here:[8] sound sleep is clearly the most concrete sign of a clear conscience, and the easiest to use in an argument. As is well known, in book 9 of *The Republic*, Plato begins his description of a tyrannical man by showing how his desires are unleashed in sleep. It is worth contrasting this with his fine description of the sleep of a wise man, 'when, I suppose, a man's condition is healthy and sober, and he goes to sleep after arousing his rational part and entertaining it with fair words and thoughts, and attaining to clear self-consciousness' (571 D). The point is that such a man 'sleeps with his heart at peace' and, enjoying repose of this kind, is spared the 'lawless visions' of dreams which can haunt others. As so often happens, Plato carries the analyses of his predecessors to a deeper level, enriching them with psychological insight, the vision of a soul divided, and the wider scope offered by his own wholly integrated system of thought. But, as also frequently happens, it is the analyses produced by those same predecessors which provide the starting-point for his own thinking, which, in this instance, further develops the ideas of a number of the Sophists.

At any rate, one cannot but be struck by the convergence of all these texts which so constantly and positively defend human virtues and moral values. Some of them establish a connection between moral values and the gods. Protagoras associates the gods with the existence of justice and respect for others—although that may be simply because he is using myth. Prodicus goes somewhat further, to judge from his apologue passed on to us by Xenophon: quite apart from

---

[8] In Critias (B 6, 15–22), the idea of moderation is extended to apply to loving and sleeping as well as drinking. But here the idea is far more limited and materialistic.

presenting a personification of Vice and Virtue, this work suggests the benevolence of the gods as one of the goals that men might set themselves, although the idea is admittedly produced as no more than a hypothetical example. Such references to the gods show that these authors professed no systematic or provocative atheism; but they certainly do not constitute the basis for their moral philosophy. The basis upon which the Sophists reconstructed morality was undoubtedly the carefully calculated interest of human beings. It is significant that the most morally inclined of all of them, the Anonymus Iamblichi, makes no mention at all of the gods and resorts to no notions of the transcendent. Nor do any of the Sophists—in contrast to Plato—suggest the possibility of rewards in a life hereafter. The period thus seems marked by a general concern to underpin morality with new bases, to compensate for those that were being undermined.

We know of one notable exception among the Sophists, however. The young Meno tells us that Gorgias, whom he had known in Thessaly, expressed scorn for Sophists who set themselves up as teachers of virtue: 'Skill in speaking is what he takes it to be their business to produce' (*Meno*, 95 c). There were probably others too who were indifferent to the entire moral issue, or could even be described as amoralists. By and large, though, the Sophists to varying degrees shared a common desire to defend virtue on rational grounds. In fact, this was part and parcel of their critique. Finally, it is clear that this movement even extended so far as to include Socrates and Plato. They may be more demanding than the Sophists: unlike these, Socrates emphasizes the fate of souls after death, while Plato insists upon the absolute existence of Ideas. To defend morality, however, they too, like the Sophists, are obliged to work out arguments that rest upon utility.

The Sophists' strategy where virtue is concerned is thus quite clear. It is even fair to say that it complemented the rest of their doctrines, forming a coherent whole. Utility was the key notion upon which all their arguments of likelihood were based ('I did not do that, for it would not have been in my interest to do so'; 'Consider the advantages that will follow if you heed what I tell you' . . .). As a result there emerged a realistic, or even pessimistic conception of psychology as exemplified in Thucydides' work, where every single person, despite the more or less altruistic appearance of his motives, always pursues his own interests. It was upon that very self-interest that, directly or indirectly, the new morality ultimately rested. And what that new morality, which everyone praised in his own fashion, boiled down to was that the individual must behave well towards others because he is bound to them.

Confirmation of the general tendency of this thinking is provided, once again, by the philosophy into which it developed. Whatever the variations from one thinker to another and even the disparities that set the more traditionalist Sophists apart from the more revolutionary, it was in this form that their legacy passed into Athenian classicism, represented, once again, by Isocrates.

Isocrates believes that it is human opinions that provide the authority in matters of morality. He is proud to teach people how to speak well, for speech provides the means for them to get together, to understand one another, and to coexist. He believes that the finest thing a man can do is proffer good political advice; and there is one particular piece of advice which provides the connecting link between all his treatises. It is that one should behave well in order to win the esteem and sympathy of other people, for in the last analysis it is that sympathy which, thanks to the unity that it engenders, creates true strength. This is his explanation for the greatness and collapse of the hegemony first of Athens, then of Sparta, and also for the overthrow of the oligarchy. His recommendation to cities and princes alike is to take care to acquire and preserve the lasting form of power which is founded upon fine actions. This may not add up to a particularly lofty moral philosophy or to politics of a particularly subtle kind. But it is a moral philosophy and a type of politics which undoubtedly developed out of the theories upon which the Sophists' moral and political ideas were founded.

As we have seen, those theories enabled the Sophists to build their defence of the virtues upon a firm and rational basis. Those virtues were essential to the life of a city, so it is hardly surprising that, as well as devoting their efforts to the reconstruction of moral values and human virtues, the Sophists frequently tried to elaborate doctrines of a specifically political nature—that is to say, doctrines directly designed to promote the welfare of cities and peoples.

8

Politics

POLITICS of two kinds played an important part in the activities of the Sophists: internal politics and politics of external relations between one people and another.

Politics within the Cities

The Sophists, who set out to teach 'the art of politics', clearly took an interest in the internal conflicts of cities and in constitutional problems. However, at least so far as internal city politics go, it would not be correct to attribute to them, as a collective group, opinions or sympathies which would place them in any particular party.

A priori, it is certainly true that the development of their teaching programme was linked with that of the Athenian democracy. The rhetorical and political training that they purveyed only made sense if the skill of public speaking truly did make it possible for individuals to play an effective role. However, their teaching was costly and aimed only at those rich enough to pay for it: the aristocrats, whose families had long been predominant in Athens and who must have been particularly concerned to retain or recover their influence. In the gatherings described by Plato, it is they who fill the stage. The *Protagoras* takes place in the house of the wealthy Callias. There, the Sophists are joined by the great aristocrat Alcibiades, not to mention Critias, who himself almost qualifies as a Sophist besides being a well-known aristocrat, and who was later to be a prominent member of the oligarchy.

However, in itself all this constitutes no reason to ascribe the same ideas and sympathies to all the Sophists. There are distinctions that need to be made. Here again, Protagoras stands a little apart from the younger Sophists. Protagoras was a friend of Pericles; and the regime which brought Pericles to power represented the very spirit of democracy. However, this was a kind of democracy which, in comparison with what followed, was to seem distinctly moderate. The very personality of Pericles ensured that his personal authority predominated in political practice to such an extent that Thucydides was prompted to remark that, under the title of democracy, it was really the first citizen who governed. Pericles managed to combine great firmness with great prestige. So long as he remained in power there was no sign of the demagogy of which, after him, the texts never cease to complain.

It is known that Protagoras acted as legislator for the Panhellenic colony of Thurii, founded at the instigation of Pericles. There has been much speculation about what kind of regime he intended to institute. On the face of it, it seems likely to have been a democracy for, in the first place, it must have been a system inspired by that of Athens, even if other cities were also associated with the enterprise. The city's acknowledged founder was an Athenian and it is hard to imagine Pericles, or the citizens of Athens, looking kindly upon a constitution that differed significantly from their own. All the evidence suggests that Protagoras himself also subscribed to such views. The myth that Plato has him expound, in which every man has a share in justice, is altogether in line with the principle according to which every individual is capable of judging for himself and coming to his own decisions. Furthermore, we know that, in real life, charges were pressed against Protagoras by a certain Pythodorus, who was later to become a member of the oligarchic government of the Four Hundred.

The Thurii constitution must have been a moderate democracy, however. Not only was Pericles, who inspired the venture, not an extremist of the kind that was to appear in Athens later on; but the very fact that the laws, which were drawn up in advance on a theoretical basis, were designed for a city intended to extend a welcome to people of different origins itself ensured a certain balance. All the indications thus suggest that Protagoras was a man who favoured moderate democracy.

In contrast, the other major Sophists—some of them, at least—seem to have inclined to more oligarchic ideas. It is impossible to say anything definite about Gorgias in this connection, except that his disciple Isocrates also seems to have defended moderate democracy. However, it would clearly be foolhardy to deduce the master's political ideas from those of one of his pupils. Our ignorance is all the more regrettable since Gorgias, who came to Athens as an ambassador from an allied town, was certainly no stranger to politics. Nor is anything known of Prodicus' political views. As for Hippias, if we are to believe Tertullian (and if the man to whom he refers truly is Hippias the Sophist—which is by no means certain), he perished in the course of political conflicts, plotting against his native city of Elis, in the Peloponnese, possibly in a democratic revolt against the oligarchy then in power there. But with such questionable evidence, we cannot be sure.

Where some of the other Sophists are concerned, however, we are on slightly firmer ground. One is the anonymous author of the *Double Arguments*, who protests against the selection of magistrates by lottery. This was one of the grounds on which the opponents of democracy frequently attacked it, and some of the proposals of moderate democrats were deliberately designed to limit the effects of selection by lot. The text, which is very brief, resorts to a number of arguments traditionally used in this controversy. One consists in comparing the situation with that of the practical trades and skills (and has a somewhat Socratic ring). Another is the idea that, by drawing lots, one might select someone who was hostile to the regime (a point which Isocrates was later also to make, in his *Areopagiticus*).

Apart from this brief piece of information, we know at least a little about some of the other major Sophists. If it were certain that the Sophist and the orator who went by the name of Antiphon were truly one and the same man, Antiphon could be included here. Antiphon the orator certainly played a major role in the oligarchic revolution of 411 and lost his life in it. But unfortunately that identification is extremely controversial.

On the other hand, where Thrasymachus and Critias are concerned, the circumstances are in no doubt. A fragment written by Thrasymachus which has come down to us constitutes the first known speech advocating the 'ancestral constitution', that is to say, a moderate regime with oligarchic tendencies. In *The Republic* (340 A), furthermore, Thrasymachus' arguments are forcefully supported by a certain Clitophon, known for his part in the revolt of 411, when he proposed an amendment which opened up the way for oligarchic reform. The association between these two names seems unlikely to have been purely fortuitous, so this piece of evidence would appear to confirm that of the fragment on the 'ancestral constitution'.

As for Critias, strictly speaking he may not have been a Sophist, but he certainly was extremely active in politics and one of the most committed advocates of oligarchy. He made his mark not in the first oligarchic revolution (in which his father was involved) but in the second, in 404.[1] He was one of the Thirty Tyrants and shared direct responsibility for the sentence and execution of Theramenes, the proponent of a 'moderate constitution'. Critias considered Theramenes too easy-going, too soft on democratic ideas. While swallowing his draught of hemlock Theramenes is supposed to have exclaimed: 'To the health of the fine Critias!' Critias has also been held responsible for the reign of terror to which Athens was for a while subjected. He was killed shortly after, in the struggles in which the efforts of exiled democrats prevailed over the oligarchy, thereby liberating Athens from this short-lived oligarchic regime. If anyone in Athens was wholeheartedly in favour of oligarchy, it was Critias.

The few Sophists who are known to us, and the slender evidence that we possess about them, thus present a wide spectrum of attitudes and political tendencies, ranging across the board from moderate democracy, through moderate oligarchy, to extreme oligarchy. The most that we can do is sketch in a rough picture of their common characteristics. It seems fair to say that, unlike some of those who claimed to be their disciples and in contrast to men such as Callicles,

---

[1] He was exiled between the two revolutions and seems to have spent some time in Thessaly, helping the oligarchs. However, in Xenophon (*HG* 2.3.15; DK A 10), Theramenes presents him as having served the cause of social revolution. It seems rather strange. However, the case of Critias is perfectly clear without taking this doubtful testimony into account.

the Sophists were fundamentally concerned for the human group. They did not approve of anarchy (which Antiphon, for one, severely condemned) any more than of tyranny imposed by a single individual. What they favoured were regimes worthy of the name *politeia*.

It is tempting to believe that they shared a common inclination towards the 'ancestral constitution', for this would certainly tally with the principle of order founded upon concord. In fact, that would be the most likely of suppositions were it not for the fact that, among them, two extreme cases constitute, or appear to constitute, exceptions: the first is Antiphon—if, that is, Antiphon the Sophist is to be identified with Antiphon the orator; the second—and here there can be no doubt—is Critias. Remarkably enough, these two happen also to be the only native Athenians in the group. Not being foreigners, they were no doubt more likely to take part in political action and better placed to express their views without fear. That being so, their ambitions, social relations, or simply the force of circumstances may well have carried them along. But in truth all this is pure speculation. What emerges most strikingly is the way that the best reasoned and most carefully structured reflection may, depending on the moment or the individuals involved, lead to different practical choices.

In this domain, at least as much as in that of philosophical analysis, it is pointless to ask whether these men were 'for' or 'against' any particular measure or any particular regime. Unlike in the domain of philosophy, as individuals they surely must have been committed to one side or the other, prepared for action and ready to take risks. But they did so in different ways and we do not know enough to be any more specific.

However, nearly all of them shared an interest in political thinking, and this led them to introduce yet another new science, founded upon the definition of moral principles in conjunction with concrete comparison. On this point the evidence is incontrovertible.

We possess virtually no information about the nature of the political thought of the Sophists. But at least we know that they engaged in such thought: the titles of their works and the random evidence that we do possess suggest a wealth of activity of which no trace remains. We also know that, for some of them, at least, it constituted an essential part of their work.

After all, when, in the dialogue which bears his name, Plato's Protagoras describes the nature of his teaching, he says:

This learning consists of good judgement of [a man's] own affairs, showing how best to order his own home; and how to become most capable of dealing with public affairs both in speech and in action.

Socrates then encourages him to speak even more plainly, saying, 'I wonder whether I follow what you are saying; for you appear to be speaking of the civic science (*politikē technē*) and undertaking to make men good citizens', to which Protagoras replies, 'That is exactly the purport of what I profess' (319 A).

It is surely an injustice more or less to transpose those words, as some scholars have, construing them to mean that Protagoras aimed to teach his pupils how to pursue a brilliant career of precisely the kind desired by the gilded youth of Athens. For that is not what he says: instead, he speaks of good management, the ability to take political action, and good citizens. He also speaks of a *technē*, with the particular knowledge and rules that any *technē* implies. Rhetoric is certainly one element here, but by no means the only one. The good citizens whom Protagoras has in mind must also be capable of giving good advice and, in order to do so, must possess a general understanding of political problems.

The effects of such teaching could be far-reaching. It is not unreasonable to suppose that it prompted the extraordinary spate of maxims and analyses to be found in the literature of the day, particularly in the works of Thucydides and Euripides. The currents of feeling by which assemblies are moved and the ways in which these can be used, as well as mass psychology in crowds and armies, are subjects upon which both Thucydides and Euripides comment. But they

also write of the reasons which make alliances strong, the
dangers which arise when people are either too poor or too
rich, the role of intelligence and foresight in statesmen or
military leaders, the dangers of demagogy, the power of
public opinion, the relative importance of money and glory,
the differences and also the similarities between Greeks and
barbarians, the need for a civic spirit, and the advantages of
generosity . . . All these themes, listed here in no particular
order and in more or less haphazard fashion, imply active
thinking in every domain of politics, thinking that tended
to turn every individual into a kind of expert, capable of
clear understanding. The speeches which both these authors
incorporate in their works convey some idea of that thinking;
and the collections of fictitious speeches which survive confirm the formative impact of the Sophists' teaching.

First and foremost, though, political skill presupposed a
lucid understanding of the various aspects of city institutions
and of what might be called the city constitution. We know
that several of the Sophists worked in this area, and it comes
as no surprise to find Protagoras leading the way. Why else
should he have been chosen as the legislator for Thurii? All
the evidence indicates that he had thought deeply about
legislation, and was furthermore generally recognized to be
an expert on the subject. A list of his works compiled by
Diogenes Laertius includes a treatise entitled *On the Constitution*. It is the earliest known example of a work bearing this
title, but it is part of a double stream of development for
which there is plenty of evidence.

During this same period, an interest in political systems is
reflected in the discussion of different regimes which appears,
somewhat anachronistically, in book 3 of Herodotus and also
in a treatise written at an unknown date but probably before
the outbreak of the Peloponnesian War or during the first half
of that conflict. The treatise is entitled *On the Constitution of
the Athenians* and is mistakenly included in the works of
Xenophon (simply because half a century later Xenophon
wrote a *Constitution of the Lacedaemonians*). This kind of
thinking was probably as novel as the abstract noun used—
the word which we translate as 'constitution' but which at
the time denoted a whole collection of laws, constitutional

regulations, customs, and mores.[2] Its rapid diffusion seems to testify to a new-found awareness.

This was connected with a desire to improve political life and render it less corrupt. The measures to be taken to that end were discussed in the city's Assembly and, naturally enough, the Sophists, who set out to prepare their pupils to take part in such debates, sought to establish the bases of certain general ideas which could be of use to them. One way and another, these matters were becoming a serious subject of meditation, and this too was a subject which was already in the air. A number of philosophers, particularly the Pythagoreans, had thought and written about political life and the principles behind it. Contemporary thinkers were also concerned with political issues. Hippodamus, who took part in the founding of Thurii, was a great town planner and may have designed the plan of this new town. We know for sure that he reorganized Piraeus. In *Politics*, 2.4, Aristotle writes of him:

He was the first man not engaged in politics who attempted to speak on the subject of the best form of constitution.

No doubt he too produced a treatise 'On the Constitution'. Aristotle summarizes his ideas, which included a plan to divide the population and the territory into three, as well as his description of a system of government. Hippodamus was probably active considerably later than Protagoras, but they seem to have shared an interest in this field.

Phaleas of Chalcedon, whom Aristotle mentions just before Hippodamus, had produced a plan for a constitution which envisaged an equal distribution of wealth or measures designed to equalize fortunes. The exact dates of this thinker are not known, but he was a compatriot of Thrasymachus and one of Plato's predecessors. His activities, too, testify to the vogue for political research.

Protagoras had clearly laid the foundations for a whole new movement of thought, and treatises on political matters now seem to have appeared in great profusion. It is impossible to

---

[2] Cf. J. Bordes, *'Politeia' dans la pensée grecque jusqu'à Aristote* (Paris, 1982).

say how much they owed to Protagoras' own work for we know nothing of the contents of his treatise so, once again, are reduced to pure conjecture.

Given his taste for antilogies and contrasting arguments, Protagoras' own treatise may well have considered the pros and cons of different kinds of political system. It has even been suggested that the debate on different regimes in book 3 of Herodotus reflected the analyses of Protagoras. Considerable surprise has greeted the idea that, when Darius was on the point of seizing power, the Persian leaders calmly discussed the respective advantages and disadvantages of each of the three main types of regime (monarchy, oligarchy, and democracy), and scholars have been quick to detect the influence of Athenian debates and the work of the Sophists. Herodotus and Protagoras are both associated with the founding of Thurii, a fact that underlines the convergences in their thought. If these were an indication of direct contact between the two men—which is, however, no more than a hypothesis—they would accentuate the importance of Protagoras' role as an initiator, illustrating it in concrete fashion. Even if that is not the case, they remain extremely telling.

As a genre, such treatises 'On the Constitution' were to enjoy a remarkable popularity. After all, Protagoras' initiative was to lead straight to Plato, whose great treatise which we know as *The Republic* (from its Latin title) was in Greek entitled *Politeia* or *On the Constitution*. This is another respect in which Plato's debt to Protagoras may well be greater than is generally believed. The fact that Plato's treatise was also given a subtitle, *or, On Justice* underlines the preoccupation with ethics and the insistence on absolute values which distinguish Plato's work from that of his predecessors in general and Protagoras in particular.

These treatises 'On the Constitution' sometimes took rather different forms, as can be seen from the work of Sophists such as Critias and Thrasymachus. Critias handled the genre in various ways. Fragments of his *Constitution of the Lacedaemonians*, composed in verse, survive, as do a few brief fragments of a *Constitution of the Thessalians* and a *Constitution of the Lacedaemonians* in prose. Some elements of these constitutions are assumed to be related to a *Constitution of the Athenians*. At any rate, it is certain that Critias wrote a large number of treatises of this type. One ancient piece of testimony refers, in the plural, to the 'Constitutions' of Critias (A 38).

This series of texts testifies to a great interest in political matters; and it also reveals a marked taste for comparisons. Critias does not appear to have composed any theoretical and general works on the various constitutions or on the ideal constitution. Instead, in a spirit of curiosity similar to that concurrently displayed for ethnological and anthropological data, he looks about him and describes what he sees, he collects examples, and, at every turn, he suggests comparisons.

The meaning of the word *politeia* was extremely wide at this period, and Critias' descriptions seem to have been devoted to practical customs more than to institutions. None of the fragments ascribed to him that have come down to us are concerned with political institutions. But he was certainly interested in morality and in the conditions of life and, for a Greek of this period, these were matters which were very much part of a general system and were connected with the political regime (in the broadest sense of that term).

Whatever the exact content of these texts may have been, it is clear that they established the bases for what constituted as it were a vast socio-political enquiry of a kind that was to enjoy considerable success in the future. It is worth remembering that Xenophon too produced a *Constitution of the Lacedaemonians* and, above all, that Aristotle, in preparation for his *Politics*, made many studies of this kind. The only one that has survived is the *Constitution of the Athenians*, but the ancient catalogues attribute to Aristotle between 158 and 171 such 'Constitutions'; some sources speak of as many as 250. To these we should add the *Rules of Barbarian Life* (*Nomima barbarika*), the *Tables of the Laws of Solon*, and other studies of this kind. In this huge collection of works, now lost, Aristotle was following in the footsteps of Critias; and these studies of his explain how it is that his treatise, the *Politics*, is so much more concrete and detailed than Plato's *Republic*. The two greatest political thinkers of Greece may thus be seen as the end products of two separate currents of thought initiated

by two Sophists, Protagoras and Critias, the former with
his ideas about legislation, the latter with his comparative
studies of political systems.

There would not appear to be much left for the other
Sophists to do. Yet Thrasymachus did write a text that
survives (mentioned above several times already) and it is
one that opens up perspectives every bit as exciting as the
works of Protagoras and Critias to which we have referred.
Thrasymachus' text likewise consists of reflections on a constitution, although it is not necessarily correct to suppose it to
be part of a treatise entitled *On the Constitution*, as many
scholars do, for we cannot be sure that such a treatise ever
existed. The text could just as well come from Thrasymachus'
Deliberative Speeches, whose existence is attested by the
Suda.[3] If that is indeed the case, the genre would be similar
to that so often used by Isocrates to disseminate ideas he
believed in under the cover of a fictitious advocacy, thereby
combining a rhetorical model with political propaganda.
Thrasymachus' fragment was preserved as an example of
style; but, as Isocrates' *Plataicus* shows, these fictitious
speeches were sometimes both personal and committed.

Thrasymachus starts by justifying his decision to speak—a
rhetorical commonplace, but one which he exploits to recall
the happy times of yesteryear—thereby immediately establishing the political gist of his opening remarks. His political
drift is then made even clearer, but the spirit of his argumentation, in which moral and political themes are intertwined,
is remarkably conciliatory. Thrasymachus bewails all the
mistakes of the past and, in terms strongly reminiscent of
the Anonymus Iamblichi, he points out how war has taken
over from peace just as, within the city, hatred and strife
have superseded concord. He deplores the fact that private
ambition now prevents politicians from recognizing the
common ground that may exist in apparently opposed positions. He goes on to praise the 'ancestral constitution' as
being the one best adapted to all the citizens, that is to say,
the one most likely to make them pool their interests. (It is a
koinotatē constitution, i.e. one that is in the general interest.)

---

[3] They clearly tackled a number of different political themes.

We do not know what arguments Thrasymachus used to defend the various practical reforms whose general trends are known to us from other texts of this time. However, it is remarkable that a text only one page long should so strikingly convey a number of dominant tendencies both of tone and in modes of reasoning. Two features characteristic of the Sophists' general style are clearly detectable. The first is the method of making realistic judgements based on results rather than abstract principles, asking: 'What has the present regime done for us? What has actually resulted from it?' That is an empirical and realistic way of proceeding, and quite the reverse of Plato's method: for him, everything is governed by principles, which operate as intellectual and moral imperatives. The type of demonstration used by Thrasymachus was to serve as a model to Isocrates. He used it in *On Peace*, when assessing the imperialistic policies of Athens and Sparta; and again in the *Areopagiticus*, when contrasting the existing Athenian democracy with that of 'our ancestors'. The other procedure that Thrasymachus uses which is characteristic of the Sophists in general consists in favouring above all others such measures and principles as are likely to ensure union and agreement. Isocrates was later to adopt exactly the same line. In that same treatise, *On Peace*, he praises the democracy of the past for fostering good relations between citizens, in particular between the rich and the poor (31–2); and as the greatest achievement of democracy he singles out the reconciliation which followed the departure of the Thirty Tyrants: this would remain the very symbol of concord in the eyes of all (69). If Protagoras leads on to Plato, and certain features of Critias' work to some extent prepare the way for Aristotle, this short text by Thrasymachus constitutes an extraordinarily direct antecedent to the various treatises of Isocrates.

Although practically all the works written by these Sophists are lost, enough traces of their thinking remain for their influence upon later Greek political thought to be manifest. The whole of the fourth century, with its rich harvest of analyses and theories of many kinds, was without doubt deeply affected by the influence of these men. It owes its very impetus to the spirit of the Sophists, which, despite the divergences between them, is clearly detectable in all their research.

So far, we have considered only internal politics and constitutions, a field in which only a few of the Sophists have left their mark. But if we now look beyond the subject of different political systems and turn our attention to the relations between separate cities, it so happens that we meet with precisely those whom our enquiry appeared to have missed. The impact of the doctrines which these Sophists disseminated was to be every bit as original and important as that made by the doctrines concerned with the city's internal political system.

Beyond the Individual Cities

The Sophists, of all men, were particularly apt to consider every problem from a broad perspective, without being tied down by petty details. There were a number of reasons for this. In the first place, they were—as we have seen—travellers who hailed from every corner of the Greek world. In the course of their travels they had paused to teach in many other cities apart from Athens. The fact that Plato's dialogues, in which they are set on stage, all take place in Athens tends to make us forget that they travelled far and wide. They left occasional traces as they passed through Olympia and even Sparta. Gorgias (who came from Sicily) is known to have taught in Boetia and above all in Thessaly, where he seems to have settled at the end of his life. Conversely, it was in Sicily that Hippias (who came from Elis, in the Peloponnese) one day ran into Protagoras (who came from the borders of Thrace) . . . As for Thrasymachus (who came practically from the Black Sea), the titles of his works include that of an address *For the People of Larissa*, a city situated in Thessaly.

All these towns scattered around the Mediterranean were Greek. The belief that Protagoras was educated by Persian magi is very suspect; and if he was, he certainly constituted an exception. But what a wide range of places they covered within the Greek world! The Sophists brought a spirit of cosmopolitanism to Greece, or rather they reintroduced it there and helped it to evolve.[4]

Curiosity about other cities and other peoples was already in the air, as the case of Herodotus testifies. A native of Asia Minor, he settled for a while in Athens, then became a citizen of the new colony of Thurii, in Italy, for which Protagoras formulated a set of laws. As a historian, Herodotus had written about many Greek cities, as well as describing the customs of various barbarian peoples. The interests of the Sophists were also wide-ranging, but they concentrated above all on the towns which they knew, that is to say, Greek ones. As we have seen, Critias produced studies on many of them, including Sparta and the cities of Thessaly.

By virtue of the fact that they visited and compared different Greek cities, thereby establishing connections between them, the Sophists were well placed to appear as the very embodiment of the notion of Greek unity. It was a role that was also favoured by the times in which they lived. The idea of Greek unity had emerged and taken on reality half a century earlier during the Persian Wars, as Herodotus testifies when he notes how the Athenians valued 'the kinship of all Greeks in blood and speech and the shrines of gods and the sacrifices that we have in common and the likeness of our way of life' (8. 144).

Up until the Peloponnesian War, that spirit lived on despite rifts and minor skirmishes. Athens even tried to represent the dominion that she had gradually acquired in the Greek world as a Panhellenic confederation. No doubt such considerations influenced the founding of the colony at Thurii, and it is certainly significant that, as we have noted, the first of the Sophists had a hand in that foundation. In his life, if not in the fragments of his work that have survived, he is thus associated with a notion of union among Greeks.

Sparta, however, was not a part of this movement; and the Panhellenism of Thurii was a strictly Athenian version. Things had changed since the war against the barbarians and soon the Peloponnesian War was to set Greek against Greek in

---

[4] The archaic period witnessed similar movements and exchanges, but these did not become a subject of enquiry and comparison.

a pitiless conflict. The eruption of the war must have come as a shock to citizens who were hoping for reconciliation between Athens and Sparta and, over the years, the situation grew worse. The war lasted twenty-seven years, during which time many atrocities took place. It was not long before the Persians became involved; and plays presented from 411 onwards tend to introduce allusions to the idea that Greeks would do better to unite against the barbarians. A character in Aristophanes' *Lysistrata* thus exclaims (in 411), 'While your enemies are gathered there in arms, you are killing other Greeks and destroying their cities!' Similarly, in Euripides' *Iphigenia at Aulis* (written in about 407), we are told that it is fine to die 'for Greece'. Iphigenia herself declares forthrightly, 'It is right, Mother, that Greeks should command barbarians, not barbarians Greeks; for there you find slavery, and men here are free.' There were similar reactions on the Spartan side. Xenophon tells us that, in 406, the Spartan leader who was forced to ask the Persians for financial help remarked that 'the Greeks were truly unfortunate to have to pay court to barbarians in order to obtain their money' and went so far as to declare that 'if he returned safely, he would do everything in his power to effect a reconciliation between Athenians and Spartans'.

These were precisely the times through which the Sophists lived. Protagoras drew up his laws for Thurii in 443, thirteen years before the outbreak of the Peloponnesian War; Gorgias arrived in Athens in 427, four years after the beginning of the war; Critias came to power when the war ended; and Gorgias, who lived to be 100, survived him. In other words, the Sophists' generation saw the birth of a nostalgia for Greek unity. The year 411, in which Aristophanes expresses that nostalgia, is the very year to which Thrasymachus' fragment refers.

That very fact alerts us to a third reason why the Sophists—or at least some of them—should have been disposed to play an active role in spreading the idea of Panhellenism. Thrasymachus' text is enough to remind us of the importance of concord, or *homonoia*, in the philosophy of the Sophists. Not only was 411 the year in which we find the first specific allusion to the ideal of Greek unity, in the *Lysistrata*; it was also the year in which the word *homonoia* is first known to have been used, by Thrasymachus. Of course, this may be a chance coincidence brought about by the vagaries of the transmission and citation of texts; nevertheless, it seems significant.

That concord, which was supposed to make for the well-being and strength of cities, might also have put an end to the conflicts between cities which were dividing and destroying Greece. The doctrines promoted by the Sophists in general were, in this respect, in tune with the Panhellenic aspirations.

We know for certain that at least two of them played a positive role in this area. Thrasymachus was one, as is indicated by a single phrase that has survived from his speech *For the People of Larissa*. It would be meaningless were it not for the circumstances, which confer a striking significance upon it. In a play written in 438 but now lost, Euripides had one of his characters speak as follows: 'Shall we, who are Greeks, become the slaves of barbarians?' In the time of Archelaus, King of Macedon from 413 to 399, Thrasymachus resuscitated that quotation, no doubt a famous one, changing it hardly at all: 'Shall we, who are Greeks, become the slaves of Archelaus?' It is not known exactly when or in what circumstances he produced this flourish; but it certainly did not pass unnoticed: itself a quotation from Euripides made twenty years on, it was preserved by being cited by Clement of Alexandria no less than seven centuries later.

However, the major champion of Panhellenism, the man who was to be regarded as its embodiment and most famous advocate, was neither Thrasymachus nor any of the younger Sophists, but Gorgias. Although he was one of the oldest Sophists, his Panhellenist activities appear to have come relatively late. His great speech on the subject almost certainly dates from 392—more than ten years after the end of the Peloponnesian War.[5]

The very nature of this speech and its context are remarkable. It was delivered at Olympia, on the occasion of the

---

[5] 408 used to be suggested but that hypothesis has been, apparently correctly, abandoned.

Panhellenic Games, solemnly addressed to an audience of Greeks.[6] The setting and the occasion speak for themselves.

As the locations of the greatest sanctuaries, where people came together, and by virtue of the truce imposed by the Games, Olympia and Delphi were the major Panhellenic centres; and the Sophists seem to have been eager to perform there. Hippias, whose home was close to Olympia, was in a better position than most to exploit the facilities that it offered. But his behaviour, as described in Plato's *Hippias Minor*, does not appear to have been at all exceptional. In this dialogue, Hippias explains that he was in the habit of visiting Olympia each time the Games were held and would, as he puts it, 'entering the sacred precinct, offer to speak on anything that anyone chooses of those subjects which I have prepared for exhibition, and to answer any questions that anyone asks' (363 c–d). Clearly, however, 'exhibition speeches' such as those delivered by Gorgias, were even more prestigious.

It is not known when these 'Olympic Speeches' became a feature of the Games,[7] but two of them became famous: one delivered by Gorgias, the other, at the following Olympic Games, by Lysias, both deeply inspired by the spirit of Panhellenism. The Pythian Games held at Delphi likewise produced a *Pythian Speech*, also composed by Gorgias. Neither its date nor its contents are known; but it was in all likelihood written in the same spirit, for Gorgias was probably in the habit of making the most of these great occasions not only to display his talent but also to disseminate his ideas. Nor did the tradition stop there: Isocrates' famous speech known as the *Panegyricus* is a composition which, although designed for reading, presupposes a similar context. The *panēgureis* were the solemn meetings that these great Greek festivals constituted. It is only as a consequence of Isocrates' speech, devoted to the praise of Athens, that the word later came

---

[6] That is what the texts say; but he probably did not read his text out himself. It is hard to imagine how anyone, let alone a centenarian, could have made himself heard to such a crowd, in the open air, without the aid of a microphone.

[7] The tradition, transmitted by Lucian, claimed that the first complete reading of Herodotus' work took place at Olympia. Lucian suggests that this was a daring initiative on the historian's part.

to mean 'encomium' and that the title of his speech was, mistakenly, converted to *A Panegyric of Athens*. Isocrates had been working on his *Panegyricus* for a long time, having probably started it at the time of Gorgias' *Olympic Speech*. It appears to have been presented to the public on the occasion of the Olympic Games of 380. The principle behind it was thus exactly the same. Isocrates himself defined it, saying, 'I have come before you to give my counsels on the war against the barbarians and on concord among ourselves' (*Panegyricus*, 3).

Once again, a Sophist—Gorgias, this time—had blazed the trail, initiating what was to become a great classical tradition.

Gorgias' *Olympic Speech* was probably conceived partly to show off his skills as a rhetorician. But the scraps of testimony that have been preserved leave no doubt about the force of the ideas that he expressed and the authority that they gained. We know that the speech was composed in praise of the Games; and later writers have cited odd sentences relating to the qualities demanded by such a competition. Above all, though, Philostratus' *Lives of the Sophists* has left us a summary of Gorgias' speech. The passage runs as follows:

Seeing that Greece was divided against itself, he came forward as an advocate of reconciliation, and tried to turn their energies against the barbarians and to persuade them not to regard one another's cities as the prize to be won by their arms, but rather the land of the barbarians. (493)

This speech of Gorgias' says it all; and it is tempting to pause to comment on the text. The idea of *homonoia*, such an important feature of the Sophists' thinking, is given pride of place. There is an anecdote that Plutarch records in this connection: after delivering a speech on *homonoia* to the Greeks at Olympia, Gorgias is supposed to have been questioned by one of his listeners about the degree of *homonoia*, if any, that reigned in his own household. The word was clearly of essential importance. Philostratus' summary also contains some revealing stylistic turns of phrase which convey the assumption that Greece constitutes a unit in itself. (For example, the Greek text refers not to 'one another's cities' or 'each of their cities' but to 'their cities, between them'.) Above all, in similar vein, the expression 'internal strife' (or 'faction'), *stasis*, is used to refer to war waged between Greeks. In *The Republic*, Plato was later to devote several eloquent pages to establishing that this was the correct term to use: 'internal strife' was indeed the correct expression in such circumstances, just as if it were a case of civil war within a single city:

Whenever Greeks fight barbarians, we shall say that this is war, that they are natural enemies and that this enmity deserves the name of war. But whenever we see Greeks fighting other Greeks, we shall say that they are friends by nature, but that Greece is sick in that case and divided by faction [internal strife], and faction is the name we must give to that enmity. (470C–D; translation by J. de Romilly)

Plato was not the first to use the term which he proudly defends here. As we have seen, Gorgias had already brilliantly put it to similar use.

This striking speech was not the only one in which Gorgias set out such views. He several times returned to the same theme. One occasion was in a speech in praise of the town or region of Elis, in which Olympia was situated. And, as we have noted, he also composed a *Pythian Speech* probably in the same spirit. Above all, he also used another type of exhibition speech to purvey this kind of propaganda, injecting it with an unusual spirit of Panhellenism. This was the funeral oration, a genre designed to commemorate those fallen in war. We know of many examples, some real, some fictitious, of this Athenian practice, the most famous being the speech which Thucydides ascribes to Pericles, in book 2 of his *History*. But a funeral speech such as this, composed in the course of a war between Athens and Sparta, was bound to reflect the hostility between the two rival cities. Gorgias' speech was quite different. In the first place, it was a fictitious speech, for as a foreigner he could not be called upon officially to deliver such an address. He thus enjoyed a freer choice of themes. Furthermore, he elected to compose this fictitious speech during the second half of the war against Corinth.

In this conflict, in which the Persians were also involved,

Athens and Sparta certainly found themselves once again on opposite sides. But at this point Athens was regaining her authority in Greece and it was naturally hoped that she would co-ordinate resistance to the barbarians in a manner worthy of her earlier role. Gorgias had always placed his trust in Athens: it was the reason for his famous embassy in 427. Now that the city seemed vouchsafed a second chance, he took it upon himself to offer her advice. Philostratus tells us what form it took. According to him, Gorgias

incited the Athenians against the Medes and Persians, and was arguing with the same purpose as in the *Olympian Oration*, but he said nothing about a friendly agreement with the rest of the Greeks for this reason, that it was addressed to Athenians who had a passion for empire, and that could not be attained except by adopting a drastic line of policy. But he dwelt openly on their victories over the Medes and praised them for these. (*Lives of the Sophists*, 493)

In other words, Gorgias was adapting the themes of his *Olympian Speech* as far as possible, suggesting Panhellenic action as a goal for Athenian ambitions. The trophies to be won from the barbarians call to mind his *Olympian Speech*'s fine antithesis showing that trophies won from barbarians are to be preferred to those won from other Greeks. In his *Funeral Speech*, he produces an equally striking antithesis, which Philostratus cites:

Victories over barbarians call for hymns of praise, but victories over Greeks for dirges. (*Lives of the Sophists*, 493)

The forceful words of the *Funeral Speech* link it closely with the earlier *Olympian Speech*, firmly setting the seal of Gorgias' personality upon both.

Gorgias displayed remarkable skill in adapting his own projects to the circumstances and exploiting the ambition of one Greek city to promote the ideal of reconciliation with others. Even in this his example was emulated by his disciple Isocrates.

Isocrates never ceased to press passionately for a union of Greeks against the barbarians. But he was repeatedly forced to adapt his programme to the possibilities of the moment, always hoping to see Athens at the head of a union of Greeks, but in certain circumstances willing also to consider rulers of other cities,[8] even Philip of Macedon. He invariably proffered the same advice to whoever seemed in a position to follow it. He was prepared to vary details, so determined was he—as was Gorgias—not to jettison the principle.

We know that the second Athenian confederation, founded in 376, appeared to confirm Isocrates' hopes and crown his efforts with success. But those efforts themselves simply took over from the endeavours of Gorgias. The *Olympic Speech* almost certainly dates from 392. The *Panegyricus* was written in 380. The continuity is both manifest and remarkable.

It should not be forgotten that Isocrates had been a pupil of Gorgias' in Thessaly. He was connected with the Sophists in a number of other ways too. He had also been a pupil of Prodicus, and had married Hippias' daughter and adopted one of his sons. He did not continue to accept all their teaching; but in the political field he remained deeply influenced by Gorgias. In this domain, more than in any other, the line of thinking initiated by the Sophists leads to and culminates in him. Where political matters were concerned, the new ideas were absorbed into Athenian thought without modification or qualification.

However, the Sophists' political aspirations were never realized. Greek unity was still no more than a dream when the armies of Macedon arrived, and was still a dream later, when the Romans came. The memory of Gorgias pleading for Greek unity at the festival of Olympia is a shining image, but it was destined to fade away just as the golden statue erected at Delphi to immortalize him was to disappear.

Only the ideas, the principles, and the new discoveries remained, together with the inspiration that would for ever mark the domain of thought and theory. Though the Sophists' writings and statues have disappeared and the excitement that they aroused has long been a thing of the past, their ideas survived.

---

[8] Here and there, there are hints of possible connections. Isocrates may have been in contact with Jason of Pheres (a letter written by him to Jason's son survives); and a suspect remark by Pausanias also links the names of Jason and Gorgias. However, the information is too vague to be of much use.

Conclusion and Afterthoughts

It may seem somewhat perverse to insist on tracking down the thought of a handful of men whose works are lost, whose few preserved remarks survive without context, cited by invariably suspect intermediaries, and whose only portraits were produced by their opponents, frequently in a spirit of mockery. It is certainly a taxing quest, and also a risky one, involving a series of hypotheses which are not only open to challenge but may be quite simply erroneous. The justification for dragging innocent readers into this laborious undertaking is that what is at stake makes it worth while. We all like to try to solve riddles; and these are riddles to which it is impossible to remain indifferent.

That is firstly because of the influence that these men exercised at the most brilliant point in Greek culture. It is also because of all the ideas that the Sophists initiated—ideas which, once slightly modified and assimilated, were to survive and, as meaningful as ever, come down to the twentieth century AD.

It is true that the Sophists themselves are elusive, as are their works. As if in a dark cave, we can distinguish a few silhouettes, hear a few words, recognize a particular tone of voice, sense a particular cast of mind. But when all is said and done, we can make out little more than what Plato presents in a few brief pages at the beginning of the *Protagoras*. Here, the few lines that are devoted to each of the Sophists convey a number of impressions: a measure of respect, a little mockery, the voice of one Sophist, the gait of another. Try as we may to get closer to them, it is not possible to make real contact.

All that is undeniable. Yet we sense with awe that these half-glimpsed, shadowy figures are directly responsible for a multitude of discoveries. Of this there can be no doubt. One can argue over the respective importance of the role of this or that Sophist, as one can over the extent of their debt to developments which took place before they arrived on the scene. But there can be no question about the innovations for which they personally were, to a large extent, responsible.

The extent of their impact upon the history of Greek thought can be measured both by the reactions that they provoked within philosophical circles and by their legacy to cultural life in general. Let us make no mistake about this: whatever Plato's criticisms of them, the Sophists certainly played a decisive role in the development of Plato's own philosophy—if only by virtue of the responses that they forced out of him.

That is particularly true of Protagoras—Protagoras, who is never treated with anything less than respect; Protagoras, whose disciple and friend is a person as endearing as the young Theodorus of the *Theaetetus*, who is so loyal to his master that he increases Socrates' regard for him; Protagoras, finally, who with his doctrine on the Truth draws Plato into those long, dogged discussions in the course of which Plato elaborates his own metaphysical philosophy. But it is not just a matter of Protagoras. Dialectical definition as practised by Plato, according to which every idea is divided into two aspects, is a new version of Prodicus' method of distinguishing between synonyms. And after all, Plato's reflections on justice were themselves prompted in reaction to Thrasymachus.

Of course, Plato was above all concerned to show the deep divide between Socrates and the Sophists. The thought of confusion between them was intolerable to him. Furthermore, he wanted to establish a philosophy capable of refuting all that he condemned in their teaching. But his very antagonism turned out to be fruitful in that it brought about a double birth: for if rhetoric, as the sophists understood it, was something new, so was philosophy as Plato understood it. The two were invented side by side, and the contrast between them served to define them both.

The miracle is that one and the same city, in the course of the same period, gave birth to two kinds of thought, the one totally opposed to the other, the one humanistic and practical, the other transcendental and idealistic. We are thus presented with a twofold image of a lawgiver, a Janus, as it were: one is the legislator of Thurii, who, on the basis of experience and comparison, drew up a set of laws, now lost, for a real city; the other is the lawgiver of *The Republic* and *The Laws*, who devised an ideal system on the basis of an uncompromising analysis.

Presented thus, they may have the air of parallel and rival births. However, we are bound to recognize that it was not an equal battle and that the advantage went to philosophy. Plato's written works were preserved and his disciples continued to think along the lines indicated by him. It was not so with the Sophists.

A number of explanations may be adduced. It is reasonable to suppose that the activities and role of the Sophists were essentially linked with the concrete life of the Athenian democracy and that the demand for their teaching declined when Athenian independence was first threatened, then lost, and political life consequently lost its impetus and importance. It is also possible that, concerned as they were with day-to-day affairs and immediate effects, the Sophists (who, besides, were foreigners) left fewer works which, from a literary point of view, seemed worth copying and meditating.

Those are certainly plausible explanations and they should not be discounted. But there was a more determining factor: namely, that in their fervour and their pride in their new role, the Sophists thought they could do everything at once. The early masters to whom this study is devoted were philosophers as well as teachers of rhetoric, political advisers as well as logicians, stylists as well as scholars. Later, they lowered their sights: once the great flourish of the early days was over, the Sophists were reduced to teachers of rhetoric. In this more modest guise, the Sophists too were to live for ever.

Let us be clear that of one thing at least there can be no doubt. Even if their role came to an end and their works disappeared, the movement that they had launched opened up new perspectives in every intellectual field.

As soon as one moves outside the context of philosophical debate, their influence is manifest and now takes many positive forms. The Sophists seem to have been responsible for so many things. By virtue of the very form that their teaching took, they were the first to dispense an intellectual education designed to be of use in practical life—just as education still is today. Their teaching took the form of an education through rhetoric: this too was new, and it caused a sensation. But their methods have survived down to the present day. They established the basic procedures of rhetoric, procedures involving style and composition, but also procedures of reasoning and a sort of early logic still in its infancy. To learn how to become better speakers, they pondered deeply upon language and tried to set in order the hitherto unknown study of grammar. To provide orators with a fund of commonplaces, they produced reflections on human nature, on psychology, on the reactions to be expected in different sets of circumstances, on strategy, and on politics. They also seized upon and developed the possibilities offered by a comparative study of different societies. They created a vast array of *technai*, and those new *technai*, or human sciences, of theirs are the very ones that the modern age has taken up and continues to evolve. The Sophists were behind it all: they tried everything, created everything, inaugurated everything. But that unprecedented surge of energy resulted in a number of unfortunate consequences for them.

It seems to have made them over-confident of the powers of their art. They showed off and were boastful. So it was that the claims of skill and effectiveness that were associated with the name of 'Sophist' backfired: 'Sophists' came to mean people who were too sure of themselves, who set words above ideas, and valued captious arguments more than serious thought. Furthermore, that is the view of the Sophists that posterity has fastened upon, and as a result many modern scholars are sceptical about the importance of their doctrines. Because the Sophists tended to develop practical methods whose ultimate goal was not the Truth, some— including major scholars—have considered their doctrines to be of no more than secondary importance. Yet—as the detailed arguments into which Plato entered in themselves suggest—those doctrines were profoundly serious.

In the field of criticism, the Sophists were the first to embark upon a radical critique of all beliefs, in the name of a methodical and rigorous rationality. They were the first to try to think of the world and life purely in terms of human beings. They were the first to consider the relativity of knowledge as a fundamental principle, and to open up the way not only for free-thinking but also for absolute doubt regarding all metaphysical, religious, and moral matters. Let us not claim that they were necessarily right to do so; simply that they possessed the originality to push rationalism and scepticism to the limit. Even if the sole achievement of their critique had been to elicit responses and encourage people to defend their beliefs more carefully and think more clearly about what those beliefs implied, the Sophists' efforts would have been invaluable. They were already bearing fruit where Plato was concerned, in that they obliged him to produce a dialectical justification of the supremacy of the Good. Once the Sophists appeared on the scene, philosophy could no longer content itself with revelation: it was now forced to reason and produce proofs. But, in fact, the new lead taken by the Sophists' critique itself continued to be followed. It would surely be naïve to deny the wide popularity that it regained in the eighteenth century and still enjoys today. These days, its influence is considerably greater than that of Platonism.

That is frequently acknowledged. But what does not seem to be fully recognized is that their originality went far further: the Sophists re-created the world on a human scale and founded it upon human needs. In this world of theirs, the necessities of communal life created a new place and a new meaning for justice, concord, and the human virtues in general. All humanist systems of thought which create values within an existentialist framework sprang from the seeds sown by the Sophists' new ideas. Finally, confronted by the importance of the political group and communal life, they moved on from the invention of all the *technai* mentioned above to evolve a political philosophy which was to fuel those of both Plato and Aristotle and, through them, all the political thought that followed, from Cicero down to the present day.

There are thus plenty of reasons why these little-known men should exert a fascination upon twentieth-century minds; and to those reasons we should perhaps add another, albeit one of a rather different kind. The intellectual enterprise upon which the Sophists embarked afforded them first adulation, then hostility and mockery, as a result of which their teaching was distorted or marginalized before eventually being assimilated in a modified form. The whole sequential pattern is typical of the kind of ongoing exchange that tended to develop—and no doubt always will—between innovators and their public.

On the side of the innovators, the case of the Sophists demonstrates how the conviction of their own originality can lead to over-confidence in the field of practical application, and also how soon those who follow the newly blazed trail strive to outdo their precursors. On the side of the public, we can see how adulation may go hand in hand with hostility and irony, and how success itself brings in its wake distortion, exaggeration, and misunderstandings. Influence sometimes takes unpredictable and undesired forms.

Yet despite the misunderstandings, something got through and bore fruit. The dialogue between the Sophists and their public also shows how the twin surge of admiration in some quarters, resistance in others, precipitated the evolution of not simply philosophical reflection but the very mentality of those involved. If every thinker, in every period, owes much of his inspiration to the political, social, and cultural conditions of the day, the example of the Sophists shows that the converse is equally true. By giving precise and lucid expression to the latent aspirations of the moment, intellectuals imbue them with a virtually irresistible force. Every new technique, every new doctrine, every new word introduced by thinkers gradually, sometimes imperceptibly, changes the sensibility of all.

It truly is a matter of 'sensibility' for, as we have seen, an active and constant interchange takes place between the ideas of the intellectuals and the moral attitudes that prevail. Morality or, as the case may be, an absence of morality, engenders philosophical theories which, in their turn, sanction and foster particular types of behaviour and revolts, and may suddenly liberate particular desires. Intellectuals constantly influence the evolution of the community.

There are consequently plenty of reasons why the adventure that was played out in fifth-century Athens merits the attention even of those who are primarily interested in the present-day world and its ideas, sciences, and problems: for that adventure possesses a relevance for all periods of crisis and change. One nevertheless feels certain scruples for having singled it out in this way. For we should beware of promoting the definitely false equivalence that is sometimes suggested between classicism and rationalism. Much has been made of the incredible success of the Sophists in Athens, and they have been closely associated with the fashion for *technai* and the passion for knowledge by which Athens was gripped at this time. For those very reasons, to restore a correct perspective, we should remember that these erudite teachers, reasoners, and rationalists certainly represent only one of the faces of Periclean Athens.

In the first place, let it never be forgotten that their rationalism was—to their credit—all the more militant because it was so new and because much progress still remained to be made. To judge from the testimony of the authors of the time, the new-born Athenian democracy—which was, after all, a direct democracy—seems to have responded more readily to irrational impulses than to thoughtful deliberation. Thucydides and Euripides both lamented the fact, and Plato, for his part, likened the people to a gross animal with blind instincts to which the orators pandered. It was clearly a democracy which badly needed to learn to think. As a public principle of motivation, the very notion of justice had only recently taken over from clan vengeance. There was still much thinking to be done on this score too. Above all, credulity, belief in oracles, and shadowy terrors still loomed large. There is hardly a fifth-century text that does not, at some point, deplore the power of diviners and all their lies. Seen in this reconstructed context, the Sophists' attempts to establish rationalism were certainly timely.

But, most of all, we should remember that the Sophists' rationalism represents only half the picture. And even in the case of the Sophists themselves, we have concentrated upon lectures and analyses whose very nature inclines them to a certain theoretical dryness. However, that is a characteristic of the genre rather than of the sensibility of these men. The Antiphon of *On Concord* is the only moralist Sophist from whose hand a few fragments have survived; and those few pages reveal a most acute sense of human suffering. The passages on the disappointments of marriage sound a pathetic note: 'pleasures do not come alone but are attended by griefs and troubles'; as to the worries of paternity, when life is full of cares, the soul loses its springtime buoyancy and even a man's face is not what it was (fr. B 51). Finally, fragment 50 runs as follows:

Life is like a day-long watch and the length of life is like one day . . . in which, having seen the light, we pass on our trust to the next generation.

These reflections echo the traditional pessimism of one particular strain of Greek poetry. But here it takes on wider implications and the forceful images used make the point more acutely. In the present study we have been concentrating on the Sophists' theories and arguments, but we should remember that these thinkers were also the contemporaries of tragedy.

It is above all when we turn to Athens itself and the works that it has left us that we can appreciate the extent to which all this intellectual excitement was also linked with other tendencies. Athens was passionately committed to the powers of intelligence, but equally so to a love of beauty, an acute sense of human suffering, and the secret ferment of an idealism which was about to burgeon and flourish.

Pericles was prepared to enter into a day-long discussion with Protagoras over who (or what) was responsible for the accidental death of a young man killed by a javelin while training. But meanwhile Phidias was another of his friends, and Pericles would spend other days presiding over the constructions on the Acropolis. Beauty had its rights, alongside intelligence.

Similarly, Euripides and Thucydides, the disciples of the Sophists, wasted no time in making use of the intellectual methods that the latter had introduced. But they used them in tragedies or works of tragic implication, where they served to strengthen and emphasize a poignant sense of human suffering and the vagaries of history.

After all, the fact that the Sophists, with all their critical rationality, prompted Plato to respond with his own un-compromising idealism and fervour speaks for itself. The Sophists' influence in philosophical matters was clearly crucial but, indirectly, the need to counter it stimulated in others a keenness of perception and a tender descriptive skill of a different order.

The analyses of the Sophists made everything possible but only had the power to do so because, in Athens, they complemented other aspirations which they served to express or liberate. In Greek thought as a whole, the Sophists occupy a spearhead position, one which they themselves assumed in a methodical fashion which has sometimes led to misunder-standings. They have suffered from that lack of understand-ing to such a degree that their influence is now sometimes hard to discern. Without them, however, those who followed, with their unflagging fervour and their sense of pathos, tragedy, and history, would never have been as they were. Nor, indeed, should we be as we are today.

BIBLIOGRAPHICAL NOTES

Texts

The use of the texts is of the first importance. The texts of the Sophists, in Greek, are collected together in Diels–Kranz, *Die Fragmente der Vorsokratiker* (of which many revised editions have been published: always consult the most recent). A Greek text, with Italian translation and commentary, published by La Nuova Italia, Florence, began to appear in 1946. It is edited by M. Untersteiner, who is also responsible for most of the translation and commentary. There is a French translation of the fragments by J. P. Dumont (Paris, 1969); and there are two English translations: one is by R. K. Sprague *The Older Sophists* (Columbia, SC, 1972), the other, the *Ancilla to the Pre-Socratic Philosophers*, (Oxford, 1948), is by Kathleen Freeman.

Also to be consulted, texts which are more or less contemporary with the Sophists and help us to understand them: Aristophanes, *The Clouds*; Euripides; Thucydides; Plato (in particular *Protagoras, Gorgias, The Sophist, Theaetetus*; Isocrates, *Against the Sophists, Helen, Antidosis*. All may be found in the Loeb Classical Library, as may the testimony of Philostratus, *Lives of the Sophists* (second and third centuries AD).

General Studies

(In chronological order): F. Heinimann, *Nomos und Physis: Herkunft und Bedeutung einer Antithese im griechischen Denken des 5. Jahrhunderts* (Basle, 1945). E. Dupréel, *Les Sophistes* (Neuchâtel, 1948–9). M. Untersteiner, *I Sofisti* (Turin, 1949; English trans., Oxford, 1954). W. K. C. Guthrie, *The Sophists* (Cambridge University Press, 1971). G. Romeyer-Dherbey, *Les Sophistes*, Que sais-je? (Paris, 1985).

Also to be consulted, a number of recent collective studies: *Sophistik* (articles collected by J. C. Classen and translated into German), Wege der Forschung, 187 (Darmstadt, 1976), G. B. Kerferd (ed.), *The Sophists and their Legacy* (Wiesbaden, 1981); and (B. Cassin (ed.), *Le Plaisir de parler: études de sophistique comparée*, Proceedings of a colloquium held at Cerisy (Paris, 1986), together with a companion volume, B. Cassin (ed.), *Positions de la sophistique* (Paris, 1986).

Specialized Studies

A detailed bibliography on the Sophists, of no less than 66 pages, which will be of use to all Greek scholars and philosophers, may be found in Classen (ed.), *Sophistik*. Many of these works make a most important contribution to the discussion on the Sophists; but the list below provides instead a few more general studies which offer a framework for the themes treated here. It includes my own works, frequently echoed in the present study.

On Education and Rhetoric (Chs. 1–3)
G. Kennedy, *The Art of Persuasion in Greece* (Princeton, NJ, 1963). H. I. Marrou, *A History of Education in Antiquity*, trans. George Lamb (London, 1977).

On the Doctrines in General and their Influence (Chs. 4–6)
F. Chapouthier, 'Euripide et l'accueil du divin', *Entretiens de la Fondation Hardt*, 1 (1954), 205–37. E. R. Dodds, an edition of Plato's *Gorgias*, with commentary (Oxford, 1959). S. Zeppi, *Studi sul Pensiero etico-politico dei Sofisti* (Rome, 1974). J. de Romilly, *La Loi dans la pensée grecque* (Paris, 1971).

On City Attitudes and Political Life (Chs. 7 and 8)
E. Barker, *Greek Political Theory: Plato and his Predecessors* (London, 1918). G. Mathieu, *Les Idées politiques d'Isocrate* (Paris, 1925). J. de Romilly, *Problèmes de la démocratie grecque* (Paris, 1975, 1986). J. Bordes, *'Politeia' dans la pensée grecque jusqu'à Aristote* (Paris, 1982).

Also: C. H. Kahn's important study, 'The Origins of Social Contract Theory in the Vth Century BC', in Kerferd (ed.), *The Sophists and their Legacy*, 92–108.

CHRONOLOGICAL TABLE

Political life		Intellectual life	
		496	Birth of Sophocles
490–480	Persian Wars	490?	Birth of Protagoras
		480	Birth of Euripides
		470?	Birth of Socrates
		458	Aeschylus' *Oresteia*
443	Foundation of Thurii	443	Protagoras draws up the laws of Thurii
		442	Sophocles' *Antigone*
		438	Euripides' *Alcestis* (his first extant play)
431	Outbreak of the Peloponnesian War		
		427	Gorgias arrives in Athens on an ambassadorial mission
		424?	Euripides' *Hecuba*
		423	Aristophanes' *The Clouds*
411	Oligarchic revolution in Athens	411?	Attacks against Protagoras. Fragment by Thrasymachus
		406–405	Deaths of Euripides and Sophocles
404	Defeat of Athens. Oligarchy of the Four Hundred	404	Critias is among the Thirty (oligarchy)
		399	Death of Socrates
		c. 398	Plato's first dialogues
		393	Isocrates' school opens
		392	Probable date of Gorgias' *Olympic Speech*
		387	Plato founds the Academy

INDEX

In this work the Sophists have been considered as a group from various points of view. This index provides the particular references for each individual Sophist. Those in **bold** print relate to the more substantial analyses devoted to them.

SUPPLEMENTARY REFERENCES

For the benefit of more specialized readers who would like to trace the origin of the texts cited, the following list contains references not so far given.

TRANSLATOR'S NOTE ON
GREEK AND LATIN TEXTS

Except where otherwise indicated, I have used the following translations of the Greek and Latin texts, (with slight adaptations by
J. de Romilly where stated.) Abbreviations used in footnotes are
according to LSJ.

Kathleen Freeman, *Ancilla to the Pre-Socratic Philosophers* (Oxford,
1948), for: Antiphon, Critias, Democritus, Gorgias, Parmenides,
Prodicus, Protagoras and Thrasymachus.

R. K. Sprague, *The Older Sophists* (Columbia, SC, 1972), for the
Anonymus Iamblichi.

The Loeb Classical Library (London and New York, or London and
Cambridge, Mass.) for:

ARISTOPHANES, *The Birds*, trans. Benjamin Bickley Rogers (1968).
—— *The Clouds*, trans. Benjamin Bickley Rogers (1967).
—— *Lysistrata*, trans. Benjamin Bickley Rogers (1963).
—— *Thesmophoriazusae*, trans. Benjamin Bickley Rogers (1963).
ARISTOTLE, *The Art of Rhetoric*, trans. John Henry Freese (1975).
DIOGENES LAERTIUS, *Lives of Eminent Philosophers*, trans. R. D. Hicks
(1979).
DIONYSIUS OF HALICARNASSUS, *On Thucydides*, trans. Stephen Usher
(1974).
HERODOTUS, trans. A. D. Godley (1946).
ISOCRATES, *Against the Sophists*, trans. George Norlin (1963).
—— *Antidosis Helen*, trans. Larne Van Hook (1968).
—— *Nicocles, Panegyricus*, trans. George Norlin (1966).
LUCRETIUS, trans. Martin Ferguson Smith (1975).
PLATO, *Apology*, trans. Harold North Fowler (1966).
—— *Euthydemus*, trans. W. R. M. Lamb (1924).
—— *Gorgias*, trans. W. R. M. Lamb (1953).
—— *Greater Hippias, Lesser Hippias*, trans. Harold North Fowler
(1970).
—— *The Laws*, trans. R. G. Bury (1967).
—— *Meno*, trans. W. R. M. Lamb (1924).
—— *Phaedrus*, trans. Harold North Fowler (1966).
—— *Protagoras*, trans. W. R. M. Lamb (1924).

—— *The Republic*, trans. Paul Shorey (1946).

—— *Theaetetus*, trans. Harold North Fowler (1967).

PHILOSTRATUS, *The Lives of the Sophists*, trans. Wilmer Cave Wright (1922).

SEXTUS EMPIRICUS, *Against the Physicists*, trans. R. G. Bury (1953).

THUCYDIDES, *History of the Peloponnesian War*, trans. Charles Forster Smith (1975–7).

XENOPHON, *Memorabilia*, trans. E. C. Marchant (1965).

—— *On Hunting*, trans. G. W. Bowersock (1968).

The University of Chicago Press (Chicago and London) for:

AESCHYLUS, *Eumenides*, trans. Richmond Lattimore (1953).

EURIPIDES, *Hecuba*, trans. William Arrowsmith (1958).

—— *Helen*, trans. Richmond Lattimore (1956).

—— *Hippolytus*, trans. David Grene (1942).

—— *Iphigenia at Aulis*, trans. Witter Bynner (1956).

—— *The Medea*, trans. Rex Warner (1955).

—— *The Trojan Women*, trans. Richmond Lattimore (1958).

SOPHOCLES, *Philoctetes*, trans. David Grene (1957).